Political Reason

Also by Allyn Fives

POLITICAL AND PHILOSOPHICAL DEBATES IN WELFARE (*2008*)

Political Reason

Morality and the Public Sphere

Allyn Fives
Postdoctoral Researcher,
School of Political Science and Sociology,
National University of Ireland, Galway

palgrave
macmillan

First published 2013 by
PALGRAVE MACMILLAN

Palgrave Macmillan in the UK is an imprint of Macmillan Publishers Limited, registered in England, company number 785998, of Houndmills, Basingstoke, Hampshire RG21 6XS.

Palgrave Macmillan in the US is a division of St Martin's Press LLC, 175 Fifth Avenue, New York, NY 10010.

Palgrave Macmillan is the global academic imprint of the above companies and has companies and representatives throughout the world.

Palgrave® and Macmillan® are registered trademarks in the United States, the United Kingdom, Europe and other countries.

ISBN: 978–0–230–23898–5

This book is printed on paper suitable for recycling and made from fully managed and sustained forest sources. Logging, pulping and manufacturing processes are expected to conform to the environmental regulations of the country of origin.

A catalogue record for this book is available from the British Library.

A catalog record for this book is available from the Library of Congress.

10 9 8 7 6 5 4 3 2 1
22 21 20 19 18 17 16 15 14 13

Printed and bound in Great Britain by
CPI Antony Rowe, Chippenham and Eastbourne

For
Anne Marie Power
and
Joanna Fives

Contents

Preface

The structure and content of the final version of this book are very different from what had been planned. An even more significant change occurred to the book's main argument. The primary reason for this lies in a reappraisal of Alasdair MacIntyre's work, namely his attempt to conduct political philosophy from within a specific 'tradition', Aristotelian Thomism. The reassessment came about not so much because of a concern with MacIntyre's Thomism, an aspect of his work many have either chosen to ignore or treat as reason enough to ignore MacIntyre's arguments in total, but rather because of what came to be seen as fatal flaws in his, and indeed in any, attempt to conduct rational enquiry from within a tradition, whatever tradition that may be. I came to the conclusion that such a 'historicist' approach is deeply flawed as it creates irredeemable problems in regard to epistemology, ethics, and politics.

In earlier versions of some of these chapters, I had argued that, taking away the troubling historicism, which was the cause of the concern, in particular, regarding relativism, it should be possible to build on MacIntyre's work so as to provide an account of human flourishing that had universal application. Then there would be a basis for political reasoning in some notion of the human good that did not lead to relativism. However, I also came to see that, although it may be possible from within a moral and philosophical doctrine such as Aristotelian–Thomism broadly defined to defend such a universal conception of the human good, and Philippa Foot among others has tried to do this, morally speaking it was inappropriate as a basis for political debate. It would be morally inappropriate on the grounds that in politics we should expect to find, and we should accept when we do find, disagreement about such things as the best way to live, or the true purpose of human life, or the virtues that are expressions of our potential, and so on. But if we should not try to base political reasoning on some account of the human good held to be universally true, what then happens to the moral content of political reason?

In addition, it also became clear that the problems MacIntyre could not overcome were not so dissimilar to problems that characterize the work of post-modernists, neo-Nietzscheans, and post-structuralists, who take the view that the certainty looked for in reason and morality is continually undermined by power and difference. Indeed it seemed more and more to make sense to place MacIntyre in the same category as Foucault, Derrida, Rorty, Mouffe, Laclau, and others who take a post-modern and post-structuralist stance. It was not that my earlier papers on MacIntyre did not criticize his historicism. What had changed was my coming to the conclusion that MacIntyre and post-modernists were open to the same criticism and for the reason that they were opposed to the same heritage in moral thought, namely the Enlightenment. While accepting that post-modernists baulk at MacIntyre's stated intention of finding rational and objective answers to moral questions, and that MacIntyre has unambiguously distanced himself from the immoralism of Nietzsche and his followers with their rejection of conventional moral virtues, not least Christian virtues, nonetheless, what binds them together, and the reason both approaches are equally problematic, is their wholesale opposition to the Enlightenment.

This book adopts the view that the Enlightenment is characterized by two commitments:

1. a commitment to rational justification, i.e. scepticism with respect to validity claims, in particular moral claims; and
2. a commitment to moral equality, i.e. the contention that all should be viewed as moral equals and that all are owed equal moral consideration, in particular when offering reasons to others in justifying our beliefs and actions.

Such a statement needs some clarification, and hopefully that is what the chapters in this book provide. But briefly it is not assumed here that, for instance, if one has a strong sense of tradition, or strongly held religious beliefs, or takes a critical stance to the pervasiveness of power, then one cannot also be truly rational; nor is it assumed that if one is to be committed to moral equality one must also be a secularist or a liberal. Nonetheless, both MacIntyre and post-modernists clearly and repeatedly reject both the idea that moral issues can or should be settled by the force of the better argument as such, that is, by appeal to reason-as-such and morality-as-such, and the idea that, as others are our moral equals, then to justify moral conclusions we must offer reasons others can be expected to accept.

So if the approach of MacIntyre is no less problematic than post-modernism, what direction should political philosophy take? Perhaps the direction taken in this book was simply determined by the way in which MacIntyre and post-modernists have been criticized, for that critique, and the definition of the Enlightenment on which the critique rests, was informed by Rawls's work on 'reasonableness'. Rawls has said that reasonable citizens (i) view one another as free and equal; (ii) they offer each other fair terms of social cooperation; and (iii) they recognize and accept the consequences of 'the burdens of judgement', namely that, in politics we should not seek a rational consensus on a single comprehensive moral doctrine.

While the first part of this book locates MacIntyre and post-modernism in opposition to the Enlightenment, in the remainder Rawls's 'core conception of reasonableness' is worked up as a response to those failings. It may be argued that there is a hint of circularity in an argument that rejects MacIntyre on the basis that he does not live up to the standards of Rawls's core conception of reasonableness, and then going on to defend Rawls's core conception of reasonableness for offering just what MacIntyre did not. In an effort to show that this is not the case, the two final chapters look at the practical application of these ideas in the areas of civic education and global distributive justice. It is hoped they will illustrate that the core conception of reasonableness is superior to MacIntyre's historicism in terms of epistemology, ethics, and politics in two crucial senses, and it will be seen to be superior on the criteria that are most relevant for a political theory, namely that it shows how we are to take the moral point of view in politics and it goes some way towards showing how we are to resolve moral questions that we are forced to address in politics.

Acknowledgements

In writing this book I received support and encouragement, and comments and suggestions on the work at a very early stage, from Professor Russell Keat. Earlier versions of the chapters were first delivered as conference papers or presentations, in Manchester, London, Edinburgh, and Galway. I probably benefitted most from hearing what others think of what I have been trying to do, and hearing what they think to be its strengths and weaknesses. In this regard Keith Breen has been very generous with his time and expertise and friendship down through the years. Similarly, thanks are owed to Amy Allen, Alex Bavister-Gould, Tony Burns, Jo Campling, Emilios Christodoulidis, Bregham Dalgleish, Ricca Edmondson, Horace L. Fairlamb, Oliver Feeney, Brendan Flynn, Richard Freeman, Paul Garrett, Mark Haugaard, Jonathan Hearn, John Holmwood, Richard Hull, Kimberley Hutchings, Omar Khan, Kelvin Knight, Marian Kuna, Joe Mahon, Pete Morriss, Raymond Plant, and Marcus Woerner.

I want to thank the President of Ireland, Micheal D. Higgins, for the way he has supported me and promoted my work since launching my first book in Charlie Byrne's bookshop in 2008.

I would like to thank my colleagues at the Child and Family Research Centre, the School of Political Science and Sociology, and also collaborators on research projects from other departments and centres in NUI Galway and elsewhere.

Very special thanks to my parents, Jim and Julie Fives, my brothers and sisters, Karen, Kieran, Anne-Marie, and Aonghus, baby Joanna Fives, who had the biggest impact on the writing of the book as her imminent arrival created a new deadline for its first draft, and finally, my wife Anne Marie Power.

Several chapters in this book draw on previously published material. An earlier version of Chapter 6 appears as 'Non-Coercive Promotion of Values in Civic Education for Democracy', *Philosophy and Social Criticism* (Sage, 2011). An earlier version of Chapter 5 appears as 'Reasonableness, Pluralism, and Liberal Moral Doctrines', *Journal of Value Inquiry*, vol. 44, no. 3 (Springer, 2010): 321–339. Some of Chapter 4 appeared first as 'Reasonable, Agonistic, or Good? The Character of a Democrat', *Philosophy & Social Criticism*, vol. 35, no. 8 (Sage, 2009): 961–983. Some of Chapter 3 appeared first as 'Human Flourishing: The Grounds of

Moral Judgement', *Journal of Value Inquiry*, vol. 42, no. 2 (Springer, 2008): 167–186. An earlier version of Chapter 2 was delivered at a conference in honour of Alasdair MacIntyre at the London Metropolitan University in 2007. Parts of the Introduction first appeared as 'Aristotle's Ethics and Contemporary Political Theory', *21st Century Society*, vol. 1, no. 2 (Taylor and Francis, 2006): 201–220.

1
Introduction – Political Reason after the Enlightenment

Background

In a democracy, not only is disagreement a fact that can be observed, but it is also something that morally speaking should be accepted. But what types of disagreement should be tolerated and where instead can and should we push for agreement? This is the more pressing issue and the more difficult question to resolve. Democratic politics is characterized just as much by disagreement, conflict, and discord as it is by consensus, unity, and shared commitments. Although fellow citizens may try to come to some agreement about the proper aims and goals of a society, the distribution of its benefits and burdens, as well as the values and principles that are to be cherished and promoted, nonetheless in the political realm disagreements arise. Democratic politics is both an arena where we can seek out or express our shared identity as members of the one group or society and also a site of clashing world views; it is the realm in which we pursue common goals but also make competing claims to scarce resources; and in politics the claims we make often are incompatible and also justified with principles that are or seem to be incommensurable.

This has led some to argue that if we are to continue to guarantee individual freedom, then in our political reasoning we must accept moral pluralism.

> [The] diversity of doctrines – the fact of moral pluralism – is not a mere historical condition that will soon pass away; it is, I believe, a permanent feature of the public culture of modern democracies...A public and workable agreement on a single general and comprehensive conception [of the good] could be maintained only by the oppressive use of state power. (Rawls, 1987: 425)

What we require therefore, according to Rawls, is a 'political conception of justice', a morality of the public sphere, whose purpose is to 'specify a point of view from which all citizens can examine before one another whether or not their political institutions are just' (ibid. p. 426). The alternative view, however, is that, despite the plurality of moral points of view, a much more substantial agreement is available than Rawls recognises. There are certain 'inescapable frameworks' of moral reasoning, frameworks that incorporate qualitative distinctions, which provide us with 'the sense that some action, or mode of life, or mode of feeling is incomparably higher than the others' (Taylor, 1989: 19). Even in modern pluralist societies, Charles Taylor contends, such frameworks 'provide the background, explicit or implicit, for our moral judgements, intuitions, or reactions' (ibid. p. 26).

What this illustrates is that, in studying politics, we are concerned with both the goals that we do or should pursue as well as the principles and values that we do or should cherish and promote. We must also address the way in which we do or should deal with disagreements in politics, and so we are concerned with both reason and morality. In short, we have been set the (daunting) task of coming to an understanding of what should count as good reasons in political debate and more precisely what should count as morally weighty reasons in political debate. In particular, we ask whether we may appeal to a supposedly shared background of qualitative distinctions, a comprehensive morality made up of judgements of what is better or higher, as Taylor and others argue, or instead that, so as to respect the liberty of our fellow citizens, in politics we must limit ourselves to a more narrowly defined 'public' morality, a morality that does not presuppose the truth of any one comprehensive moral doctrine, as Rawls and others argue.

Political reasoning is one type of moral reasoning, but what is political reasoning? What makes it different from other types of moral reasoning? We could say, to begin with, that political reasoning involves the giving of reasons in deliberation and debate, reasons that are to support or justify conclusions about identifiably 'political' ideas, actions, policies, institutions, and so on. A reason for something is 'a consideration that counts in favour of it' (Scanlon, 1998: 17). When we are concerned with the 'standard normative sense' of reason we are concerned with whether something is a 'good' reason, that is, an assessment of the grounds for taking something to be the case (ibid. p. 19). Although political reasoning includes many different categories or types of reasons, it is moral reasons and moral reasoning that will be addressed here.

It may be objected that we are unused to morality playing much of a role in real-world politics, as in many if not most cases political actors (whether 'politicians' or not) do not (or do not seem to) act from moral motives and do not offer moral justifications for their actions, at least, not moral justifications that are genuine. Nonetheless, when the reasons given to support a conclusion are non-moral (concerning say economics, popular opinion, legislation, lobbying, special interests, prejudice, ideology, and so on) it is still possible to ask, what moral reasons, if any, support the conclusion and are there moral reasons to revise or reject the conclusion?

However, there is, it seems, a serious tension in current political philosophy. There are a great number of theories of social justice, concerned with the morally justified distribution of benefits and burdens in society, and also many theories of political reasoning, which address the standards, principles, and logic of morally justified political debate. For example, concerning social justice there is the disagreement between Rawls, who claims that an injustice is an inequality not to the benefit of the least well-off, and Robert Nozick, who objects that such a principle would require the able bodied and advantaged to be used 'simply as a means' for the sake of the least advantaged (Rawls, 1971: 75; Nozick, 1974: 169–172). Similar debates continue concerning the rights of young people (Harris, 1996), and the rights of the distant poor (Pogge, 2008). When we consider political reasoning itself, there is disagreement between historicists, such as Alasdair MacIntyre, who believe that we need a hierarchical ordering of goods, with one overall good, something that a 'tradition in good working order' (MacIntyre, 1988) provides, and liberals, such as Rawls, who believe that although 'to subordinate all our aims to one end does not strictly speaking violate the principles of rational choice..., it still strikes us as irrational, or more likely as mad' (Rawls, 1971: 554). In addition, post-modernists have entered the debate on social justice and political reason. They contend that conflicts around our identity are as important if not more so than those concerning the distribution of resources, and also that political interaction is and should be about the 'contestation of identity'. 'Hence the importance of leaving this space of contestation forever open, instead of trying to fill this gap through the establishment of a supposedly "rational" consensus' (Mouffe, 2000: 56).

This plurality of approaches concerning both social justice and political reasoning is such that not only is there no agreement about what justice requires of us as political actors (for instance, as citizens of a democracy), but there is also no agreement about how disagreements such as these are to be rationally resolved in democratic debate. In political debate, should we reason from within a traditional horizon, as MacIntyre argues? Or establish what has intrinsic value and worth, as MacIntyre believes and as Taylor does with his 'qualitative distinctions'? Or appeal to universal moral principles, as is the case with Nozick's social contract approach? Or seek out reasons that can be shared by fellow-citizens, as Rawls argues? Or instead should we see this process as a type of conflict, as post-modernists claim? Furthermore, what claims can disadvantaged fellow-citizens make, and what claims can be made by disadvantaged non-citizens? Do the distant poor have the same claims on us as our fellow citizens, as cosmopolitans argue? And what is the moral status of children and young people, do they have rights and duties, and do they have many if not all of the rights that adults have, as is claimed by the children's rights movement?

Political philosophers do not agree about these issues. Indeed, there are a variety of different approaches within political philosophy, offering different, often seemingly incommensurable, accounts of moral argumentation in politics. But if that is the case how can political philosophers provide any help when we try to rationally resolve disputes such as these?

Despite the appearance of irresolveable conflict, it is nonetheless possible to bring a considerable degree of order within current politics and political philosophy. That, at least, is the thesis of this book, and it rests on an analysis of the nature and cause of the disagreements among political philosophers. There is a clear distinction to be made, it will be argued, between those who reject the heritage of Enlightenment philosophy, thinking of it as a failed and/or dangerous project, and those whose political philosophy incorporates many basic premises and commitments of the Enlightenment while nonetheless retaining a critical attitude to the failings of other Enlightenment philosophers or Enlightenment political projects. It is also the thesis of this book that any wholesale rejection of Enlightenment philosophy, a rejection which post-modernists and historicists engage in, creates a barrier within political philosophy to the rational resolution of the moral disputes arising in political debate.

It will also be argued that, although distinctively 'liberal' versions of the Enlightenment heritage are less than completely successful here, many of the conceptual and moral resources needed for this purpose can be found within the heritage of the Enlightenment itself. In particular, what the Enlightenment heritage helps show is that the idea of 'public reasoning', or 'reasonableness', along with commitment to scepticism and to the moral equality of fellow citizens that reasonableness presupposes, are the prerequisites of morally justified political debate concerning issues of social justice.

The argument of this book

Enlightenment philosophy is by no means a single, uniform school of thought, and a greater number of commitments can be identified with it than will be presented here. Nonetheless, for the purposes of this discussion, it is possible to take the following two features as characteristic of Enlightenment political philosophy:

1. a commitment to rational justification, i.e. scepticism with respect to validity claims, in particular moral claims; and
2. a commitment to moral equality, i.e. that all should be viewed as moral equals and that all are owed equal moral consideration, in particular when offering reasons to others in justifying our beliefs and actions.

A note of caution is required before proceeding further. There are many who are committed to moral equality in some form and/or scepticism in some form who nonetheless would not be characterized as Enlightenment thinkers. This is the case as the terms 'scepticism' and 'moral equality' are open to multiple interpretations. First, scepticism can be either an extreme or a moderate position.

1. The extreme position involves scepticism either 'about whether anything ever "counts in favour of" anything else..., or about whether we are actually capable of making judgements about when this is the case' (Scanlon, 1998: 19). This is scepticism about the very possibility of rationality, that is, scepticism about the existence of reasons and scepticism about our capacity to give such reasons.
2. Alternatively, one can be sceptical in the 'moderate' sense of not taking beliefs or convictions on trust from others; and in the sense of being willing to look for reasons to hold the beliefs one already has. Moderate scepticism is an approach to reasoning that stands opposed to MacIntyre's historicism, and also to Hans-Georg Gadamer's hermeneutics. Gadamer contended that reasoning must always proceed from what is not put to the question, our presuppositions or 'prejudices', and that such prejudices form our inescapable 'horizon' of understanding (Gadamer, 1975: 271 ff.).

Although such a hermeneutic position involves commitment to rational justification, this is rational justification *within* a horizon or worldview or tradition, and therefore it is not sceptical. Such a tradition may be informed by accounts of human flourishing and human perfection and/or religious belief, and it is just such commitments that are *not* put in question by rational argumentation. These rather are the first principles of all genuinely rational argumentation (see MacIntyre, 1988: 118). In contrast, the moderate view of scepticism is that, in principle, all accepted truths are open to rational analysis and that, in principle, it is possible to look for reasons for such truths. One is not required to doubt that there is such a thing as rationality or to doubt that it can ever be attained. It is this second, moderate, version of scepticism that will be employed here when referring to the Enlightenment.

The commitment to moral equality can be interpreted in a number of ways as well. It can either be about the way others should be treated generally speaking, or it can be about the way others should be treated when offering moral justifications.

1. A commitment to moral equality in the treatment of others generally can be developed in a number of different ways. One can be committed to moral equality in the sense that one believes the interests of all should be given equal consideration when any decision is made that affects others, as utilitarians argue (Mill, 1861), or that all should be treated with equal concern and respect, as liberals argue (Dworkin, 1985), or that all are equally valuable and equally capable of living a meaningful life, as perfectionists argue (Hurka, 2001), or that as humans we are all equally weak and sinful and in need of moral aid, as Christians argue (Tawney, 1921). This would suggest that not everyone committed to moral equality is also an 'Enlightenment' thinker. While the utilitarian commitment to equal consideration of interests and the liberal commitment to equality of respect are recognizably Enlightenment positions, this is not the case with many perfectionist or Christian accounts of moral perfection and/or moral weakness, insofar as they are anti-sceptical in the moderate sense above.

2. The commitment to moral equality can also be about the way others should be treated when offering moral justifications. For

Rawls, we must be willing to give an account of ourselves and our actions to others and in doing so acknowledge the moral equality of others (1993a). It would seem, one can be committed to moral equality in the first general sense without being committed to moral equality in the second more specific sense. This is the case with some utilitarian thinkers who insist on two levels of moral reasoning, a level of philosophical justification and a level of everyday deliberation. At the level of justification we can justify acts that ensure all are treated with equal consideration; but we are not required to disclose to those affected what the actual justifying reasons were. As the level of justification is separate from everyday moral deliberation we need not treat others as moral equals in the justification of those acts (this is discussed in Chapter 7). And it will be argued that it is the commitment to moral equality in offering moral justifications that has most significance for political action and political philosophy. As political philosophy is concerned with the proper way in which to address moral issues in political debate and action, then the central moral concern will be the way we view our fellow participants in that political debate and action. So the commitment to moral equality in the treatment of others generally is necessary but not sufficient for the definition of the Enlightenment: one must also be committed to moral equality in regard to the way others should be treated when offering moral justifications in political debate.

Coming now to contemporary political philosophy, it can be said to be *after* the Enlightenment in one of either two senses. Philosophical analysis can be *after* the Enlightenment in the sense that it continues 'in the manner of' or 'in accordance with' or 'in conformity to' the Enlightenment.[1] For such an approach, philosophical analysis does and should remain true to certain principles or commitments characteristic of the Enlightenment, even though it should jettison some of the premises and/or conclusions of some Enlightenment philosophers. The two commitments in question are, firstly, the willingness to view others as our moral equals, i.e. the commitment to moral equality, and secondly, the willingness to offer justifications for the claims we make and to judge the claims made by others on the merits of the justifications that can be offered in their defence: that is, the commitment to scepticism. An approach to political philosophy can be said to be 'in the manner of' the Enlightenment not only because of its content but more because of its style of doing philosophy.

To take just one example, Kantians argue that a maxim can be accepted as a moral principle only if it is compatible with the Categorical Imperative. That is, the maxim must be universalizable and also it must require that humanity be treated as an end in itself. The two relevant formulations of the Categorical Imperative are: 'act only on that maxim through which you can at the same time will that it should become a universal law'; and 'act in such a way that you always treat humanity, whether in your own person or the person of any other, never simply as a means, but always at the same time as an end' (Kant, 1785: § 51, 66–67). In these requirements of moral justification we can see the twin commitments to moral equality and scepticism. They express the view that we should view others as moral equals, and that is why we must treat the humanity of others 'always as an end' and never simply as means to our ends, and also that we should be willing to offer justifications to others with considerations that they as our equals should be able to accept, and that is why the maxims we put forward must be such that all persons could will that they be made into universal laws.

Similar commitments can be found in the works of the other major philosophers of the Enlightenment era and before. For example, Thomas Hobbes, in the 1650s, based political philosophy on the 'passions' of the ordinary or 'natural' person: read thyself, he urged us, for whoever looks into himself when he thinks, reasons, hopes, opines, etc. 'and upon what grounds; he shall thereby read and know, what are the thoughts, and passions of all other men, upon like occasions' (Hobbes, 1651: introduction, 3). Although Hobbes's State, or Leviathan, was to exercise absolute power, its purpose was to guarantee the security and liberty of each. So not only must political reasoning proceed from the passions of each, political practice must be for the benefit of each. Again, David Hume, in the 1730s, called for a politics based on a general sense of common interest, but also a philosophy based on 'experience and observation', rather than 'Principles taken upon trust, consequences lamely deduced from them' (T introduction: 41).

The reality of politics may seem far removed from the standards of the Enlightenment, but that in itself is not reason enough to conclude that the problem lies with Enlightenment thought. Politics may well involve domination and power, but the point is that political debate should be based on nothing more than the force of the better argument, that is, the *unforced* force of the better argument (see Habermas, 1990: 88–89). In our deliberations and debates we may be deeply swayed by unquestioned presuppositions, but once again the point is that, when called on to do so, we can and should drag ourselves back 'from the particular to the general' and thus put ourselves in a position to offer reasons for our conclusions that others can at least understand and see as genuinely moral reasons (see Dworkin, 1985: 219–220).

Furthermore, the Enlightenment as a style of doing political philosophy cannot be confused with, or reduced to, specific political revolutionary movements in history that were rightly or wrongly categorized as 'Enlightenment' projects, in particular, the French and Russian revolutions and subsequent totalitarian rule. It may be that Enlightenment ideas or premises were used to motivate or justify many political projects that rightly deserve more blame than praise; but it can still be the case that it is from within the inheritance of the Enlightenment that we are best placed to analyse such projects and resolve the moral disputes to which they give rise. For example, the Soviet system may have been justified by its proponents on the basis of a socialist social science free from bourgeois ideology, and therefore a genuinely sceptical or objective science, and also on the basis of the unrelenting march of history towards a classless, and therefore truly equal, society. Marx himself understood the communist political goal in much this way (see Marx, 1859). Nonetheless, the moral resources of the Enlightenment also provide us with the material needed for a close moral analysis of the abuses of the Soviet regime, namely that it treated people simply as means, in that it killed millions of its own people, and that it perverted truth and reason and morality in efforts to justify itself, in particular by representing such mass murder as a necessary stage in the process towards emancipation (see Grossman, 1964; Solzhenitsyn, 1973). That is, the commitments to scepticism and moral equality provide the moral resources needed to take a critical stance to politics, even when the political projects we analyse are said to be exemplars of Enlightenment ideals.

So political philosophy can be and is *after* the Enlightenment in the sense that it wishes to carry on in the same spirit as, or in accordance with, the Enlightenment. There is a second, quite different, way in which philosophy can be *after* the Enlightenment, however. For some, the Enlightenment is a project in philosophical analysis (and social practice and political ideology) that has come to an end but also the project itself was a failure right from its inception. For this school of thought, the Enlightenment is a period of failure, although not necessarily in the sense that it has been surpassed or improved upon by a successor. Rather, it is a period of failure in that it could never have succeeded in its stated goals, its unintended consequences were disastrous, and also many of its followers are yet to relinquish their faith in this failed and dangerous project. Political philosophy therefore, it is argued, must be *after* the Enlightenment in the sense that this is a philosophical approach that must be consigned to the past. Such a claim is part of the otherwise opposed positions of, on the one hand, Friedrich Nietzsche and his followers, often simply referred to as post-modernists (including the work of Michel Foucault, Jacques Derrida) and, on the other hand, various historicist thinkers, such as Martin Heidegger, Gadamer, and MacIntyre.

Although the Enlightenment is said to be based on a commitment to scepticism, historicists believe the Enlightenment actually failed to provide objective and impartial criteria of moral judgement. According to MacIntyre, Enlightenment philosophy failed, and was destined to fail, because of its hubris. It was thought that philosophy could be based on nothing but reason in itself, a pure, ahistorical, and universal philosophical perspective. This conception of 'ideal rationality', MacIntyre contends, 'ignores the inescapably historically and socially context-bound character' that any substantive set of principles of rationality 'is bound to have' (1988: 4). In contrast, what the historicist claims to show is that philosophers should not be fearful of how their context (their community and tradition, and the settled conviction they provide) influences their reasoning, for such contexts are actually the very conditions of its possibility. What MacIntyre sees as the disastrous consequences of Enlightenment philosophy include the weakening or atrophy of tradition in the modern world and in consequence a loss of moral certainty and identity. He believes 'political, economic and moral structures of advanced modernity ... exclude the possibility of realizing any of the worthwhile types of political community' (1991: 91). This is disastrous, according to MacIntyre, as political reasoning by rights should be immersed within tradition(s), proceeding from the moral commitments of tradition(s).

Such a historicist analysis of the modern condition owes a great deal to developments in continental thought in the early twentieth century, in part the work of Wittgenstein, but in particular the path taken by some followers of Edmund Husserl's phenomenology, most notably Heidegger and Gadamer. The latter contended that Enlightenment thought is guilty of a 'prejudice against prejudice', an unquestioned presupposition that unquestioned presuppositions must be done away with (1975: 271ff). Gadamer's critique perhaps best expresses the historicist view that human reasoning is always situated within a 'horizon' and also the danger posed by the Enlightenment's desire to see through and dispel such 'prejudices'. Therefore, the Enlightenment was and remains dangerous as it weakens the non-rational foundations of rationality and morality.

There is another dimension to anti-Enlightenment thought. If the historicist view is that community, tradition, and history can and indeed must be acknowledged as the sources of our moral and rational certainty, the post-modern perspective is that all moral and rational certainty is continually undermined and displaced by the inescapable factors of 'power' and 'difference'. Post-modernists are engaged in an act that is both destructive and creative here. They hope to destroy what we have wrongly taken as sources of moral certainty but they also hope to create new approaches to politics and ethics that can be engaged in without the need for such certainties.

Political actors, according to Chantal Mouffe (2000) and Richard Rorty (1989), should accept not only that human rationality and morality are historically situated and embedded within contexts, as the historicists contend as well. The post-modernist also develops Nietzsche's insights concerning the 'lowly' beginnings (Foucault, 1971: 79) of what we take to be our noble motives and abstract theoretical categories. The distinctions between 'true' and 'false', and between 'good' and 'bad' have their origins not in the things themselves, but rather they express nothing more than a 'will to power' in our struggle for survival and domination over nature and over other humans (Nietzsche, 1888: 65). This is

> the endlessly repeated play of dominations. The domination of certain men over others leads to the differentiation of values; class domination generates the idea of liberty; and the forceful appropriation of things necessary to survival and the imposition of a duration not intrinsic to them account for the origin of logic.
> (Foucault, 1971: 85)

However, if the political actor is aware that every moral judgement is nothing but an act of violence, then, according to the post-modernist, the excesses of human domination resulting from Enlightenment hubris can be curtailed and, instead, spaces opened up for a kind of liberty and democracy that do not need to lay claim to illusory foundations in 'reason' or 'morality'. It does not erect new foundations to replace those it has undermined. Instead, 'it disturbs what was previously considered immobile; it fragments what we thought unified; it shows the heterogeneity of what was thought consistent with itself' (ibid. p. 82).

Michel Foucault, in his later work, wanted to retrieve the Enlightenment as a style of doing philosophy, namely 'a philosophical ethos that can be described as a permanent critique of our historical era', but he also refused 'the blackmail' of the Enlightenment, that is, the requirement to be either 'for' or 'against' the Enlightenment (1984: 42). What Foucault does continue to reject is any set of principles or commitments, such as the 'themes' of 'humanism', themes that he sees even in National Socialism and Stalinism (ibid. p. 44). For post-modernism, it is the assumption of rational and moral certainty, the 'blackmail' of having to be for or against the Enlightenment, that is in itself dangerous:

> It is not desirable for a society to be ruled by a single democratic logic. Relations of authority and power cannot completely disappear, and it is important to abandon the myth of a transparent society, reconciled with itself, for that kind of fantasy leads to totalitarianism. A project of radical and plural democracy, on the contrary, requires the existence of multiplicity, of plurality, and of conflict, and sees in them the raison d'etre of politics (Mouffe, 1989: 41).

The horrors of the Russian gulag and German concentration camp are not antithetical to the Enlightenment heritage, for post-modernism. Rather, they are the logical consequence of the Enlightenment's implausible account of human nature and the possibilities for rational certainty about such things as justice, freedom, historical progress, equality, happiness, and so on. When humans believe in the absolute certainty and integrity of their objectives they are more likely to commit horrendous crimes in pursuing those aims, and the Enlightenment only fosters and encourages this dangerous hubris, it is argued, by its commitments to scepticism and moral equality.

The hypothesis of this book is that the current impasse in political philosophy can be represented as a debate around the heritage of the Enlightenment. It is also argued that political philosophy can and should be *after* the Enlightenment in the first sense discussed above: contemporary political philosophy should be 'in accordance with' the basic principles and commitments of the Enlightenment. The argument has three main components:

1. Efforts to reject the Enlightenment as a failed experiment themselves fail, and the manner of their failure suggests the continued validity of just those Enlightenment principles and commitments said to be no longer tenable, namely moral equality and scepticism;
2. Those who defend the Enlightenment project now sometimes do so in ways that are unjustifiably one-sided, tied as they are in

particular either to liberal morality or to liberal politics. Nonetheless, it is possible to separate the Enlightenment project, specifically the concept of reasonableness, from this narrower liberalism;

3. Political philosophy based on the concept of reasonableness can be applied to practical issues, in particular global distributive justice and civic education, in ways that show the viability of this approach.

One way in which political philosophy can be in accordance with the Enlightenment, and the commitments to moral equality and scepticism, can be seen in the concept of reasonableness. What will be referred to here as 'Rawls's core conception of reasonableness', derived from John Rawls's later work (1993a), but with important qualifications to be discussed later, can be defined as follows: Reasonable citizens (i) view one another as free and equal; (ii) they offer each other fair terms of social cooperation, agree to act on those terms provided others do, and do so even at the cost of their own interests in particular situations; and (iii) they recognize and accept the consequences of 'the burdens of judgement', namely that, as differences between comprehensive moral doctrines have a morally innocent source, in politics we should not seek a rational consensus on a single comprehensive moral doctrine. The core conception of reasonableness can be applied to morally justified political debate and in particular political deliberation about issues of social justice. A reasonable political debate is marked by the willingness to offer justifications for proposals in moral terms, and to do so with reasons that should be acceptable to all free and equal fellow citizens. Reasonableness is also a requirement of social justice, as principles of justice can be valid only if they too can be justified with reasons that should be acceptable to all free and equal citizens.

In the history of Western philosophy there have been various different and perhaps incommensurable approaches to political reasoning. Each one has attempted to answer questions that are of vital importance to political activity in all its forms: how do we distinguish good from bad and right from wrong; and how do we make such judgements in the political sphere? We have mentioned the Enlightenment approach, which is based on a commitment to moral equality and scepticism. However, Enlightenment thought itself, the philosophy of Hume, Jean Jacques Rousseau, Kant, and Jeremy Bentham, among others, saw itself as a reaction to and an effort to move beyond that of its predecessors, namely the philosophy of Classical Greece and Medieval Christianity, in particular the work of Aristotle, Plato, and Aquinas. What the latter shared was a series of commitments that will be referred to here under the heading 'the function of man' argument, and Enlightenment thought is best illustrated in juxtaposition with this approach.

Aristotle's 'function of man' argument

Although 'the function' in question was conceptualized in different ways, as different accounts were given of the *telos* of human life, that is, the ultimate good or purpose or end of human life, nonetheless, throughout this lengthy period of Western culture it was not unusual to claim that political deliberation and debate had one point or purpose: the pursuit and attainment of man's *telos*.

As MacIntyre explains in *After Virtue*, the 'moral scheme' preceding the Enlightenment was characterized by a 'teleological' approach to morality. It consisted in an account of human nature as well as the purpose (*telos*) that humans can attain, and it conceptualized ethics as the means by which one can transform human nature so as to attain the purpose or end of human life. Ethical deliberation involved considerations of how human nature in its 'untutored' state is to be transformed so as to attain this goal. Ethical deliberation also involved a logical structure that required one to argue from what 'is' the case to what 'ought' to be, from premises about one's situation as well as human nature to conclusions about what actions are right and what character traits are good given our human nature and given our *telos* as humans:

> Within that teleological scheme there is a fundamental contrast between man-as-he-happens-to-be and man-as-he-could-be-if-he-realised-his-essential-nature. Ethics is the science which is to enable men to understand how they make the transition from the former state to the latter. (MacIntyre, 1985: 52)

Political reasoning, therefore, was only possible with the following four components: a metaphysics of the nature of man, a teleological account of man's ultimate good or purpose, ethical premises and conclusions concerning what is right and good, and a form of logic in practical reasoning where moral conclusions may be inferred in part at least from non-moral premises.

What then was the content of morality and the nature of moral deliberation in the political sphere, according to 'the function of man' argument? Virtue was of utmost importance, with respect to both what was considered morally valuable but also moral deliberation itself. Firstly, then, virtue was morally valuable. To deliberate well we must 'put in order' our desires on the basis of ethical precepts discovered through reason, and also by forming habits of thought and action that are prescribed by 'the study of ethics': 'reason instructs us both as to what our true end is and as to how to reach it' (MacIntyre, 1985: 53). So reason was to discover the character traits that should be fostered if one was to live a good life: those character traits have included the virtues of justice, practical wisdom, courage, moderation, and many others in Athenian thought, and also faith, hope, and charity in later Christian thought. For instance, for the virtue of moderation, desires and emotions are 'put in order' when the virtuous person does not desire too much or too little but instead desires what reason has taught should be desired and when it should be desired. Note that moderation is rightly thought a virtue in part because of views concerning human nature, in particular concerning the benefits of controlling our desires, the difficulty of doing so, and the possibility of developing habitual responses to what is desired. Therefore, the moral conclusion that moderation is a virtue is inferred in part at least from many non-moral premises about human desire and motivation and habit.

The virtue that should be the most conspicuous in political debate, indeed the virtue that must be present always, is practical wisdom (*phronesis* in Greek, *prudentia* in Latin). It is a valuable character trait and therefore a virtue we should foster, but also, it needs to be present and active whenever we deliberate about what is right and good. In the case of practical wisdom, the desires are 'put in order' so as to ensure that we wish for the ultimate human good (*telos*) and that it is the first premise of our practical deliberation. So the virtuous person reasons correctly about practical issues because he or she has the virtuous habit of deliberating in this way. The virtuous person accepts as a first premise that such and such is the human *telos* (for instance, Aristotle's life of civic and political virtue, or Plato's life of philosophical wisdom, or Aquinas's beatific vision, and so on), and so always begins deliberations from this *telos*. However, it follows that the virtuous person also accepts the whole teleological scheme of ethics with its account of human nature and the human *telos*, and also the logical structure that allows moral conclusions to be inferred in part at least from non-moral premises.

The 'function of man' argument can best be illustrated through a brief overview of Aristotle's ethics and politics. In *The Nicomachean Ethics*, Aristotle begins with the question: what is the human good, what is the purpose (*telos*) of man? It is important to note he assumes not only that there is such an ultimate good, although it may be composed of a plurality of goods, but also that moral deliberation requires such a *telos*.

Aristotle conceptualizes the human good as an 'end'. There are as many ends as there are actions, arts, and sciences, he contends, but each is rightly desired for the sake of a final end:

> If, then, there is some end of the things we do, which we desire for its own sake (everything else being desired for the sake of this), and if we do not choose everything for the sake of something else (for at that rate the process would go on to infinity, so that our desire would be empty and vain), clearly this must be the good and the chief good (EN, I. 2, 1094ᵃ 19ff).[2]

The 'human good' is that for the sake of which other goods are desired. There is a good appropriate to each activity, and Aristotle is here engaged in 'political science' (what we would call political philosophy) (I. 2, 1094ᵇ 3–4). It is not simply an empirical science, for its end is 'the good for man' (ibid.). But political philosophy must address itself to the right audience, those who are to engage in political action, and the right audience is not necessarily a particular social class or race or gender (although there are good reasons to think Aristotle believed this to be the case as well) but rather it is simply people who have the appropriate habitual responses, that is, virtues. In Aristotle's terms, the student of political philosophy is an 'educated man'. He is not just an expert, a good judge of some one subject (economics or rhetoric, for instance). Rather, '...the man who has received an all-round education is a good judge in general' (I. 3, 1095ᵃ 1). The 'educated man' is also said to be 'experienced' in the sense that he exercises virtues: 'things in virtue of which we stand well...with reference to the passions' (II, 5. 1105ᵇ 24). While knowledge of the human good is of no use to the 'immature', those who pursue 'each successive object, as passion directs', in contrast, '...to those who desire and act in accordance with a rational principle knowledge about such matters will be of great benefit' (I. 3, 1095ᵃ 7–10).

The mature person, the person who has received an all-round education, is the ideal citizen in Aristotle's scheme. Such a person is not carried away by passion, desire, or self-interest. When the good citizen engages in politics, it is as a 'good judge in general'. In effect, however, what this means is the good citizen accepts that the goods in life are hierarchically ordered. Some things are desirable only as means to some other end, and all goods are valuable as a means to the final end. Honour, wealth, wisdom, and pleasure are desirable as ends, Aristotle believes, but also as a means to *eudaimonia* (happiness or flourishing), which alone is desirable for its own sake, and never as a means to anything else. For that reason, it is an end of action that is 'final without qualification' (I. 7, 1097 a 32). The function of a human being, *eudaimonia*, is 'an active life of the element that has a rational principle' (I. 7, 1098ª 2). It is within 'the soul' we have a rational principle, and the active life of the soul is the exercise of virtue. 'Human good turns out to be the activity of the soul exhibiting excellence, and if there are more than one excellence, in accordance with the best and most complete' (1098ª 15).

So the good citizen is the person mature enough to realize both that there are many goods worth pursuing but also they are pursued for the sake of one overriding good. This is reflected in the good citizen exercising the virtue of practical wisdom (*phronesis*). Practical wisdom is not the same as 'mere smartness'. The latter is akin to the reasoning of a modern-day self-interested utility maximizer, for it is the ability 'to do the things that tend towards the mark we have set before ourselves, and hit it' (VI. 2, 1144ª 3), regardless of what the 'mark' or objective is. It is virtue alone that ensures the objective is good. Therefore, it is by exercising practical wisdom that we deliberate well about ethical questions, and it is through practical wisdom that we engage in political deliberation and debate. When we think about the proper objectives of a political community, or the means we should use to attain them, although we are moved to pursue pleasure, wealth, and honour, we also rightly believe that such things are valuable only if they are pursued for the sake of a life of virtue, and indeed they will be dangerous if pursued for other reasons. The good citizen has these ethical objectives to the forefront when deliberating and debating. In other words, if citizens justified themselves merely by pointing to how their proposal or plan will make people happier or more wealthy, then such considerations would be rejected not only as morally vacuous and even morally deplorable but also as irrational. To think morally and rationally just means starting from the commitment to the human good.

How is this virtue of practical wisdom to be exercised? Aristotle makes a distinction between two types of practical reasoning: 'excellence in deliberation in the unqualified sense... which succeeds with reference to what is the end in the unqualified sense' and 'excellence in deliberation in a particular sense... which succeeds relatively to a particular end' (EN, VI. 9, 1142ᵇ 29ff). Exercising the virtue of practical wisdom may well lead to success as a participant in some one activity or in pursuit of some one good (say the good of a sport or of an occupation). However, practical wisdom must contribute to what is an end in the unqualified sense, namely, human flourishing. As Philippa Foot has noted, virtues are related 'only to good ends' and 'to human life in general', rather than to the ends of particular activities (1978: 5). And so it follows that excelling as an artist, for instance, is no guarantee that one will lead a good life. Perhaps unkindly, but not unfairly, Gauguin's decision to leave his family for the sake of his art is often taken as the perfect illustration of this point (see MacIntyre, 1985: 201).

The practical wisdom needed for political engagement is directed always by what is the good or end of the activity, but there can be many activities and therefore many different goods. Aristotle is enough of a pluralist to recognize this and therefore acknowledges the diverse purposes that we strive to serve and the many ends or goods we pursue. Nonetheless, this plurality is held together by the one single end of life that we as humans have as our function or *telos*, namely the life of virtue. This then shapes the type of considerations that are appropriate in political deliberation and debate. In engaging with others, and offering reasons for our claims or arguments, it is necessary to show how the reasons offered are derived from or entail the good or end that we as participants in this activity are pursuing. Something counts as a reason in this teleological scheme insofar as it is derived from or entails the end or good of the activity or pursuit. In political engagement, the 'end' is a political community shaped by the civic and political virtues of its citizens, which include practical wisdom, justice, moderation, courage, magnanimity, and liberality. Our arguments can be considered relevant only if they are based on reasons that a virtuous person would give, which is to say they reflect commitment to the good(s) of our political community.

Aristotle is aware that, in reality, political communities take various forms, each with their own, appropriate, set of aims and goods. In *Politics*, he notes that the aims of a democracy differ from the aims of an aristocracy or an oligarchy. The best practicable model of political society may well be a mixture of each of these (the 'polity'), although Aristotle's preference is for an aristocracy of virtue. It is therefore the case that political morality will be to some extent 'relative' to the type of political community in question: morality requires different things of citizens in a democracy than it does in an aristocracy. Nonetheless, whatever the particular system, political reasoning is teleological. When we give reasons to others we do so from within a teleological scheme where there is an end or good being pursued in the activity and it is only in light of this end or good that we can distinguish what is right and good.

The Enlightenment of David Hume

For the 'function of man' argument, as we have seen, the reasons we use in political deliberation are part of a teleological framework. Some consideration can properly count as a reason, it is rationally compelling, to the extent that it plays a part in a chain of reasoning that incorporates premises about human nature, the *telos* of man, and the moral virtues and rules of action required to get from the former to the latter. Although in many respects the Enlightenment approach to political reasoning is diverse, and such variety is only to be expected, nonetheless it is possible to discern a set of shared characteristics, which comes in part at least from a rejection of the teleological approach to political reasoning. We will focus here on the work of David Hume, but the same purpose would have been served with a discussion of Kant or Bentham or Rousseau, among others. What they have done is call into question each of the various components of 'the function of man' argument: they have questioned theses about human nature, they have thrown into doubt the very notion of a human *telos*, traditional accounts of moral virtue and rules of right action have been reconceptualized and/or revised, and finally the logic of arguments that infer moral conclusions in part at least from non-moral premises has been put under scrutiny.

One dimension of what we have been calling the Enlightenment approach is scepticism, and Hume's scepticism can be seen from his preoccupation with the precise limits of rational certainty and rational analysis, or 'human understanding' (Hume, T introduction: 41).[3] Hume criticized philosophers he believed to have 'drawn disgrace upon philosophy itself':

> Principles taken upon trust, consequences lamely deduced from them, want of coherence in the parts, and of evidence in the whole, these are everywhere to be met with in the systems of the most eminent philosophers, and seem to have drawn disgrace upon philosophy itself. (T introduction: 41)

In contrast, 'experience and observation' will be the foundation for Hume's new 'science of man' (T Introduction: 43). In rejecting 'principles taken upon trust' as a basis for rational analysis, he has his sights set partly on Scholastic philosophers such as St Thomas Aquinas, who are worthy of criticism, Hume believes, for taking some premises as self-evident or unquestionable truths because of their source in Christian thought, in particular the premise that all humans have one and the same *telos* or purpose (T 2.2.7: 349). In rejecting medieval Scholasticism, Hume is also rejecting the work of Aristotle, or at any rate the way in which Aristotle was accepted as the one authority among pre-Christian thinkers. The importance of Aristotle for Aquinas, but more importantly the importance of authority for medieval thought, can be seen in Aquinas referring to Aristotle simply as 'the Philosopher'. Such a rejection of authority on Hume's part reflects his commitment to the need for, and possibility of, rational justification of all validity claims, namely, scepticism.

Hume's scepticism is evident again in his understanding of the precise role played by reason in morality. For 'the function of man' argument, not only was reason to discover the one true purpose of human life, our *telos*, the correct course that needed to be taken to pursue that end, namely a life of virtue, involved the subjection of the emotions to the ruling hand of reason. For Hume, in contrast, 'Reason is, and ought only to be the slave of the passions' (T 2.3.3: 462). This claim is based on the following two lines of thought. First, Hume argues that although morality is to be a guide to action, reason can never be a motive to any action of the will. Rather, due to the prospect of experiencing pleasure or pain from an object, we feel passion, either aversion or propensity, and as a result of the passion we are carried to avoid or embrace the object. We are not moved by reason as such. Reason merely discovers the best ways to attain the ends given to us by our passions: it 'comprehends whatever objects are connected with its original one by the relation of cause and effect' (T 3.1.1: 511). Second, reason is incapable of preventing volition. We are moved originally by passion rather than by reason, and nothing 'can retard the impulse of passion, but a contrary passion' (T 2.3.3: 462). If reason has no original influence, "tis impossible it can withstand any principle, which has such an efficacy, or even keep the mind in suspense a moment' (T 2.3.3: 462).

Morality is to be a guide to action. However, if reason is, and ought only to be the slave of the passions, then and as a consequence morality is not based on reason. As Hume puts it, morality does not consist in relations of ideas (i.e. a priori propositions of logic and pure mathematics) and nor does it consist in any objective matter of fact discovered by observation of the world around us (i.e. empirical experience of good or bad 'things'). On the one hand, this a sceptical position for it makes explicit the limits of our rational powers: reason alone cannot provide the foundations for morality. There is a second way in which this a sceptical position, for Hume is rejecting the traditional method of moral reasoning associated with 'the function of man' argument.

Hume's conclusion here has subsequently come to be discussed as the 'is-ought gap' (Hudson, 1983: 249ff). This is a gap of logic, as it concerns the logical distinction between different types of statements: synthetic statements of fact and analytic statements of logic and mathematics on the one hand and moral evaluations on the other. As Hume states,

> In every system of morality, which I have hitherto met with, I have always remark'd, that the author proceeds for some time in the ordinary way of reasoning, and establishes the being of God, or makes observations concerning human affairs; when of a sudden I am surpriz'd to find, that instead of the usual copulations of propositions, *is*, and *is not*, I meet with no proposition that is not connected with an *ought*, or an *ought not*. The change is imperceptible; but necessary that it should be observ'd and explain'd; and at the same time that a reason should be given, for what seems altogether inconceivable, how this new relation can be a deduction from others, which are entirely different from it. But as authors do not commonly use this precaution, I shall presume to recommend it to the readers; and am persuaded, that this small attention wou'd subvert all the vulgar systems of morality, and let us see, that the distinction of vice and virtue is not founded merely on the relations of objects, nor is perceiv'd by reason. (T 3.1.1: 521)

The argument is that morality does not consist 'merely' in a matter of fact or in rational principles. Rather, it is a matter of sentiment, disapprobation and approbation, and it is an object of feeling, not an object of thought. Hume gives as an example the case of wilful murder. In observing the case you cannot

> find that matter of fact, or real existence, which you can call *vice* ... You never can find it, till you turn your reflection into your own breast, and find a sentiment of disapprobation, which arises in you, towards this action. Here is a matter of fact; but 'tis the object of feeling, not of reason. It lies in yourself, not in the object. (T 3.1.1: 521)

There are two different interpretations of the implications of Hume's account of what we now call the 'is-ought gap'. Some believe he is arguing that an 'ought' statement can never be inferred from premises that are statements of fact or reason, what 'is' the case. For instance, we cannot conclude that justice forbids theft of property by simply stating factual premises about human nature and factual premises about the situation under consideration. Those factual statements do not by themselves support the moral conclusion as there is nothing unjust in the facts themselves (whatever they may be). And so the 'vulgar' systems of morality are properly called vulgar for 'lamely' deducing moral conclusions from non-moral premises.

However, others believe that Hume does not reject absolutely the legitimacy of arguing from 'is' to 'ought'. Indeed, Hume's own account of moral deliberation seems to involve making some such link. As we saw above, Hume observes sentiments of approval or disapproval; he believes that these are 'facts', although they are observed within oneself. We can also say that from these observations he infers moral judgements. For it seems to be his argument that something ought to be valued (i.e. it is good) because of the existence (i.e. the observation) of a passion. As we shall see presently Hume seems to suggest that the reason why 'justice' is a moral virtue at all is dependent upon the confluence of certain social and historical facts that, when they are observed and when we learn from them, we, as a result, develop the passions of a just person. Therefore, the more accurate understanding of Hume's argument would seem to be that, for Hume, the 'vulgar' systems of morality (including Aristotle's) have given a faulty account of moral deliberation as they have accepted premises 'on trust', premises about what 'is' the case, and 'lamely' deduced conclusions from them. Hume's position marks a radical departure for the reason that he will instead show, through observation and experiment, both what premises can be accepted and how to infer conclusions from them. What Hume does not do, therefore, is reject outright the approach to logic that allows moral conclusions to be inferred from statements that are non-moral.

In short, Hume has shown we cannot take 'on trust' the nature of human motivations and impulses, or that we have such a thing as a *telos*, and we cannot assume that moral deliberation simply involves inferring what is required in a specific situation given our *telos*. How then is moral deliberation to be understood? In particular, how do we make moral judgements in politics?

Hume begins with an analysis of why some character traits are virtues. According to Hume, a virtue is any quality which, if we detect it in others, tends to produce love for them, and the human capacity for 'sympathy' explains why this love is produced for what he refers to as 'natural' virtues (Hume, EPM[4] 2.1: 18; see Mackie, 1980: 120). Through human sympathy, we each have 'a lively idea' or impression of ourselves; and this communicates liveliness to any idea associated with it. Because we can see that, for instance, beneficence pleases and is useful to others, we feel 'love' for the beneficent person even when we ourselves are not benefited directly. Such natural virtues arise in us because of our human nature. In contrast, what Hume calls 'artificial' virtues, which include justice, allegiance, and promise-keeping, the virtues needed for the political sphere, cannot be explained simply by the operation of sympathy. The ideas of 'right' and 'obligation' and 'property' emerge only as the 'convention' of justice itself becomes established. Justice is a virtue because it is a quality which, if we detect it in others tends to produce love for them, but also the feeling of love in this instance is explained by the dual action of sympathy and self-interest. This is Hume's explanation for why justice is a virtue:

> It is only a general sense of common interest; which sense all the members of society express to one another, and which induces them to regulate their conduct by certain rules. I observe, that it will be for my interest to leave another in the possession of his goods, *provided* he will act in the same manner with regard to me. He is sensible of a like interest in the regulation of his conduct. When this common sense of interest is mutually express'd, and is known to both, it produces a suitable resolution and behaviour (T 3.2.2: 541).

Note that every single person is 'sensible' that the principle is in their interest. Note also the importance attached to the fact that 'all the members of the society express to one another' the general sense of common interest. Both of these points are characteristic of Hume's Enlightenment commitment to moral equality. The interests of each individual are relevant in determining that the principle is a moral principle. There is also the Enlightenment commitment to offering moral justifications for ourselves, our actions, and our proposals. Each person is said to 'express' this common interest, and it is 'known' to all. Therefore, moral principles in politics are those that we know to be in our self interest and which we explicitly express to each other in the collective effort of governing ourselves.

Convention is 'a general sense of common interest' and the convention of justice emerges only in so far as each person's self-interest ('love of gain'), operating indirectly, restrains the competitive expression of that self-interest (Hume T. 3.2.2: 544; see Mackie, 1980: 84; Hardin, 2007: 81 ff). When we come to see that justice is in each person's self-interest we are motivated by self-interest to restrain the operation of our self-interest, thereby establishing the convention of justice.

Nonetheless, Hume does not say that justice is a virtue simply because we each recognize being just as something that is in our self-interest. He accepts that in making such a moral judgement we adopt a distinctively 'moral' point of view, that is, a 'general' point of view. How can Hume explain our adopting this general point of view without relying, as Aristotle and others did, and Hume does not want to do, on some notion of the one true purpose of human life?

Justice is an artificial virtue, Hume is arguing, as the motivation and the reasons to be just arise only through 'experience' and 'education' (T 3.2.1: 535). What we experience is that many goods necessary for life are also scarce, and we also observe that although humans are generous this generosity is limited in its scope, usually extending to family and friends. Scarcity of goods and limited generosity are 'the circumstances of justice': they are the conditions of human existence that make justice necessary but also possible (see Rawls, 1971: 126). If humans were perfectly generous or if there was no scarcity of needed goods, there would be no need for rules of justice: the issue of the 'just' distribution of benefits and burdens simply would not arise, as abundance combined with the natural virtues of generosity and beneficence would suffice (T 3.2.2: 546). At the same time, both self-interest and sympathy combine to make justice *possible*, Hume believes. Once convention is established, we can see that justice serves the public interest, humans are moved by sympathy with others to act from the public interest, and humans can be motivated by the public interest when this is combined with their self-interest (T 3.2.2: 550–551). Also due to convention, in thinking justly we are thinking from 'some steady and general points of view', rather than each of us thinking from his or her own sentiments of pleasure and disgust, sentiments which tend to vary (T 3.3.1: 632). Nonetheless, moral virtues are rightly valued, and therefore rightly considered moral, for the reason that they are both pleasing and useful to ourselves and others, that is, because we have a propensity towards those who are virtuous. It is through experience and education that we come to adopt the artificial virtues and therefore come to love those who are just.

In summing up, justice is a virtue and moral approbation should attach to just motives. Crucially justice is a virtue *not* for the reason that it is the necessary means to attain 'the good life for man' (whether it is the good life of Plato, Aristotle, Aquinas, or any other 'authority'), but rather it is a virtue only insofar as it is pleasing and useful to others and to ourselves and also that that we can know this to be the case by observing our own passions. The content of political engagement for

Hume will have to reflect this reality. Political proposals can be morally justified only by showing that they are just, but this in turn means that they are or will be pleasing and useful, to ourselves and to others. It is no longer the case that in politics we must show how the pursuit of wealth and happiness will serve 'the' final or ultimate end, for principles can be shown to have moral force only in so far as they promote what is pleasing and useful.

Hume is attempting to derive morality from considerations that should be acceptable to anyone, as morality is to be based on nothing more than our own observations and experiences. However, is his position such that he cannot separate morality itself from what are mere interests and passions? It could be argued that Hume simply never clearly distinguishes between two ideas. On the one hand, he wants to show that our moral sentiment of justice arises from self-interest, as it is an automatic, unconscious attempt by each to keep all others in order, but on the other hand, he wants to show that our moral sentiments stem from our tendency to take, as a result of sympathy, a distinctively moral point of view, the point of view of the 'impartial spectator' (Mackie, 1980: 85; see Norton, 1993: 175). For one line of criticism, Hume has smuggled a moral point of view into his scheme without ever giving a justification for its inclusion. Hume accepts that moral judgements are made from a general point of view, but by what means can such a general point of view be brought about except on the basis of principles and premises known to be true independently of our pleasures and interests? For this critique, the suspicion is that, whereas 'the function of man' argument relied on unquestioned assumptions about man's *telos*, Hume is relying on unquestioned or unjustified assumptions about the content of morality.

Another apparent problem in Hume's work is that he does not call into question prevailing views of his day concerning the content of justice, views which restricted its scope considerably. John Mackie wonders whether the rules of property are as obvious and as uniform, or so inflexible, as Hume thought. Hume himself acknowledged that, in a 'besieged city' rules of justice can rightly be suspended, allowing for the commandeering of property, rationing, and the public purchase of property. Mackie's observation is that, despite Hume's apparent blindness to this possibility, 'it may turn out that even in normal times our relation to some resources is rather like that in the besieged city' (1980: 94). If this is a failing in Hume's thought, perhaps it is best seen as his failure to carry to their logical conclusion the commitments of the Enlightenment that have provided the foundations of his work. It is the failure to be sufficiently sceptical when faced with social mores and shared common-sense assumptions, and it is the failure to accept the implications of a commitment to moral equality when such commitments would disrupt the privilege and advantage enjoyed by the few at the expense of the many. If that is the case, then the solution to these failings on Hume's part perhaps can be found within the Enlightenment itself, in a more thorough application of Enlightenment commitments than we had seen hitherto.

However, an alternative view is that this failing on Hume's part in fact reflects a deeper problem within the Enlightenment approach itself. Were Enlightenment thinkers too quick to assume that they had found the proper basis for certainty and validity, in this case moral certainty? Is there at the heart of the Enlightenment project a naivety, or hubris, about the difficulties in making moral judgements? Or indeed are there ideological commitments and prejudices that are to blame for such hasty moral judgements, ideological commitments that are inseparable from the Enlightenment itself?

If Hume was too quick to accept and condone a system of social stratification that greatly disadvantaged the vast majority of his fellow humans, his moral equals, perhaps other Enlightenment thinkers were too quick to reject the whole of modern society as inherently corrupt and therefore rightly deserving to be destroyed through violent revolution. The latter can be sensed in Hume's one-time friend Rousseau, or at least in those whom he inspired.

The thought of Rousseau could motivate and give some justification to the excesses of the French Revolution, the 'Terror', and it is equally plausible to see the French Revolution and Robespierre's Committee of Public Safety as Enlightenment projects. Rousseau's political philosophy required that, because we are moral equals and because the moral law applies equally to all, in politics we must act on the basis of the 'general will' alone, the will that comes from all and is applied to all. Indeed, we can only be truly free by acting in accordance with not our passions and self-interests but rather this moral law. But Rousseau assumed the moral law to be in principle knowable; he assumed also that the general will was infallible. As a result, he concluded that any one individual could be legitimately forced to follow the general will but in doing so he or she was being 'forced to be free' (Rousseau, 1762: Book I, Ch. 7). We can be truly free only if we accept and act from within the moral point of view, but also the individual may be forced to be free when he or she would otherwise have pursued their own interests and pleasures. In particular for conservative commentators such as Edmund Burke, the French Revolution represented an attempt to regenerate the whole human race on the basis of rational principles, thereby rejecting all existing traditional beliefs and practices, but to do so required force. People were to be forced to be free in the sense of forced to be 'virtuous'. Robespierre wrote that if 'the basis of government in the time of peace is virtue, the basis of popular government in the time of revolution is virtue and terror: virtue without which terror is murderous, terror without which virtue is powerless' (Burke, 1790, in Nisbet, 1967: 34, 42). Thus, during the Terror, the Committee of Public Safety could insist that those who were not thinking and acting from morally pure motives in the public sphere could and should be coerced. The political implications of Rousseau's Enlightenment thought are diametrically opposed to those of the politically conservative Hume. Nonetheless, perhaps they both arise from the too hasty assumption that moral certainty has been attained thanks to the twin commitments of scepticism and moral equality.

Political philosophy after the Enlightenment

The revolutionary nature of Hume's work is obscured if in focusing on his political conservatism we lose sight of just how much it calls into question the moral and political thought of the Western tradition. Indeed, it can be said that morality was turned on its head by the work of Hume and others in what we are referring to here as the Enlightenment critique of 'the function of man' argument. And this was a revolution in moral thinking just as radical as the Copernican revolution in astronomy (see Kuhn, 1957). Before the Copernican revolution, the prevailing outlook was that the earth was at the centre of the universe, and the planets, the sun, and the stars revolved around the earth. Similarly, before the Enlightenment, man's *telos* was at the centre of morality, and moral argumentation could and had to revolve around it. Before the Enlightenment, man's pleasures and interests were subordinated to man's *telos* in the sense that the moral significance of pleasures and interests were determined by their place within a system of value that had the human *telos* at its centre. With the advent of the Enlightenment, however, suddenly it becomes possible for Hume to contend that a character trait is morally praiseworthy only insofar as it is pleasing and useful to ourselves and to others, and, what is more, we can know this to be the case simply by observing our own passions. What we take to be pleasing and useful now moves to the centre of our moral universe.

The defining characteristics of Enlightenment political thought as discussed above include commitments to scepticism and moral equality. Such commitments can be seen in Hume's insistence that no one fundamental end of human life should be taken on trust, and also that justice is a virtue to the extent that it is pleasing and useful to ourselves and others, that is, to the extent it is based on convention, a general sense of common interest. In justifying ourselves to others in political debate we offer reasons to our equals and reasons that are not to be taken on trust but instead based on our observations and experiences. Enlightenment thinkers developed scepticism and moral equality in various ways, which unfortunately cannot be explored here in the depth called for. Rousseau's insistence that political morals must be based on a social contract which in turn reflects the general interest, Kant's accounts of the moral imperative to always treat humanity as an end in a kingdom of ends (Kant, 1785), and utilitarian arguments that acts are right in proportion as they tend to promote happiness and that the happiness of each is to be given equal consideration (Mill, 1861), each in their own way reinforce, but also reinterpret and take in new directions, the twin commitments of scepticism and moral equality. There was or is something called 'Enlightenment political thought', therefore, even though there was much disagreement on how best to treat others as moral equals or how best to rationally justify the moral claims we make. Furthermore, when anti-Enlightenment thought emerges it is characterized by hostility to the core commitments of the Enlightenment that we have listed, rather than specifically a rejection of the thought of Hume or Kant or Bentham or Rousseau, or any one individual thinker. While the Enlightenment included a diversity of approaches, its opponents were in agreement in reacting against these two central commitments.

A number of developments in Western philosophy at the end of the nineteenth century and the beginning of the twentieth century made possible what now can be seen as an outright rejection of Enlightenment thought. They include the work of Nietzsche, Wittgenstein, and Heidegger, and they reflect the serious challenges faced by any consistent application of the commitments to moral equality and scepticism. Whether or not it is thought that these challenges provided a fatal blow to the Enlightenment, or instead that the Enlightenment can effectively respond to them, defines the two opposing strands of contemporary political philosophy that will be addressed in this book.

Nietzsche's genealogy of morals is a history of morality unlike any other. It is a history of the hidden sources of our moral commitments, and Nietzsche concluded that the distinctions we make between 'truth' and 'falsity' and between 'good' and 'bad' are nothing more than our own constructions and reflect nothing more than our 'will to power' (1888: 65). This is the case for Judaeo–Christian morality as well as its secular successors, liberalism, democracy, humanism, and so on. Of course this is not how truth and morality are conceptualized from *within* these moral systems. For our purposes, however, the crux of Nietzsche's point is that Enlightenment thinkers are no different from 'the function of man' philosophers of Medieval Christianity. As morality and truth have these 'lowly' beginnings (Foucault, 1971), Enlightenment philosophers were guilty of the shortcomings they themselves ascribed to the Schoolmen of the Middle Ages. That is, to use Hume's own terms, Enlightenment thinkers were guilty of taking principles on trust and lamely deducing conclusions from them. 'Observation' or 'reason' came to be seen as unquestioned sources of authority for the Enlightenment, in much the same way as 'God's law' or 'human nature' were for 'the function of man' philosophers.

Nietzsche's own account of good and bad, that is, what he took to be the content of morality, explicitly rejected the moral commitments of the Enlightenment, along with the whole Judaeo–Christian tradition. If the will to power is behind all that we think and do, what should the content of morality be? It should be a morality of vitality and strength that will approve of all that is cold, harsh, and pitiless, and it should approve of these hard character traits as that which furthers our will to power; and it should be a morality that condemns pity and compassion as that which enervates and sickens, that which prolongs the misery of the wretched and saps the vitality of the strong (1887: §269). What is good is that which strives to dominate and survive, that which has vitality and life. The will to power also extends to our deliberations and discussions. When we justify ourselves we do nothing more than dominate others. The act of justifying is just one more exercise of our will to power, a violent attack, for the conclusion that is justified is nothing more than the conclusion that has power on its side. It is for that reason power and knowledge are always joined together in the one 'nexus': 'all knowledge rests upon injustice', 'the instinct for knowledge is malicious', and knowledge 'creates a progressive enslavement to its instinctive violence' (Foucault, 1971: 95–96).

The influence of Nietzsche can be seen in various schools of thought: deconstruction, post-Marxism, post-structuralism, Foucault's genealogy, and post-modernism. According to each, as Nietzsche would have agreed, morality is what we make it through our struggles and conflicts, but also we are dominated just as much by the well-meaning liberal universalist as we are by the malevolent tyrant: they both strive to impose their truth and morality upon us (see Foucault, 1971, Mouffe, 2000). Each of his followers, however, must face up to what appear to be serious contradictions in Nietzsche's thought. For if Nietzsche (and his followers) is making a statement about the world that is to be accepted as true or justified, is this itself nothing more than one more violent act? If the answer is yes, then why is it any different from what he is rejecting; why should we accept it as a genuine insight into, and illumination of, the world? If the answer is no, Nietzsche's statements are not simply one more series of violent attacks, then there seems to be a self-contradiction: this is a statement that all statements are nothing more than violent acts which is not itself just one more violent act.

Two other sources of anti-Enlightenment thought can be mentioned here as well: Wittgenstein's later linguistic philosophy and Heidegger's phenomenology. In Wittgenstein's later work, the notion of 'language games' plays a central role in his attempt to show both that there is no universal system of rationality and also that being rational is a matter of knowing the different rules suited to their own 'language game' (1953: §54). To reason well is to know how to play the rules of the game, Wittgenstein concludes, and this is the case whether the 'game' is chess or whether it is instead politics. If 'anyone utters a sentence and *means* or *understands* it he is operating a calculus according to definite rules', Wittgenstein argues (ibid. §81). There may well be some similarity between the games we play (what Wittgenstein refers to as a 'family resemblance') and therefore some overlap between the rules we should use in different games, but when we reason, including when we reason about politics, we do so not on a universal basis but on the basis of a game, or on the basis of many inter-related games (1953: § 66, 67). Thus it may seem that all reasoning, including political reasoning, is relativistic: something is correctly said to be rational only 'relative to' the game we are playing and its rules. It is and can never be rational-as-such, or rational universally, as there is no 'as such' or universal when it comes to reason. The attractiveness of Wittgenstein's work can be explained by observing that, so far in human history, it has not been possible to find one system of moral principles accepted by all as valid, despite the attempts of religious zealots, socialists, liberals, democrats, and many others to do just that. However, one can accept this observation without agreeing with Wittgenstein that reason is relative in the sense he claims. Indeed, Hume himself shows how in the political sphere moral considerations emerge from specific historical and social circumstances, namely with the establishment of convention, and yet he does not also embrace relativism more generally.

Heidegger's work also involves a similar rejection of universalism, and move towards relativism. Heidegger began as a follower of the phenomenological method of Husserl. For Husserl, whereas natural science takes for granted the possibility of cognition, philosophy, through phenomenological orientation, puts in question the possibility of cognition. Philosophical thinking involves 'bracketing' the empirical and metaphysical presuppositions of science's 'natural attitude', which is done through a process of 'phenomenal reduction', a return to transcendental immediacy (Husserl, 1907: 13–15). Heidegger's philosophy arises from doubts about the possibility, and desirability, of such phenomenological abstraction or reduction. Instead, it is argued that, due to the finite and historical state of our human condition, our being-in-the-world, there is no presupposition-less perspective. Heidegger insists that the human condition is one of 'becoming' and 'thrownness', a moving towards and a proceeding from (1927: 135ff). For instance, a Catholic speaks from within a tradition of thought and a history of values and practices, and also it is just this richness of the historical horizon that makes understanding and insight possible now and in the future. If we are always starting from a perspective or horizon it is folly to try to get beyond, to 'reduce', all such partial and limited perspectives.

Current political philosophy can be understood only against this backdrop of efforts to undermine, or move beyond, the Enlightenment, to carry out philosophy in an anti-Enlightenment mode. This anti-Enlightenment approach to political reason can be seen in MacIntyre's historicism. Historicists claim that all rational enquiry is constituted by traditions, that traditions are incommensurable, but also nonetheless that it is possible to reach rationally justified moral conclusions that are both objective and impartial. What is being referred to here as 'historicism' is derived in large part from the work of MacIntyre but also from Gadamer's hermeneutics. Both are attempting to combine a largely Aristotelian approach to practical reasoning with the historicist thesis that all such reasoning is historically constituted. What this means, therefore, is that this reaction to Enlightenment thought in many ways is a reversion to 'the function of man' argument. The history of political thought, in this instance as in many others, does not travel in a straight line.

The post-modern approach to political reasoning mirrors that of historicism to a significant extent. Post-modernists draw on Wittgenstein's claim that to have agreement in opinions there must first be agreement in language used which in turn implies agreement in 'forms of life' or 'language games'. There is no 'view from nowhere', or Archimedean point, or universal language of rationality. What is more, historicists accept much of the post-modern Nietzschean ('genealogical') analysis and deconstruction of contemporary morality. However, while MacIntyre has praised Nietzsche's analysis of the 'lowly' origins of modern moral utterances, for Mouffe and other committed post-modernists, morality and politics is and will always be and should be 'lowly', or in Mouffe's terms 'agonistic' (2000: 80ff). Even democratic interaction is always violent and exclusive (Mouffe, 2000: 48). It is agonistic, or competitive, rather than rational and consensual. Of course it also follows that post-modern philosophy and post-modern politics can be no different from what they describe, although perhaps it is different by being conscious of its own violent and exclusionary nature.

In contrast, theories of reasonableness, or public reasoning, draw heavily and explicitly on the Enlightenment heritage. Just as the Enlightenment required scepticism, theories of reasonableness require that citizens offer each other justifications for the proposals made in political debate. Just as the Enlightenment entailed commitment to moral equality, theories of reasonableness require that the reasons given to others are reasons it is reasonable to expect others to accept. In Rawls's work, democratic debate is based on or restrained by moral requirements. We should view one another as free and equal and offer each other fair terms of social cooperation. There is the further requirement that we bracket the truth or falsity of comprehensive moral doctrines. So even if, for instance, proposals for support for the needy are inferred from basic Catholic premises, in democratic debate it would be unreasonable to support these proposals with nothing more than Catholic theology, proceeding as if Catholic theology provided every citizen the moral framework needed to reach moral conclusions. Catholics must at some stage in democratic debate present their proposals supported by considerations that have a reason-giving quality for their non-Catholic fellow-citizens.

What is it that provides the required reason-giving quality, according to this approach? A consideration is *prima facie* compelling if it entails or implies acknowledgement of the moral equality of others. To put the same point another way, a consideration cannot be compelling for participants in a democratic debate if it is antithetical to the moral equality of fellow citizens. Considerations that would have no place in democratic debate include proposals for racist segregation, sexist restrictions on opportunities and rights, and denial of civil liberties to religious or linguistic or cultural minorities. However, it is not clear whether other proposals would also be unreasonable, including those concerning market freedom and economic inequality, immigration controls, aid and trade deals with developing countries, children's rights, abortion rights, and animal rights. Indeed, while reasonableness provides a moral basis for democratic participation, it leaves undetermined the resolution to the disputes that characterize contemporary democratic debate. For its detractors, the theory of reasonableness is either incapable of supplying genuine guidance in democratic debate or else it will tend to privilege considerations and arguments more in tune with liberal individualistic commitments obviously shared by authors such as Rawls and Mill (see Dryzek and Niemeyer, 2006; McCabe, 2000; Hare, 1973). However, what its supporters say in its defence is that the theory of reasonableness creates a space for dialogue that can lead to morally justified decisions but that it is not intended as a decision-making procedure for the inference of the one correct answer to a social problem. The reasonable conclusion is what could not reasonably be rejected by all those committed to seeking out a solution that can be justified with reasons others should be willing to accept (Freeman, 2000: 410; Scanlon, 2002). There are many possible reasonable responses to political disputes and it is up to reasonable citizens themselves to find their own solutions.

Book structure

In the next two chapters (Chapters 2 and 3) we begin our look at anti-Enlightenment thought with an exploration of Alasdair MacIntyre's political philosophy. In Chapter 2, we look at the argument that political reason is practice-based and, in turn, community-based and tradition-based. MacIntyre's specific political commitments and proposals are discussed along with what he has to say on critical rational enquiry. His is a politics of the margins, a politics of the local community where a moral consensus on the hierarchical ordering of goods is possible. One question is whether this would be a conservative, insular politics hostile to pluralism and individual freedom. A further question concerns a drift towards moral relativism, where standards of morality are relative to traditions, and also an abject view of reasoning, where at some point the giving of reasons come to a halt and instead we insist on a superior (because virtuous) perception of particulars. The argument of the chapter is that, to avoid incoherence, MacIntyre must make a choice. He could choose to accept that we can arrive at standards of rationality that are independent of any specific traditions, and therefore standards that can be used in a critical rather than an insular fashion, but this would entail rejecting historicism. The only alternative is to retain historicism but accept that he cannot avoid the charges of relativism, abjectness, and conservatism.

In Chapter 3 we look at the Catholic, Thomist influence on MacIntyre's thought. Our interest here is both in the way his religious belief shapes the content of his political theory, including his defence of a demanding ethic of just generosity, but also the role to be played by religious belief in political reason itself. The argument of this chapter is that MacIntyre's mix of Aristotelian and Thomist philosophy is not sufficient to answer the questions posed of MacIntyre in Chapter 2: namely, that MacIntyre's is a conservative politics and that his historicism is undermined by relativism, an abject view of reasoning, and incoherence. Indeed, it will be argued that MacIntyre still defends a version of historicism; it is just that 'his' tradition now is that of a Thomist. For that reason, MacIntyre's political theory remains caught in a dilemma whereby he must either accept relativism, and refrain from making claims about how progress can be made, or else relinquish the commitment to historicism, and accept that rationality is not simply constituted by tradition.

Although Chantal Mouffe wishes to defend liberal democracy she also wants to reject the 'universal rationalism' of liberal theory. In Chapter 4 we see that, for Mouffe, there is no such universal rational framework waiting to be discovered or created. Instead, politics is a contextualist task as it is pursued within a 'form of life', and also it is based on considerations that are 'contestable' and 'undecidable'. Rather than consensus she calls for 'agonism'. It will be argued that Mouffe's account of agonism swings back and forth between relativism and perspectivism. Her claims can be rational only 'relative to' some context, a form of life. At the same time, however, she assumes the terms of social cooperation are contestable hegemonic constructions, and so all we have are different, complementary perspectives. As liberals have argued, moreover, it cannot avoid a performative contradiction. In stating the post-modernist case, the post-modernist must assume just its opposite.

Having found anti-Enlightenment thought to be unconvincing, in Chapter 5 Rawls's account of political reason is discussed. Having seen the Enlightenment commitments of moral equality and scepticism rejected by historicism and post-modernism, Rawls's work can be seen as a reformulation and defence of these commitments. This chapter provides a qualified defence of what will be referred to as Rawls's 'core conception of reasonableness'. Rawls is successful in his endeavour to describe political reasoning that does not rely on the justifiability of one comprehensive moral doctrine. His core conception of reasonableness is an attempt to represent the moral requirement to justify ourselves *in* political debate. However, in contrast to Rawls himself, this chapter concludes there are no sufficiently strong grounds to accept that perfectionist considerations, judgements of what is better or higher, are and must be unreasonable. There is no reason to assume that perfectionist ideas are not or can not be shared by citizens regarded as free and equal, or that perfectionist ideas must rely on the justifiability of a particular comprehensive moral doctrine. Indeed, consideration can legitimately be given to such perfectionist ideas in the debate over civic education, and the question of what values it may promote and how such a programme of civic education could be justified.

Chapters 6 and 7 provide practical applications of the arguments developed in the first five chapters of the book. First, we look at what values, if any, should be promoted in civic education and also how the promotion of values is to be non-coercive. Rawls believed civic education should promote the values of reasonableness, mutual respect, and fairness, but also that at some point public, political reasons should be used in any attempt to justify the content of civic education. However, we will also ask whether the content of civic education may legitimately be broader than this. Is it possible to offer public, political reasons to justify promoting the 'liberal' values of autonomy, integrity, and magnanimity, as well as the 'social' values of truthfulness and generosity? Although the question of *which* values to promote is important, it is often pursued at the expense of asking *who* we should address with these arguments. If civic education programmes are to live up to the requirements of a political approach, is it sufficient to address arguments only to adults, or instead must we also address young people and do so with reasons it is reasonable to expect them to accept?

The focus of Chapter 7 is our obligations to the distant poor. The question asked is, whether minimalism regarding the content of human rights ('substantive minimalism') is required by minimalism regarding the considerations that may rightly be offered to others ('justificatory minimalism', i.e. reasonableness). Rawls gave an affirmative answer to this question, that is, he believed that political reasons require that we adopt a minimalist approach to what the distant poor can claim from us as a right of justice. However, it is argued, the rationale of his own position on both justice and political reason calls that conclusion into question. So as to avoid the operation of a double standard in the engagement between 'liberal' and 'decent hierarchical' societies, it will be argued, it is not possible to conclude that the poverty of non-citizens is not a matter of distributive justice.

2
Reason and Tradition

Anti-Enlightenment political philosophy takes a number of different forms. The first of the challenges to Enlightenment thought to be discussed here is found in the work of various historicist thinkers, most notably Alasdair MacIntyre, but similar commitments are shared with those sometimes referred to as communitarians along with the broader philosophical approach known as hermeneutics. Historicism involves the following commitments concerning rationality and morality. The first contention is that rationality is neither universal nor neutral. It does not provide the one and the same standpoint at all times for all people. Its content, its methods of analysis, its standards of validity, and even its logical rules can and may righty alter. All rational enquiry, including political theory and moral theory, is infused with and constituted by the particularity of social contexts, including practices and activities, political communities, and traditions. However, according to MacIntyre, it does not follow that rationality is for that reason weakened or undermined. Although rational enquiry is 'context-bound' and 'tradition-constituted', it is from within such social contexts that we have access to standards of rational justification, and so it is *only* within such social contexts that we can deliberate and debate rationally at all.

Furthermore, to ever hope to rationally resolve political disputes, we must do so from within the moral consensus of a community or tradition. However, there are many different traditions of enquiry, and, MacIntyre also argues at some length that such traditions are incommensurable. There is no tradition-neutral, universal standpoint; there is no 'view from nowhere' from which to analyse each separate tradition; there is no universal set of rational standards with which to determine whether one tradition represents progress over its rivals. Instead, the only rational way to approach a rival tradition is to attempt to learn its language as a 'second first language', to adopt its perspective on the predicament faced by one's own tradition.

MacIntyre also contends that practical reason and moral goodness are inseparable. This is an insight we find in Aristotle as well, who argues that the practically wise person is able to deliberate well about what is conducive to the good life in general (NE, VI. 5, 1140^{a}25). To be a practically rational person one must be a morally good person. This is the case as the first premise in any practical chain of reasoning is an account of the ultimate good: 'since the good and the best is such and such,....' As a perfectionist, MacIntyre believes it is possible to distinguish what we *take* to be good from what *is* the good and the best unqualifiedly. And of course, such value judgements can be rationally justified only from within social contexts. In particular, genuinely rational political debate requires a moral consensus of a particular kind, a consensus on the overriding good and the hierarchical order of all goods within the community or tradition. And MacIntyre's Aristotelian Thomism is a tradition of enquiry that provides a consensus of a particular kind for just such a community, a consensus where the goods of Catholic moral teaching, namely the virtues of faith, hope, and charity, are at the apex of the hierarchy of all goods.

In drawing us back into an argument about virtues and goods, and in arguing that there must be a hierarchical ordering of goods and a moral consensus on this ordering, MacIntyre is re-articulating 'the function of man' argument, the argument of Aristotle and Aquinas, the argument that Hume rejected. MacIntyre's contention is that rejecting 'the function of man' argument was a mistake, but also that it can be retrieved now, if only on the margins of mainstream society. However, 'the function of man' approach to political reason is one which gives great importance to virtues in reasoning itself. Indeed, it is a sign of a virtuous character to be able to perceive what morality calls for in the particular situation, and it is only those with the virtues who have this perception. One possible criticism of such an approach is that it entails taking an 'abject view' of reasoning. That is, it involves or leads to a view whereby reasoning as such is called into question. This is the case as, when offering justifications for ourselves, at some point the giving of reasons comes to a halt; at some point, the virtuous person can no longer explain why a particular judgement is called for in a particular situation; it just is what morality calls for.

Are there any further reasons to be concerned with historicism? It has been argued quite forcefully that historicists cannot avoid relativism and/or a conservative politics. Relativists need not deny the importance and authority of moral considerations. However, a relativist could go on to argue that 'different people could, quite reasonably, attach this kind of importance to different forms of conduct' (Scanlon, 1995: 233). This follows from the fact that relativists assume that moral judgements can only ever be rational-relative-to some specified conditions or parameters, never rational-as-such. Relativism is problematic as it entails that, as each judgement is justified according to its own specific parameters, conflicting judgements may be equally justified. It is also problematic with respect to our interaction with strangers, those individuals who do not share 'our' parameters, as it does not provide us a way to justify our actions to strangers in terms that should be acceptable to those strangers.

According to his critics, MacIntyre's political theory is conservative as well. As he believes that critical rational enquiry is something 'we' undertake from within 'our' shared mode of practice (1999a: 157), MacIntyre does not ensure that political debate is in fact critical, that is, that it can call into question accepted beliefs and theories. As he assumes that there must be a moral consensus on the overriding good and the ordering of all goods, he is furthermore hostile to moral pluralism. Finally, as he believes one can have rights only as the member of a particular community and against the background of a particular tradition, he is hostile to the concept of universal human rights, and therefore does not accept that strangers have rights of justice against us.

This book is broadly in agreement with MacIntyre's argument that we should not exclude 'goods-talk' from political debate. Consideration of what is good for us as participants in a practice, as members of the same community, and as fellow humans, is an acceptable feature of critical rational enquiry in the public sphere, it will be argued. Nonetheless, it will also be argued that MacIntyre has not done enough to secure himself against the charges of abject rationality, relativism, and conservatism. Despite his best efforts to rebuff these charges, and for the very reason that he never completely leaves historicism behind, ultimately MacIntyre's position is compromised. Its approach to political debate is deeply problematic, and this is the case as it is guilty of either of the following. Either debate proceeds explicitly on the basis of a tradition that is incommensurable with its rivals, and therefore no rational progress can be made in such debate; or MacIntyre must abandon historicism and concede that, in fact, reason is *not* constituted by tradition.

The critique of a neutral and impartial philosophy

MacIntyre offers both a negative and a positive thesis in support of historicism. The *negative* thesis is his rejection of universalist moral and political theory, which he refers to as 'modern mainstream theory'. Its view of rationality, according to MacIntyre, insists on a 'neutral, impartial, and, in this way, universal point of view' (1988: 3). This so-called 'disinterestedness' in fact presupposes one conception of justice, he contends, 'liberal individualism' (ibid.). Moreover, this conception of ideal rationality 'ignores the inescapably historically and socially context-bound character which any substantive set of principles of rationality, theoretical or practical, is bound to have' (ibid. p. 4). Therefore, political theory cannot be based on a universal neutral rationality. First, such a conception of rationality in fact presupposes liberal morality, but also, second, all theories of rationality and justice arise from contexts: they are 'context-bound'.

This leads on to MacIntyre's *positive* thesis in support of historicism. We can and should turn away from 'mainstream academia', MacIntyre believes, and 'participate in the life of one of those groups whose thought and action are informed by some distinctive profession and settled conviction with regard to justice and practical rationality' (ibid. pp. 4–5).

MacIntyre wants to reconnect rationality with 'settled conviction'. He must reconnect rationality with traditions, he concludes, as principles of rationality are bound to such social and historical contexts. However, anticipating the objections such a proposal will attract, MacIntyre insists that tradition is not antithetical to reason. Rationality is constituted by tradition, but also, in turn, it constitutes tradition:

> Standards of rational justification emerge from and are part of a history in which they are vindicated by the way they transcend the limitations of and provide remedies for the defects of their predecessors within the history of that same tradition. (ibid. p. 7)

MacIntyre himself is engaged in the Aristotelian tradition, which, from the time of *Whose Justice? Which Rationality?* is developed in and through Thomism. It is also from within this tradition that MacIntyre's perfectionism is developed. In *After Virtue*, MacIntyre draws on what he calls 'the tradition of the virtues', from which he derives a 'core conception of the virtues'. In *Whose Justice? Which Rationality?* MacIntyre explains how a 'tradition in good order' provides a hierarchical ordering of goods (ibid. p. 337) as well as insisting that such traditions are incommensurable (ibid. p. 166). Therefore, 'the function of man' argument is being rearticulated within an historicist framework, as MacIntyre is arguing it is traditions alone that provide us with certainty about our *telos* or function.

The need for moral consensus

As a perfectionist, MacIntyre believes it is possible to distinguish what we *think* is good from what *is* good, and what is good *relative* to us here and now from the good and the best *unqualifiedly* (1988: 30). As an historicist, MacIntyre emphasizes that such perfectionist judgements are made possible by social contexts, they are context bound, and the first such context to be analysed is the practice.

In *After Virtue* MacIntyre defined a practice as follows:

> By a 'practice' I am going to mean any coherent and complex form of socially established cooperative activity through which goods internal to that form of activity are realized in the course of trying to achieve those standards of excellence which are appropriate to, and partially definitive of, that form of activity with the result that human powers to achieve excellence, and human conceptions of the ends and goods involved, are systematically extended. Tic-tac-toe is not an example of a practice in this sense, nor is throwing a football with skill; but the game of football is, and so is chess. (1985: 187)

MacIntyre is not just interested in practices as social phenomena. He also emphasizes the centrality of practices for moral judgement. A virtue is a morally admirable character trait, and, in the first instance, it is 'an acquired human quality the possession and exercise of which tends to enable us to achieve goods which are internal to practices....'; and moreover, we can attain these internal goods only by striving to attain the standards of excellence appropriate to the practice (ibid. p. 191). This is the case with justice, truthfulness, and courage, among other virtues. It is not just that virtues *do* enable us attain the internal goods of practices. To be a virtue, at this first level, a character trait *must* enable us to achieve the internal goods of practices.

However, MacIntyre is well aware that, in pursuing the goods of a practice, one may easily do what is morally wrong. He gives the example of Paul Gauguin, who, in pursuing the goods of artistic excellence (the goods internal to the practice of art), deserted his wife and children (and therefore neglected the goods of family life) (ibid. p. 201). For that reason, we need the capacity to reflect on and evaluate practices and their goods. Each individual must be able to evaluate the virtues, rules, and internal goods of his or her practice(s), and we can do so by exercising the virtues needed to write a life narrative. The intellectual virtue of wisdom (*phronesis* in Greek or *prudentia* in Latin) in particular is needed to determine how to combine the pursuit of different goods within different practices, or how to resolve tensions arising between the goods of different practices. Through writing the narrative of his or her actions, the agent also establishes the unity, or *telos*, of his or her life (ibid. p. 219). Crucially, MacIntyre also believes that it is in this way that a moral agent can give an intelligible account of his or her actions, and therefore can be held to account:

> To identify an occurrence as an action is ... to identify it under a type of description which enables us to see that occurrence as flowing intelligibly from a human agent's intentions, motives, passions and purposes. It is therefore to understand an action as something for which someone is accountable, about which it is always appropriate to ask the agent for an intelligible account. (ibid. p. 222)

However, just as the moral person must step back from and reflect on his or her practical pursuit of goods, such reflection is required as well in the writing of one's life narrative. This becomes possible because all such moral reasoning is, on MacIntyre's view, tradition-based. Both practices and life narratives are situated within traditions, and this is the case as 'all reasoning takes place within the context of some traditional mode of thought ... ' (ibid.). MacIntyre here praises 'the virtue of having an adequate sense of the traditions to which one belongs or which confront one', and also 'a grasp of those future possibilities which the past has made available to the present' (ibid. p. 223). However, he rejects what he calls the 'ideological', conservative, use of tradition, in particular associated with the Irish philosopher Edmund Burke (1790). We should not, MacIntyre insists, contrast 'tradition with reason and the stability of tradition with conflict' (ibid. p. 221). 'For all reasoning takes place within the context of some traditional mode of thought, *transcending through criticism and invention* the limitations of what had hitherto been reasoned in that tradition' (ibid. p. 222; emphasis added). So all enquiry is constituted by traditions, but reason (and conflict) is not incompatible with tradition. MacIntyre also goes on to argue that not only can we reason intelligibly about goods within such contexts, we can reason intelligibly about the hierarchical ordering of goods. In *Whose Justice? Which Rationality?* MacIntyre gives a detailed account of the hierarchy of goods, a hierarchy that ultimately reflects his own religious and philosophical journey from Aristotelianism to Aristotelian–Thomism.

Some changes can be seen in the material that appears in the later book. An apprentice in an 'activity' ('practice' in his earlier terminology) must learn to distinguish 'what is good relative to us here and now' from 'what is good or best unqualifiedly' (MacIntyre, 1988: 30). While some judgements of goodness are relative to a time and a place in an activity, we can also judge what is 'good as such'. Furthermore, riches, power, status, and prestige are merely 'external goods', and to achieve them one requires qualities of effectiveness alone (ibid. p. 32). However, external goods should be pursued for the sake of 'goods of excellence' ('internal goods' in his earlier terminology), and to do so requires the qualities needed 'to perform and to judge well' in regard to 'what is good or best unqualifiedly' (ibid. pp. 107–108, p. 30). That is, the instrumental goods of an activity are pursued not for their own sake, but for the sake of the goods of excellence of that activity. His meaning is that if we are to be true to the nature of such goods of excellence they must be seen as that for the sake of which external goods are pursued. At the same time, the good of an activity is distinguished from the good of the *polis* [the political community of classical Greece]. The *polis* provides 'an integrated form of life', a life in which each practice and its goods has its proper place (ibid. p. 90). To bring this about, in politics we take 'the good and the best' as our first premise, and we secure 'the overall good' of the community, not simply the good of any one practice (ibid. p. 44). For Aristotelians, the over-riding good is the exercise of moral and political virtues in pursuing the good of the political community. However, as MacIntyre is a Thomist as well, he concludes that such moral and political goods are pursued *for the sake of* the beatific vision, or friendship with God, i.e. the good of a Catholic community, and that entails exercising the theological virtues of faith, hope, and charity (ibid. p. 192).

For MacIntyre, the *polis* is based on a moral consensus concerning goods of excellence and the hierarchical ordering of those goods. A consensus is required concerning what is meritorious and deserving of reward, and it is on that basis that we answer questions of distributive justice. There must be a 'common enterprise' to which all contribute, as well as 'a shared view of how such contributions are to be measured and of how rewards are to be ranked' (ibid. pp. 106–107). If individuals make claims against society, claims to certain scarce goods, those claims can be justified only by appealing to this moral consensus. Therefore, it is on this basis of a moral consensus that political reasoning takes place. When we engage with each other in political debate the reasons we give to others are reasons that are acceptable to those others as members of this community with its own moral consensus on the hierarchical ordering of goods. For instance, parenting and teaching may satisfy the requirement of being practices (activities) in MacIntyre's terminology: this is the case only *if* they provide practitioners with internal goods (goods of excellence) that can be pursued only within these very activities by pursuing standards of excellence peculiar to these activities, and only if internal goods are given priority over the external goods that can be attained through these activities. In turn, in political debate, fellow-citizens address the question of the relative worth of these different activities and their internal goods and the performances of their practitioners. What will be at issue is the extent to which such practice-based activity does or does not contribute to a shared good for the members of this political community.

Our entitlements therefore are dependent upon what we do, our performance, within practices, and the relative worth of those practices and their internal goods as judged by the members of our community. Does it follow that those who have made no contribution to the shared goods of the political community have no entitlements to scarce goods from that community? MacIntyre remarks that, for Aristotle, '[s]eparated from the *polis*, what would have been a human being becomes instead a wild animal' (1988: 97–98). MacIntyre is not receptive to the view that individuals can claim rights simply in virtue of their humanity. Natural or human rights are 'fictions': 'they purport to provide us with an objective and impersonal criterion, but they do not' (MacIntyre, 1985: 70); and there is as much reason to believe in them as there is to believe in witches and unicorns, as 'every attempt to give good reasons for believing that there *are* such rights has failed' (ibid. p. 69). Instead, we can claim rights only as members of a community where that claim makes sense in terms of our past contributions to the community and its shared goods. Nonetheless, in particular in his later work, MacIntyre assumes that the virtuous person should be beneficent and generous, and therefore, should give to the needy, including needy strangers (1999a). However, although the needy stranger should be helped, MacIntyre is not saying that the needy stranger has rights of justice to such help. The virtuous are obliged to care for the needy stranger but it does not correspond with a right of justice for those in receipt of that care. We return to MacIntyre's account of just generosity in the next chapter, and in the final chapter we examine arguments for global distributive justice.

The first two criticisms: relativism and conservatism

For now, we ask can MacIntyre defend his virtue-based and practice-based approach as a political theory? First, it is not clear that one can hierarchically order all goods, and that any such hierarchy could serve as a basis for political debate. It may be acceptable to argue that external goods should be pursued *for the sake of* internal goods, but it is not clear which, if any, has priority among the various internal goods available to us. MacIntyre claims to be able to answer this question, but his Aristotelian–Thomist set of priorities are highly contentious. For instance, for parenting to be a good, must it be pursued for its own sake *and also* for the sake of the shared goods of a Catholic community? Further, is scientific detachment and evidence-based reasoning a good only if combined in some way (if such combination is possible) with the Catholic virtues of faith and humility? At the very least, it must be the case that the implication of MacIntyre's thought is *not* that one can flourish as a human only if one does so as a Catholic within a Catholic community. However, MacIntyre will have great difficulty avoiding the charge that, for his position, what a Catholic ought to do is fully determined by the moral consensus of his or her Catholic community. This is important as MacIntyre is laying himself open to a number of serious charges.

The first such charge is relativism. As we saw at the start of this chapter, the relativist assumes that conclusions can be justified as rational-relative-to some tradition (or some other parameters), never rational-as-such. Although MacIntyre rejects relativism, and spends much effort defending himself against the charge of relativism (1985: 264–278; 1988: 352ff.), nonetheless, some commentators continue to argue that MacIntyre can only show how conclusions can be justified for those belonging to a tradition, not justified-as-such (Bakhurst, 2003: 166, 168). Again, as we saw at the start of this chapter, a relativist can accept the importance and authority of moral considerations, yet go on to argue that 'different people could, quite reasonably, attach this kind of importance to different forms of conduct' (Scanlon, 1995: 233). This is the case if judgments such as 'being true' or 'being justified' 'cannot be assigned absolutely, but only relative to certain conditions or parameters', and so, for this reason, 'conflicting judgments can be equally correct or equally justified' (ibid. p. 219, 220). A non-relativist, by contrast, can accept that different cultures generate different norms, but also try to establish '"definitional criteria" which limit the content of anything that could be called morality' (ibid. p. 230; Cf. Foot, 2001: 86, 110, 113). A non-relativist can also note that although there are standards of evaluation that are appropriate to specific activities, we should also accept standards of evaluation that apply to all such activities. Such a non-relativist approach is in fact found in Aristotle:

> Excellence in deliberation in the unqualified sense, then, is that which succeeds with reference to what is the end in the unqualified sense, and excellence in deliberation in a particular sense is that which succeeds relatively to a particular end. (NE, VI. 9, 1142^b 29 ff)

Why is relativism problematic? The first reason for concern is that, if the relativist thesis is true, it is possible for people to arrive at competing and incompatible moral judgements about an issue without either of the judgements being mistaken. To take an example from the activity of parenting, is the use of artificial contraception morally permissible, and one can ask the question of people belonging to a socially liberal tradition and also of people belonging to a socially conservative tradition. If moral judgements are relative to some parameters, say the traditions to which people belong, and if people in the liberal tradition should come to the conclusion that artificial contraception is permissible, and should do so based on their moral sources within that tradition, and people in the conservative tradition should come to the conclusion that the same act or acts are wrong, and again should do so on the basis of their moral sources within that tradition, then although the two conclusions are incompatible neither is wrong. That is, neither of the two protagonists, who concluded that using artificial contraception is wrong and that it is permissible, is incorrect. If the relativist position is correct then moral reasoning will not be such that it could resolve disagreements about issues such as artificial contraception for the reason that mutually antithetical conclusions can each be rationally justified.

The second reason relativism is problematic is that it seems to be incoherent. Insofar as relativists 'assert that their thesis is correct, and that anyone who denies it is mistaken, they are making a claim to unconditional validity that is inconsistent with relativism itself' (Scanlon, 1998: 330). That is, the relativist states that every judgement is relative, but the relativist presumably does not mean that *this* judgement is relative. It may be possible to avoid incoherence. However, to do so the relativist must provide some non-relative reasons for why a set of reasons should be morally compelling, and non-relative reasons for why such morally compelling reasons may rightly differ in different circumstances. For example, it may be argued that belonging to a tradition explains why a set of reasons should be morally compelling to you, that is, the reasons provided by your belonging to the tradition and also that different traditions will rightly provide different sets of morally compelling reasons to those belonging to these traditions. This may be one way for MacIntyre to escape the charges of relativism and incoherence. Whether MacIntyre can make such an argument, and in that way avoid incoherence, is discussed later in this chapter.

The second serious charge raised against MacIntyre is that his is a politically conservative position. This criticism follows on from the observation that MacIntyre's political theory is, according to one line of interpretation, a political theory for a specific type of community, i.e. an Aristotelian–Thomist community. MacIntyre believes that critical rational enquiry is something 'we' undertake from within 'our' shared mode of practice (1999a: 157). For that reason, it could be argued MacIntyre does not ensure political debate is in fact critical. That is, he does not ensure debate can call into question shared beliefs, the prevailing structure of organizations, or even the philosophical, scientific, and theoretical findings of the tradition. For that reason MacIntyre's work will be unable to avoid insularity and also intolerance as it will not give a premium to critical detachment in reasoning (see Keat, 2000). A further and related criticism is that, as he assumes that there must be a moral consensus on the overriding good and the hierarchical ordering of all goods, he is hostile to moral pluralism. Although he accepts that there are and should be different goods in life, he assumes that all such goods can be ranked according to one set of commitments and principles. The charge of conservatism can be extended further. As he believes one can have rights only as the member of a particular community and against the background of a particular tradition, it would seem he is hostile to the concept of universal human rights, and therefore does not accept that 'strangers' have rights of justice against 'us'. This charge may also apply even if MacIntyre's political theory can be applied to communities that are not organized around a Catholic *telos* but nonetheless are organized around a moral consensus concerning the hierarchical ordering of *their* goods. Famously, MacIntyre's example of this kind of community is the small fishing villages of Donegal in Ireland, and it can be argued plausibly enough that such a community would be conservative *if* it is based on a single hierarchical ordering of goods.

MacIntyre has been defended against the charges of relativism and conservatism by those who argue that his is a radical politics with universal moral implications. This claim rests on the idea that MacIntyre's ethics in fact is one of 'radical self-transformation' in pursuit of what is 'the good as such' (MacIntyre, 1994c: 225; Breen, 2007: 396). 'Disciplined apprenticeship' in specific activities is required only so as to attain this radical and universal goal, MacIntyre believes:

> [B]ecause initially we lack important qualities of mind, body, and character necessary for both excellent performance and informed and accurate judgement about excellence in performance, we have to put ourselves into the hands of those competent to transform us into the kinds of people who will be able both to perform and to judge well (1988: 30).

It is unfair to say that MacIntyre simply reduces standards of evaluation to 'what are taken to be' the standards in a given practice (Cf. Miller, 1999: 116 ff.). Of course, MacIntyre has also shown how the virtues are exercised in writing a life narrative and in political engagement, and on such a basis we can reflect on and evaluate any one specific practice from a position of critical detachment (MacIntyre, 1985: 187). However, it is worth noting, MacIntyre believes, that when it comes to moral reasoning, 'those who lack the relevant experience' of 'participating in the practice' in question 'are incompetent thereby as judges of internal goods' (ibid. 188–189).

In *Whose Justice? Which Rationality?* MacIntyre concludes that rationality requires us to 'conform' to the rational standards of activities. Rationality also requires that we accept that it is 'only within those systematic forms of activity' that rational standards directing us towards the good and the best are embodied:

> A hockey player in the closing seconds of a crucial game has an opportunity to pass to another member of his or her team better placed to score a needed goal. Necessarily, we may say, if he or she has perceived and judged the situation accurately, he or she must immediately pass... It exhibits the connection between the good of that person *qua* hockey player and member of that particular team and the action of passing... It is thus only within those systematic forms of activity within which goods are unambiguously ordered and within which individuals occupy and move between well-defined roles that the standards of rational action directed toward

the good and the best can be embodied. To be a rational individual is to participate in such a form of social life and to conform, so far as is possible, to those standards (1988: 140–141).

In this illustrative passage, does MacIntyre mean that as a matter of fact we will discover standards of rationality and of ethical judgement in specific activities? Or does he mean that specific activities should determine for us what to accept as standards of rationality and of ethical judgement when engaged in this activity? Is something rightly judged good because it is required of us in conforming to the standards of this specific activity (for example, hockey), and/or because the experts in such activities come to this conclusion? There are two issues here for us: first, the relation between practical rationality and moral goodness; and second, the relation between experience of virtuous activity and knowledge of virtue.

The third criticism: an abject view of reason

As the criticisms of his work have focused in large part on the supposed deficiencies in the historicist approach to rationality, MacIntyre needs to be able to provide a robust account of practical rationality. He needs to show that, in a political debate, we can in fact rationally defend the kinds of conclusion that he has made about goods. In the first instance, MacIntyre gives what can be called a 'particularist' account of practical reasoning and wisdom. Practical reasoning is 'non-rule-governed', he claims, for it is instead a matter of virtue or wisdom more precisely (1988, p. 117). The practically wise person must apply virtues and rules in different particular situations, but there are no general rules or criteria for the application of virtues and rules.

> For in exercising *phronesis* we understand why this particular situation makes the application of some particular moral virtue or the application of some particular rule of justice in acting in some particular way the right thing to do. And there are no rules for generating this kind of practically effective understanding of particulars. (ibid. p. 116)

For MacIntyre, the practically rational or wise person is more than a rule-follower. Although we use maxims to characterize what, at some stage, is the highest standard of achievement in an activity, nonetheless, 'knowing how to apply these maxims is itself a capacity which cannot be specified by further rules' (ibid. p. 31). However, his position entails as well that practical rationality is *not* bound by general rules that are independent of each and every activity. MacIntyre's position is reasonable if, as David Wiggins argues, 'the subject matter of action ... is inexhaustibly indefinite' (2004: 481). The 'practical cannot be treated with, handled, mastered or managed by means of precepts that are at once general and unrestrictedly correct' (ibid.). While Wiggins accepts that some moral principles 'impinge *independently of any context* on those who are possessed of the ethical virtues', nonetheless, 'it takes *phronesis* ... to shape, determine and validate their application in this, that or the other set of circumstances' (ibid., emphases in original).

In defending particularism, MacIntyre explicitly rejects the position diametrically opposed to it, 'generalism'. 'Rule following will often be involved in knowing how to respond rightly, but no rule or set of rules by itself ever determines how to respond rightly' (MacIntyre, 1999a: 93). The particularist assumes that 'grounding reasons' can make a difference in one place and not in another. One supposed example is that 'my having borrowed a book from you' is a reason for my returning it to you, but also, it is not a reason for my returning it to you 'since it turns out that you have stolen it from the library' (Crisp, 2003: 36). That is, although having borrowed a book from you is a 'grounding reason' for my returning it to you it is a grounding reason only in some particular situations, and this suggests practical reasoning is not a matter of applying general principles. However, a different possible interpretation of this example, one that does not support particularism, can also be seen as equally plausible. On this second interpretation, while 'my having borrowed a book from you' is indeed *a* grounding reason, we should be moved by the 'ultimate reason', and what morality requires provides us the 'ultimate reason' (ibid. p. 37). Moral principles such as the principle of justice also satisfy the generalist insistence that 'a property cannot make a difference in one place without making the same difference everywhere else' (ibid. p. 34). It does not follow that, for the generalist, justice requires the same actions in all situations. Judgment is needed so as to appreciate what justice requires given the particulars of the case. In the above example, the person should depart from what he or she normally ought to do, that is, return borrowed books. However, justice has a compelling power in our deliberations because it applies generally. Indeed it is its generality that justifies the decision not to return the book in this instance, for the particular case (and any and all cases like it) is one where to return the book would be an injustice.

Not only is particularism not required by the differences in particulars between each specific situation, particularism also involves an unappealing, abject view of rationality. For it is based on the assumption that when we try to explain ourselves, to ourselves and to others, the giving of reasons, at some point, comes to a halt and we can do no more than 'shrug our shoulders' (Crisp, 2003: 35). This is an especially problematic approach to political issues and political debate. If the giving of reasons can and must come to a halt, the space is opened for the resolution of conflicts by non-rational means: whether sophism, deception, manipulation, intimidation, threats, violence, or any of the other many ingenuous means that have been invented. For MacIntyre, it is the wisdom of the good person that is needed in such a moment, for it is only he or she who knows how to apply a general principle in the correct way and why this is the case. But if no reasons can be given to explain this, to explain the decision, how is the wise person's decision distinguished from the decision of the fool or the knave?

It might be said that this argument against particularism is itself unjustified. This is the case if particularists could and do accept that moral considerations have generality, but merely reject the claim that precepts are 'general and unrestrictedly correct'. Particularists can accept that if maxim M applies in a particular way M_s in situation S, then we should accept the general precept that if any other circumstance is similar to S in all relevant respects, M should apply here too in the particular way M_s. So, it is argued, particularists are not rejecting the generality of moral precepts, but rather they reject the extreme view that ideal or theoretical principles can be applied in the same way in all circumstances (see McKeever and Ridge, 2006, ch1). However, this does not undermine the generality of moral principles. For the particularist is implicitly appealing to a general principle, namely what to do in situation S (and all S-like situations). Further, the particularist is not offering us an accurate account of generalism here. The generalist is not saying that general precepts are not in need of application. What the generalist is saying is that, if I propose to apply a precept in some particular way, I should be willing to offer general reasons in justification of *this* decision. In contrast, it is particularists who are saying that, at some point, such reason-giving (i.e. the giving of general considerations) comes to a halt.

The fourth criticism: circularity and paradox

So far we have looked at three criticisms of MacIntyre's account of practical rationality. The first and second criticism is that, because of the priority given to tradition, practices, and the moral consensus of a community, both relativism and conservativism may follow. The third criticism is that MacIntyre is a particularist, and that particularism may entail an abject view of rationality that opens the way for non-rational forces in political debate. However, MacIntyre may be able to escape unscathed from these criticisms, as he himself claims. This is the case because of the many different factors that, in his view, are involved in practical rationality. Practical rationality is not *just* a matter of reasoning from the shared norms of a community, nor is it *just* a matter of there being no rules for the application of rules. According to MacIntyre, to derive 'rational beliefs' about specific goods, the wise person must exercise the following 'abilities': the ability (1) to 'characterize' a 'situation'; (2) to understand his 'good *qua* participant in a variety of activities'; (3) to reason (by dialectical methods) from knowledge of what are 'goods for him' to a 'more or less adequate conception of the good as such'; as well as (4) to reason from his understanding of the good in general, 'the unqualifiedly good', to a conclusion about which of the specific goods which it is immediately possible for him to achieve he should in fact set himself to achieve as 'what is immediately best for him'; and finally, (5) to deploy these other four abilities in conjunction, which 'is exhibited in the exercise of the virtue *phronesis*' (1988: 126).

So far we have focused only on the first two abilities listed above: the ability to characterize the particular situation, and the ability to identify and pursue the goods of an activity. Now we can ask, how according to MacIntyre do we reason from our knowledge of what are goods for us to an adequate conception of the good as such (ability 3), and from the latter to what is immediately good to achieve from among the various goods we set ourselves to achieve (ability 4)?

MacIntyre does not give one account of practical rationality and another separate account of moral goodness. To be practically rational one must also be good or virtuous, as other Aristotelians and Thomists have argued (see Foot, 2001). He uses the same term (*phronesis* or *prudentia*) to refer to both. MacIntyre assumes that to judge and act rationally one must have an 'adequate conception of the good and the best' as this is the first premise of any practical chain of reasoning. However, I think it can be argued that his position appears circular and paradoxical. It appears *circular* as it seems that someone may be defined as rational only if they are morally good as well, but they may defined as morally good only if they are rational as well. It appears *paradoxical* for the following reason: if one cannot reason correctly without first having the correct conception of the good and the best, how is it possible to reason to the conclusion that 'such and such' is good and best? One strategy to avoid circularity and paradox is a biographical one: it could be argued that at various stages in our lives (initial socialization, entering an activity as an apprentice, and so on) we derive our conception of the good, in the first instance, from the 'wise' person. Before we have the capacity to judge what is good for ourselves, we take the viewpoint of the wise person as authoritative for us, and in that way gain experience of right action and judgement before we can be said to be rational or practically wise ourselves.

Such an answer does provide an explanation of how it may come about that one can develop rational abilities by first accepting certain beliefs about moral goodness. However, this simply introduces a new form of circularity and paradox. It can be represented as follows: W can claim to be wise *because* he/she aims at the good and the best, G; but also, we rightly take G to be the good and the best *because* W does aim at G. This is unacceptable as we still must ask, how can we rationally conclude either that W is wise or that G is good? It seems that we cannot rationally conclude that W is wise without being able to establish that G is good, but the only method open to establish that G is good is that it is aimed at by W.

Nonetheless, MacIntyre insists, 'the appearances of paradox and circularity are deceptive' (1988: 118). This is the case because it is *not* the function of 'practical' reason to justify or discover the first premise in all reasoning, the good and the best. Rather, it is the goal of theory to search out these first principles (*archai*) from which the good person should act. This is where we find the need for the ability to use 'dialectical' methods, as mentioned above. At the same time, theoretical enquiry is constituted by tradition, in MacIntyre's view. Social and philosophical tradition constitutes our theoretical enquiry concerning the good and the best; in particular, the tradition of the virtues (the Aristotelian and Thomist traditions) constitutes our enquiry into the good and the best. It is for this reason MacIntyre can state that 'Retrospectively surveyed, the judgements and actions of the *phronimos* [the wise person]...will turn out to be such as would be required by an adequate conception of the good and the best' (ibid.). That is, a person who is truly wise, participating within practices and a *polis*, will in fact have the good and the best as a first premise in all practical reasoning, and when theoretical enquiry within this tradition has perfected itself, when it has attained its goal, it will have successfully searched out these first principles.

What this means is that traditions of enquiry will provide the link between practical rationality and moral goodness, dispelling the appearance of circularity and paradox. The perfected theory of a tradition will establish exactly what conception of goodness the rational person should accept. Therefore, the plausibility of MacIntyre's account of practical rationality rests on his account of tradition. This is crucial because what lies in the balance is MacIntyre's defence of his whole approach to practical reasoning against the criticisms introduced above. Can MacIntyre dispel the appearance of relativism and conservatism, and can he show that the practical rationality of the wise person does not result in an abject view of reasoning, where rationality must succumb to non-rational means of persuasion?

Traditions are incommensurable

Tradition is not incompatible with reason and conflict, MacIntyre has been claiming. It is time to explore MacIntyre's epistemology and moral theory in more depth and especially the role played by tradition in moral reasoning. As MacIntyre believes all rational enquiry is context-bound, his is an 'historicist' position. His claim is that each moral theory 'principally and ultimately originates out of a *particular* community's *moral* imagination, beliefs, practices, and institutions' (Kuna, 2005: 253; emphases in original). However, MacIntyre does not deny that 'there are universal standards of moral value true for all human beings or universal principles of moral duty and obligation binding on all' (ibid.). Although enquiry is context-bound, the goal of theory is to seek out the first principles from which the good person should act, namely, 'an adequate conception of the good and the best'. Crucially, starting from within a tradition is in fact necessary if we are to move towards and grasp 'universal' moral truths. This is the case as we must proceed from the virtue of the wise person, what he/she takes to be the good and the best, and then, through 'dialectical' argumentation we can test a proposed universal against opposing conceptions of the good and the best (MacIntyre, 1988: 91). 'Without those moral particularities to begin from there would never be anywhere to begin; but it is in moving forward from such particularity that the search for the good, for the universal, consists' (MacIntyre, 1985: 221).

For MacIntyre, tradition is not antithetical to reason and disagreement. 'A tradition is an argument extended through time in which certain fundamental agreements are defined and redefined in terms of two kinds of conflict' (ibid. p. 12). There is an external conflict with those who 'reject all or at least key parts of those fundamental agreements', and there are 'internal interpretative debates through which the meaning and rationale of the fundamental agreement come to be expressed' (ibid.). MacIntyre here is mindful of the criticisms a historicist position such as his will draw. As we saw, according to their critics, historicists cannot avoid relativism. This is the case because they do not accept that political theory must 'struggle' 'against all the impulses that drag us back into our own culture, toward generality and some reflective basis for deciding which of our traditional distinctions and discriminations are genuine and which are spurious ... ' (Dworkin, 1985: 219–220: in reference to Micheal Walzer's arguments).

However, what MacIntyre actually claims is that he can and does struggle against such impulses, but also, and more fundamentally, it is *only* through conceding that enquiry is context-bound that he can do so. That is, it is he who can successfully avoid relativism, not his mainstream critics still pursuing the ideal of a value-neutral, universal theory. Also he goes on to outline in some detail how, in his eyes, he does avoid relativism.

MacIntyre rejects both relativism and perspectivism. For the relativist, a claim 'can be rational relative to the standards of some particular tradition, but not rational as such' (MacIntyre, 1988: 352). For the perspectivist, 'no one tradition is entitled to arrogate to itself an exclusive title; no one tradition can deny legitimacy to its rivals', and so, the perspectivist understands rival traditions 'as providing very different, complementary perspectives for envisaging the realities about which they speak to us' (ibid.). 'The relativist challenge rests upon a denial that rational debate between and rational choice among rival traditions is possible; the perspectivist challenge puts in question the possibility of making truth-claims from within any one tradition' (ibid.).

Relativism and perspectivism together entail 'that no claim to truth made in the name of any one competing tradition could defeat the claims to truth made in the name of its rivals' (ibid. p. 367). Although rejecting relativism and perspectivism, MacIntyre does assume theory is constituted by tradition. Therefore, the question that must be put to MacIntyre himself is, 'how then is it possible to make "truth claims" from within any one tradition and yet also to rationally choose among rival traditions?'

Truth is a matter of 'correspondence', but it is not judgements, statements, or mental pictures that do or do not correspond with their objects, MacIntyre contends. Rather, it is 'intelligent thought which is or is not adequate in its dealings with its objects, the realities of the social and natural world' (MacIntyre, 1988: 356). MacIntyre employs a conception of 'mind as activity' and he conceptualizes truth in terms of successful action (identifying, collecting, classifying, and so on, by means of touching, grasping, calling to, and so on). 'The mind is adequate to its objects insofar as the expectations which it frames on the basis of these activities are not liable to disappointment' (ibid.). As truth is conceptualized in terms of successful action; a tradition enters a period of what he calls 'epistemological crises' when its members can no longer act effectively, and solve problems (ibid. p. 362). At such a time, the use of traditional methods and arguments simply discloses 'new inadequacies, hitherto unrecognized incoherences, and new problems for the solution of which there seem to be insufficient or no resources within the established fabric of belief' (ibid.).

To avoid the charges of perspectivism and relativism, MacIntyre needs to show that claims to truth made in the name of one tradition could (rationally) defeat those made in the name of another: i.e. that it is possible to make truth claims but also to rationally choose among rival traditions. He tries to do so with the idea of 'the rationality of traditions'. The rationality of traditions accounts for the way in which practically rational and morally good people confront and engage with the alien perspective presented to them by the rival tradition. It is less a set of rules and methods and more a description of the dispositions and character traits required by the wise and good people faced with such a situation. The 'only rational way for the adherents of any tradition to approach intellectually, culturally, and linguistically alien rivals' allows that the rival tradition 'may be rationally superior to it in respect precisely of that in the alien tradition which it cannot as yet comprehend' (ibid. p. 388). We can proceed as follows:

> The protagonists of each tradition, having considered in what ways their own tradition has by its own standards... found it difficult to develop its enquiries beyond a certain point... ask whether the alternative and rival tradition may not be able to provide resources to characterize and to explain the failings and defects of their own tradition more adequately than they, using the resources of that tradition, have been able to do (ibid. pp. 166–167).

For the adherents of the first tradition, a second, rival tradition may provide ways in which to act more effectively. Nonetheless, although a 'rational way... to approach' rival traditions is possible, MacIntyre contends that traditions are incommensurable: 'there is no neutral way of characterizing either the subject matter about which they give rival accounts or the standards by which their claims are to be evaluated' (ibid. p. 166). For that reason, those who approach rival traditions in a rational way require 'rare' qualities. They need 'gifts' of 'empathy as well as of intellectual insight ... to view themselves from such an alien standpoint and to recharacterize their own beliefs in an appropriate manner from the alien perspective of the rival tradition' (ibid. p. 167).

To sum up therefore we can say that, for MacIntyre, (i) all enquiry is tradition-constituted; (ii) traditions in good working order enable adherents to act effectively and solve problems; (iii) when one tradition ceases to do so its adherents have the option of trying to learn to see their predicament from the perspective of a rival, incommensurable tradition; and, in turn, (iv) recharacterize their own beliefs from that perspective. This therefore is MacIntyre's outline of the way in which rational engagement with rival traditions is possible.

By 'incommensurability', MacIntyre seems to refer to 'global' incommensurability between rival traditions as well as both 'thin' and 'thick' incommensurability between particular elements within traditions (see the discussion of incommensurability in Simmons 1994: 120–121). Not only are there no standards internal to two traditions to determine which tradition is superior, as is the case with global incommensurability, MacIntyre also assumes that the 'thin' elements of each tradition are incommensurable, for example, claims about the nature of practical reasoning, the goods sought in human action, moral dilemmas, and the relationship between practical reason and action. The same is true of the 'thick' elements of traditions, such as substantive claims like those concerning sexuality and reproduction. For MacIntyre, moreover, it is because of global incommensurability, the incommensurability of traditions, that we experience incommensurability at the local level, whether thin or thick. That is, as rationality is tradition-constituted, traditions will determine the development of incommensurable thin accounts of practical rationality and incommensurable thick moral commitments.

The fifth criticism: incoherence

Some of his critics have concluded that MacIntyre's position is not coherent. If all rational standards are tradition-constituted, how can the decision to adopt the viewpoint of a rival tradition be rationally justified? Does MacIntyre not require some account of the 'nature of traditions' that is not itself the product of any one tradition, on the basis of which he can judge such decisions to be rational (Haldane, 1994: 104; see Allen, 1997: 511)? However, if it were possible to provide a tradition-neutral account of the nature of traditions, presumably then he could no longer state that all enquiry is tradition-constituted.

Those striving to defend MacIntyre do so by claiming that, in the engagement with the rival tradition, 'it makes sense for the inhabitants of the first tradition to acknowledge *that by their own criteria of judgement*, the second tradition offers the possibility of a more adequate grasp of reality...' (Porter, 1993: 521; emphasis added). However, if traditions are incommensurable, the reasons given from within the first tradition to accept the solutions provided by the second tradition are not commensurable with the reasons one now accepts as a member of the second tradition. If that is the case, MacIntyre himself is exposed to the charge of relativism, just the charge that the 'rationality of traditions' was meant to dispel. It appears that the reasons given for the judgement are rational relative to a tradition, but not rational as such (as relativists claim). How can MacIntyre continue to claim both that tradition constitutes rationality and that there is a rational way to approach rival traditions?

In his defence, it has been argued that MacIntyre discovers 'tradition transcendental' rational standards (Herdt, 1998: 538). The principle of 'the rationality of traditions' requires the following: members of the first tradition should acknowledge the superior rationality of the second tradition because the latter offers an illuminating explanation of the crises of the former and does not face similar crises itself (ibid. p. 535). For Herdt, this is not a tradition-independent principle, but it is also not tradition dependent, as 'such a theory of rationality [is] presupposed by, implicit in, *every* tradition of enquiry' (ibid. p. 539; emphasis in original). Nonetheless, she concludes that MacIntyre's position

> merits the designation 'historicism' because it is only within and through history that human beings become *fully conscious of* and *fully justified in holding* even those principles or conclusions of enquiry that are presupposed by the practice of enquiry at the outset (ibid. p. 541; emphasis added).

However, in the italicized text, it could be argued that Herdt, and by extension MacIntyre, is guilty of conflating an argument against 'neutralism' with an argument against 'absolutism'. It may be the case that, without participating in a tradition, we cannot become 'fully conscious of' its principles, and for that reason it may be possible to reject 'neutralism'. The neutralist position rests on the claim, 'You can see that there are good arguments whether or not you are within a given tradition' (Irwin, 1989: 52). However, disposing of neutralism does not suffice to reject 'absolutism'. The absolutist claims that 'These are good arguments, and their goodness consists not in their counting within a tradition, but in their adequacy to the subject matter' (ibid.). The absolutist position is that we can only be 'fully justified in holding' a principle because of its 'adequacy to the subject matter'. If it is fair to say that MacIntyre rejects absolutism and embraces 'contextualism', therefore it can be said that he assumes 'that the tradition determines whether the argument *is* good' (Irwin, 1989: 53; emphasis in original), not just whether we can be 'fully conscious of' its being good. However, this contextualist account presumably would apply to MacIntyre's own defence of Aristotelian–Thomism as well (Irwin, 1989: 55), and this is self-defeating: 'Hence, he [MacIntyre] ought in consistency to mean only that, from the point of view of the Thomist tradition, the Thomist tradition is superior to others' (ibid.). If that is the case, however, MacIntyre cannot effectively reject relativism, the position that a claim can only ever be rational relative-to some parameters.

There are two possible ways in which MacIntyre can respond, and both will be looked at here. The first is to argue that, although for MacIntyre rationality is relative, truth is not. The second argument is that Thomism as a tradition will be shown to be superior, but first there must occur an empathetic engagement between Thomism and its rivals (i.e. the doctrines or traditions of Kant, Mill, Hume, Rousseau, Nietzsche, Heidegger, Rawls, and so on).

Christopher Lutz contends that 'MacIntyre embraces relativity while rejecting relativism' (2004: 67). Although MacIntyre states that 'the only available standards of rationality are those made available within traditions', (MacIntyre, 1988: 352) according to Lutz, MacIntyre also assumes that truth, 'adequation of the mind to its object', 'has its own existence and imposes its own limits on the reasonableness of theories' (Lutz, 2004: 69). Although rationality is relative, truth is not. However, this response does not suffice to dispel the problems already discussed. First, it does not do enough to rebut the charge of relativism. Lutz claims that MacIntyre's preferred approach is 'to prescind from discussions of truth in order to focus on the problems of rationality' (ibid.). If that were the case, the factor that could be analysed (rationality) would be analysed in a way that presupposes relativity, but nothing could be said of truth, the element that is to prevent relativity from slipping into mere relativism. It may well be the case that there is something called truth that we as humans cannot gain understanding of through mere rationality, but then we are conceding that everything in the sphere of human rational powers is relative. Secondly, Lutz's response is not an accurate portrayal of MacIntyre's approach, for MacIntyre does have a lot to say about truth. MacIntyre has stated explicitly that truth is the *telos* of enquiry, and enquiry is tradition-constituted. He insists that theoretical enquiry should take tradition as its starting point: the 'practice of the moral and intellectual virtues ... will provide the kind of experience from which ... sound theoretical arguments about practice can be derived' (MacIntyre, 1990: 177). He also believes theoretical enquiry is never grounded on anything other than tradition: 'particularity can never be left behind or obliterated. The notion of escaping from it into a realm of entirely universal maxims which belong to man as such ... is an illusion' (MacIntyre, 1985: 221).

The second approach open to MacIntyre is to engage in an inter-traditional dialogue with other, rival traditions. For some observers, MacIntyre's position is very similar to Hans-Georg Gadamer's hermeneutics and the latter's argument concerning the 'historicity' of all reasoning: 'Although we become who we are largely through membership of communal networks, our ability to imagine alternatives to given realities and distance ourselves from received opinion allows us to disengage and critique the moral limitations of those networks' (Breen, 2002: 190).

In engaging with other, rival horizons, we can seek a shared perspective, what Gadamer calls a 'fusion of horizons' (1975: 306), because we can distance ourselves from our own perspective. In doing so we hope to attain 'completeness', a better understanding of ourselves and the world. Through dialogue about, for instance, the worth of the cultural products of different traditions we can attain a 'fusion of horizons' as the basis for a communitarian politics of recognition. However, Gadamer's hermeneutic approach has the following weakness. As Charles Taylor notes, a fusion of horizons provides us with an understanding of what constitutes worth 'that we couldn't possibly have had at the beginning' (1992: 67). However, it follows that, while traditions provide incommensurable perspectives of evaluation, dialogue creates new perspectives of evaluation that are, again, incommensurable. Gadamer himself assumed that 'the experienced person proves to be ... radically undogmatic ... The dialectic of experience has its proper fulfilment not in definitive knowledge but in the openness to experience that is made possible by experience itself' (1975: 355).

Therefore, Gadamer can only say that an understanding, perspective, or tradition is better if it is more open. But openness does not entail discrimination of better and worse, even if it is shown that openness is necessary for right judgement. To judge that a tradition is more open than its predecessor or a rival is not to determine that it is, in Irwin's terms, more 'adequate to the subject matter' (1989: 52).

Nonetheless, MacIntyre believes he can explain the progress made as a result of an empathetic and dialectical engagement between traditions. MacIntyre's thesis, he claims, is different from what Thomas Kuhn referred to as paradigm shifts in science. MacIntyre sees Kuhn's 'paradigm' as something 'conservative and essentially unitary', and the transition from one paradigm to another is a 'conversion experience' (MacIntyre, 1977: 465). In contrast, MacIntyre offers a 'narrative' of rational progress towards truth. It is a 'progress from a condition in which the mind has not yet freed itself from the limitations of one-sidedness and partiality, towards or to adequacy of understanding' (MacIntyre, 1994b: 215). A tradition is superior in so far as it can solve problems common to all traditions that cannot be solved from within those other traditions. However, for MacIntyre, a tradition is a 'language in use', and, in dialectical enquiry, one must learn the language of the alien culture as 'a second first language' (MacIntyre, 1988: 374). Also, part of this process involves coming to realize 'where and in what respects utterances in the one are untranslatable into the other' (ibid. p. 375).

MacIntyre is right that, to understand any word, in the full possibility of its meaning, a person must become immersed in the relevant language and culture. However, he is also making a more substantial claim, namely, that standards of rational justification may be radically different in different 'languages in use', and, for that reason, traditional points of view are incommensurable. Such a claim, as Donald Davidson points out, is logically incoherent: 'Different points of view make sense, but only if there is a common co-ordinate system on which to plot them; yet the existence of a common system belies the claim of dramatic incomparability' (Davidson, 1974: 184). To avoid incoherence, MacIntyre must make a choice. He could choose to accept that we can arrive at standards of rationality that are independent of any specific traditions, but this would entail rejecting historicism. The only alternative is to retain historicism but accept that truth is relative to specific traditions and that he cannot provide a narrative of rational progress.

Politics on 'the margins' and the charge of conservatism

As we have seen, for MacIntyre, political reasoning requires a moral consensus about what is good. Fellow citizens in political debate should have a shared view on how to rank contributions to their shared enterprise. Is such political debate rationally justified? Does it avoid relativism, conservatism, circularity and paradox, an abject view of reason, and incoherence? As he has been unable to resolutely defend himself against these charges concerning tradition-constituted enquiry, the same problems may arise at the level of political debate.

In a worthwhile community, MacIntyre argues, we participate in politics so as to integrate the many different practices and the goods pursued in those practices. Nonetheless, on his account, when debating these issues in politics, we do not adopt a standpoint that is detached from practice. Politics is never independent of practices, and it is itself a practice, according to MacIntyre. First, the goods of political communities and of an individual's life are understood 'as integrative of and partly structured in terms of the goods internal to practices'; and secondly, 'the work of integrating those goods into individual and communal lives itself has the structure of a practice' (1994a: 288). Therefore, practical reasoning at the level of politics is not governed by rules or precepts that are independent of practice. How can practical reasoning lead to morally justified political conclusions?

MacIntyre is sometimes categorized as a 'communitarian' along with Charles Taylor, Michael Walzer, and Michael Sandel (Fives, 2008a, Ch. 7; Mulhall & Swift, 1992, Ch. 2; Cf. Breen, 2002; Knight, 2007). Just as communitarians believe that political theory has as its objective to understand or interpret the shared horizon of its community, i.e. the social meaning of its goods (Walzer, 1983) or its moral sources (Taylor, 1989), MacIntyre argues that 'critical rational enquiry' 'is something that *we* undertake from within *our* shared mode of practice' (MacIntyre, 1999a: 157; emphasis in original). In critical rational enquiry we do not take 'the view from nowhere'; rather, we presuppose the moral consensus of a community. However, MacIntyre insists that he is *not* a communitarian, despite the similarities that others have observed. MacIntyre's rejection of the communitarian label however is a very important indicator of the precise nature of his political theory. His first argument is that he believes 'political, economic and moral structures of advanced modernity... exclude the possibility of realizing any of the worthwhile types of political community'; and secondly, he takes 'fundamental moral conflict to be... widespread and... politically debilitating' (1991: 91). That is, in contrast to what is presumed to be the beliefs of communitarians, MacIntyre is claiming that mainstream modern institutions are not suited to a communitarian politics understood as the pursuit of the goods of the community; and modern society lacks the moral consensus needed for such communitarian political engagement. For that reason, 'attempts to remake modern societies in systematically communitarian ways will be either ineffective or disastrous' (ibid.; 1995a, p. 35). State-based communitarian politics would either lead to authoritarianism, the coercive imposition of one moral view point where there is in fact deep moral pluralism, or else it would be ineffective, as it would be no different from mainstream, 'liberal', politics because it would lack a consensus on the good.

Communitarians either assume that a basic ethical consensus can be discovered, usually at the level of the nation, or else they assume that through dialogue and mutual learning (a fusion of horizons) a new shared horizon will be created under which the worth of distinct cultures can be 'recognized'. Both approaches can be found in the work of Charles Taylor. On the one hand he claims that, within modern culture, there is a 'background framework' of 'strong evaluations', that is, a shared cultural heritage composed of evaluative distinctions. In particular, modern culture entails value commitments to individual 'separateness' and also the goods of 'productive life' and 'family life' (1989: 13; 1994: 105). Taylor's second communitarian policy is to engage in a mutual dialogue and on that basis 'recognise' the worth of different traditions, communities, and forms of life (1992: 42). A communitarian politics of recognition allows the modern state to actively promote the shared goods of specific cultures within the nation state, and in doing so depart from the uniform treatment of its citizens.

Communitarians are assuming both that political reasoning ought to make use of ideas of moral goodness, but also that such reasoning is possible in modern mainstream society. MacIntyre accepts the first but rejects the second premise. For MacIntyre, communitarians are mistaken in their belief that the resources needed for such practical rationality are available in mainstream academia and politics. Modern mainstream society and moral theory encourage 'passive tolerance, that is, public indifference to the good' (Hibbs, 2004: 360). As modernity removes questions of the good life from the political agenda, because of the commitment to 'neutrality', it deprives citizens of the opportunity to engage in genuine and rational public debate about what are or should be their common goods. Further, it is not just a contingent fact that no genuine analysis of goods occurs in modern academia and politics. Such analysis is prevented by the phenomenon of 'compartmentalization'. Where society is compartmentalized, each 'distinct sphere of social activity' has 'its own role structure governed by its own specific norms in relative independence of other such spheres' (MacIntyre, 1999c: 197). A modern citizen has access to standards of evaluation, for instance, as the manager of a private company, as a parent, as a Christian, as a member of a local bridge club, and the values appropriate in one sphere may be inappropriate in or deeply incompatible with the values of another sphere, but also, he or she does not have access to standards of evaluation equally applicable in each and every sphere of life. Therefore, it is not possible in modern compartmentalized societies to form a rational consensus on matters of values and goods.

Compartmentalization itself is not an accidental feature of modern society, MacIntyre insists. Rather, it results from the nature of 'moral language' in modernity. MacIntyre believes that, in modern society, moral debates are rationally irresolveable. This is the case because modern 'moral utterance' does not, indeed cannot, employ objective and impersonal considerations to determine whether some course of action is right or some character trait valuable and good. This has happened because the link between practical reason and moral goodness has been broken. As a result, different people, or the same person at different times, can reason quite coherently to conclusions that are nonetheless diametrically opposed. This has come about, first, as the modern moral theorist, following the lead provided by David Hume, believes that it is desires and preferences alone that determine what is good, and reason does no more than establish how to attain such so-called goods for oneself and others. There can be no shared starting point in modern moral debate, that is, a shared view of the good and the best, for we actually begin from our incompatible desires and preferences.

MacIntyre also claims that modern philosophers rely on 'moral fictions' because they have lost the social and philosophical context that could have made sense of notions such as 'right' and 'duty' and 'good'. The missing context is the tradition of the virtues. MacIntyre believes his account of practices and internal goods is illustrative of the tradition of the virtues, and also a re-articulation of 'the function of man' argument. To illustrate this point, MacIntyre addresses the debate among liberals concerning welfare rights and property rights. He notes that, in the debate between those who defend the rights of the least well off to income and wealth and those who reject such rights as incompatible with property rights, no rational resolution has been forthcoming. Not only that, modern philosophers are incapable of resolving such a debate. The language of morality is in 'a state of grave disorder' and moral conflicts in modernity cannot be rationally resolved (1985: 2). This is the case because they believe the meaning of their concepts is clear when in fact it is not (ibid. p. 70). The evidence in support of the claim that the meaning of 'right' is not clear in modernity is the fact that some liberals can defend welfare rights and others can reject them, and because liberals do not have the resources to resolve this dispute. What is more, the required resources would be available only within the tradition of the virtues, where rights would be justified on the grounds that they contributed to the pursuit of goods, and therefore human flourishing (ibid. p. 53). In turn, MacIntyre proposes to retrieve this lost context by engaging with and in 'traditional' groups close to or on the 'margins' of modern society. In American society, such groups include Irish Catholics, Orthodox Greeks and Jews, and Protestants from the Southern states (ibid. p. 252).

Nonetheless, MacIntyre disassociates himself from the 'conservative' political philosophy of Edmund Burke and others, as we have seen (ibid. pp. 221–222). For MacIntyre, there must be a 'milieu' for individuals 'to step back from ... [their] roles ... and to scrutinize themselves and the structure of their society from some external standpoint' (1999c: 197). For that reason, MacIntyre's *polis* is 'a society of rational enquiry'; it is not a pre-rational *Volk* (1997: 241). Such a rational society also is not 'compartmentalised'. MacIntyre insists that the norms of each sphere, in fact, can be judged with higher standards. Specifically, a moral agent is accountable in respect of natural law and 'the human virtues' (ibid. p. 196; Cf. Hibbs, 2004: 362). And positive law derives its legitimacy from its conformity to natural law, which can be discerned by 'plain persons' (1995b: 49, 54; 1992, passim). These commitments to 'rational enquiry' and a 'natural law' discerned by plain persons informs MacIntyre's account of political debate and engagement. Has MacIntyre safely avoided conservatism here? He is proposing standards of rational justification that differ from those that are appealed to, or are implicit in, much of contemporary Western politics, and therefore are radically different from mainstream politics and philosophy. Nonetheless, if MacIntyre will not draw a clear distinction between Thomistic natural law on the one hand and the moral consensus of a Thomistic community on the other, should the suspicion of conservatism (and relativism) remain?

Despite the suggestion of conservatism that hangs over his work, MacIntyre was once explicitly committed to Marxist politics (see MacIntyre, 1968). Kelvin Knight argues that MacIntyre's politics is still revolutionary, a reading which MacIntyre himself describes as 'accurate and perceptive' (1997: 235). MacIntyre criticizes what he believes is the 'ideological' role played by the modern state. The nation state is united in partnership with the capitalist market, he claims (1999b: 210), but modern ideology is so successful that we attribute '"democracy" to the state' (Knight, 2007: 176). What is more, MacIntyre believes we can pursue internal goods (goods of excellence) now only by 'resisting' the state and the market's prioritization of external goods. For that reason, MacIntyre praises the 'virtues exemplified in cooperative resistance to and subversion of institutional power', namely, 'goods of conflict' (ibid. p. 186). MacIntyre also claims that his conception of practice parallels what Marx called 'objective activity'. In a practice, individuals can pursue 'something of universal worth' and do so by transforming their desires, skills, and character traits (MacIntyre, 1994c: 225). His is not a politics of conservative acquiescence or insularity; his is an ethic of 'radical self-transformation' (ibid.; Breen, 2007).

However, there is good reason to wonder whether MacIntyre's position can explain or justify a revolutionary transformation of social life. First, he does not account for our major social systems. This is most evident with respect to the modern state. Although MacIntyre insists that the state is 'necessarily debased', 'he praises the "Americans with Disabilities Act"' (Breen, 2005: 494; 2002, passim). As Keith Breen notes, this shows that 'state corruption is a question of contingent fact, not theoretical generalization' (2005: 494; see also Keat, 2000: 131). MacIntyre also deprives the Aristotelian–Thomist of ethical resources needed to engage with the modern state. MacIntyre advises Aristotelian–Thomists to adopt an attitude of suspicion and pragmatism with respect to the state (Breen, 2005: 495), and he believes that genuine, virtuous political engagement is possible only at the level of the local community. It follows that MacIntyre does not provide an account of how the state can be harnessed to attain the goals he aspires to: in particular, meeting the needs of the needy, and praising and rewarding the virtuous. Finally, at the end of *After Virtue*, MacIntyre rejected 'modern systematic politics' as a 'systematic rejection' of 'the tradition of the virtues' (1985: 255). Therefore, even if MacIntyre does retain the revolutionary aspirations and commitments of his earlier work, he cannot explain or justify the revolutionary transformation of society that is called for by such aspirations.

MacIntyre's somewhat ambiguous relationship with conservatism is perhaps best illustrated by his arguments concerning Holocaust denial. He concludes that Holocaust denial 'precludes a rational evaluation of an important range of human goods' (1999b: 220). However, MacIntyre believes that it is only the local community that can justifiably not tolerate Holocaust denial. As there is not a moral consensus at the level of the nation state, the state's decision not to tolerate Holocaust denial cannot be morally justified. However, is it possible to establish that a community can justify intolerance on the basis of its own moral consensus? Intolerance is actually a virtue, according to MacIntyre, 'just in so far as it serves the purpose of a certain kind of rational enquiry and discussion, in which the expression of conflicting points of view enables us through constructive conflict to achieve certain individual and communal goods' (ibid. p. 233).

Can MacIntyre both defend 'rational enquiry and discussion' but do so on the basis of the moral consensus of a community? Why is the expression of conflicting points of view something that is good, and therefore something to be protected when faced with, for example, holocaust denial? To stand over such claims is it not the case that he would have to argue that some viewpoints should not be tolerated when they are obstacles to the 'expression of conflicting points of view' *and* that the latter is a good irrespective of one's tradition or community?

3
Reason and Faith

The previous chapter explored historicism by and large through an examination of Alasdair MacIntyre's moral and political theory. According to the historicist, the Enlightenment is a failed project for the reason that, pace Hume and others, all rational enquiry must in fact be constituted and bound by traditions. Enlightenment scepticism is unattainable as an ideal because genuine rationality must be tradition-constituted, and it also follows that Enlightenment scepticism is destructive and dysfunctional in practice because it undervalues and undermines traditions. We also saw that, in MacIntyre's politics, a moral consensus is necessary, and this is a consensus on the hierarchical ordering of all goods, and in this way MacIntyre has tried to re-articulate 'the function of man' argument from within historicism. In political engagement, then, we need to agree about what is good and therefore also about what is better and worse and on that basis who is more and less deserving. Moreover, we learn to make such moral judgements by taking the insight of the wise person as our standard of what is good, before then developing the ability to reason for ourselves. Therefore, any commitment to moral equality in historicism is tempered by the acknowledgement of distinctions in worth. This is most significant when it comes to political debate and political engagement. In giving reasons to others, according to the historicist, we should acknowledge that some contributions to society are better than others and deserve greater praise and higher rewards. In debating moral issues, we should also acknowledge the superior insight of others, namely the wise and morally good person.

This historicist rejection of Enlightenment moral and political theory raises objections of course, and these have been discussed in some detail. It seems that MacIntyre will have real difficulty showing that he is right to insist all rationality is context-bound, and nonetheless that his is not a position that can be criticized as relativistic about rationality, conservative in its politics, circular in its explanation of our knowledge of good, incoherent in its account of rational progress, and tied to the abject view that the giving of reasons will ultimately come to a halt and at that point the 'wise' person's judgement must be accepted.

MacIntyre's historicism is closely bound up with his Catholicism. However, so far, his Catholicism has been the focus of analysis only insofar as it was a manifestation of his historicism. That is, his Catholicism was of interest only insofar as it happened to be the defining characteristic of the tradition in which MacIntyre's moral and political philosophy is based, the context that constitutes his rational enquiry. Indeed, MacIntyre has seen himself as constituted by quite different traditions during his academic career, most significantly for our purposes an Aristotelian tradition of the virtues and then, after his conversion, an Aristotelian–Thomist tradition. Although the precise nature of MacIntyre's historicism has varied, and this variation is largely due to his conversion to Catholicism during the 1980s, it is also the case that his was an historicist philosophy before and after that conversion to Catholicism. So, to repeat, the analysis of historicism in the previous chapter was only an analysis of Catholicism in a secondary, derivative sense.

However, the religious nature of the tradition to which MacIntyre belongs, and the religious nature of that belonging, is of interest in itself. On the one hand, as a Catholic historicist, MacIntyre gives great significance to faith as one of the theological virtues and also believes that religious 'conversion' itself plays a crucial role in practical reasoning. On the other hand, the substance of Catholic thought comes to exert greater influence over the content of MacIntyre's own moral and political theory, not least in the importance his later work gives to natural law and an ethics based on human biology. This chapter explores first the idea of religious conversion and its implications for a theory of political reasoning. After that, the content of MacIntyre's more recent ethical and political writings are analysed, in particular his turn towards an ethics based on human biology and his defence of a demanding ethic of what he calls just generosity. Although this is an engagement with MacIntyre's Catholicism, historicism is ever-present and therefore still of interest. We will be forced to return again and again to the conflict between historicism and the Enlightenment and the significant criticisms of historicism that have been raised.

Conversion and rationality

MacIntyre's work on the life and philosophy of Edith Stein provides a valuable addition to his moral and political theory and by extension to his account of political reasoning. However, it is also the case that, on the face of it, much of what MacIntyre has to say in this later work, in particular concerning religious conversion, is hard to reconcile with his earlier discussion of 'the rationality of traditions'. Whereas before he had criticized Kuhn's account of paradigm shifts for the reason that they were made to seem akin to religious conversions, now he speaks of conversion (whether religious or not) as the process by which radical shifts in belief and commitment *do* occur and *should* occur. However, the question we must ask is whether this is nothing more than a change in MacIntyre's use of the term conversion. There is a strong sense in which the MacIntyre of *Edith Stein* uses the term conversion in precisely the same way as the MacIntyre of *Whose Justice? Which Rationality?* uses 'the rationality of traditions'.

In describing Stein's conversion to Catholicism in the 1920s, MacIntyre notes that a conversion need not involve the acceptance of religious beliefs. He gives the example of Georg Lukacs' adoption of Marxism, and characterizes it as 'a deliberate act of faith' (MacIntyre, 2006: 159). MacIntyre also insists that a conversion itself (religious or otherwise) need not be antithetical to reason. For St Augustine and those like him, 'because they now believe, they now are able to understand certain things' (ibid. p. 144). This way of presenting the situation should be familiar from the previous chapter. There we explored MacIntyre's view that tradition was not incompatible with rationality or indeed rational disagreement, and also his insistence that rationality needed to be reconnected with 'settled conviction'. Concerning the conversion to Catholicism of Edith Stein, herself a follower of Husserl and his phenomenological method, MacIntyre tries to show that this understanding of conversion is not necessarily incompatible with philosophical enquiry as it is understood by the phenomenologist. For the phenomenologist asks, 'What must be changed in me, if I am to perceive and understand things as they are?' (ibid.). In that sense, then, a conversion experience is not antithetical to rational enquiry, given the assumption that the consequence of the conversion is indeed that we 'perceive and understand things as they are'.

How did Stein characterize her own conversion, in MacIntyre's view? We saw how MacIntyre emphasized that, in a time of epistemological crises, and when we approach a rival tradition in search of a solution to these crises, rare human qualities are needed, in particular the quality of empathy. Similarly, MacIntyre describes Stein's conversion as arising out of her 'empathetic' perception and understanding of the experiences of another person's suffering, her newly widowed friend:

> She saw, felt and understood what it was to which Anna Reinach was responding...Jesus presenting himself to her, as to Anna Reinach, as both human and divine, as someone to be trusted unconditionally, as someone whose gift is an inner peace that comes only as a gift, as something that cannot be willed or otherwise contrived and that has no psychological explanation in purely natural terms. (ibid., p. 164)

It is in virtue of her capacity to empathize that Stein could have Jesus presented to her; and yet this gift of inner peace cannot itself be willed. MacIntyre notes as well that Stein also refers to the experience of 'resting in God', which 'she enjoyed after her encounter with Anna Reinach's devout grief' (ibid. p. 165). This is a 'feeling of being safe, of being relieved from anxiety and responsibility' (ibid.).

Stein also drew on the writings of St Teresa of Avila to account for this experience. MacIntyre here emphasizes how close St Teresa's views were to Stein's own (mature, evolved) phenomenology. The 'experience of God's presence has a history, the history of a life of prayer', and a life of prayer is a life of learning, of identifying our limitations; it involves conflicts, and in particular the conflict needed to overcome our strong attachments to what in the worldly environment 'prevents us from acknowledging God's presence' (Ibid. p. 167). Unlike what St Teresa called a 'false spirituality' (ibid.), she believed that 'God discloses himself through embodied human nature to our embodied humanity' (ibid. p. 168). And finally, her account of how we must guard against delusion is similar to the phenomenologist's insistence that we must distinguish genuine 'phenomenological attention' from what we bring to it 'from our natural and worldly prejudices' (ibid.).

Elsewhere MacIntyre defends the idea of a hierarchy of goods, as we have seen. That is, we pursue some goods 'for the sake of' other higher goods, and we pursue what is good and best for us as humans always as an end in itself and never for the sake of some other good(s). Similarly, according to MacIntyre, the consequence of Stein's conversion was a re-ordering of the goods in her life, the emergence of a new hierarchical ordering of goods (ibid. p. 170). What place did rational enquiry have in this hierarchy of goods? Or more to the point, what form did rational enquiry take after her conversion to Catholicism? MacIntyre points out that, at the time of her conversion, and for some time after, Stein gave up philosophy altogether. He believes that her 'philosophy of embodied consciousness' had gone beyond what phenomenology could offer, but Stein as yet had no philosophical resources to employ in the ongoing development of her thought. 'It was becoming clear that her phenomenological enquiries, that any phenomenological enquiries needed to be complemented and perhaps corrected by work done from some alternative philosophical standpoint' (ibid. p. 173).

She would later return to philosophy, but only through studying the work of Thomas Aquinas. MacIntyre stresses that Stein did not think phenomenology to be an obstacle to her religious conversion (ibid. p. 174). Nonetheless, in regard to the question of what form rational enquiry should take, Stein had to ask herself the question, 'Of what communities should I make myself a part?' (ibid.). The answer to that question was, resolutely, not the community of academic philosophy, for her answer was to join the community of St Teresa of Avila, the Carmelites.

The issue that will be focused on here is what shape political reasoning takes for someone like Edith Stein, or more to the point for MacIntyre himself, who has come through such a religious experience. The concern is with the way in which a Catholic can and should engage in political reasoning. Can they, and do they feel they should, offer reasons to non-Catholics that those non-Catholics can be expected to accept? Or instead are they and should they be concerned only with addressing arguments to those who have already accepted a Catholic philosophy, and is 'a Catholic approach' such that no reasons can be given for its adoption (or rejection) to the non-Catholic? To put the same point in the terms used in the previous chapter, is MacIntyre once more stuck on the horns of a dilemma: either he rejects his own fundamental and foundational belief that all enquiry is constituted by traditions (in this case a specific Catholic tradition), or he accepts what he has tried to refute, namely that his position leads to relativism, conservatism, and an abject view of human rationality. To set about answering this question we will first consider what it is to be a member of a tradition, whatever this tradition may be.

Catholicism is not the only tradition to which one may belong. It could also be said that Marxism provides something akin to a community and tradition to sustain practical reasoning. If the commitment to Marxism has parallels with Catholic belief, this is so for at least two reasons. The first concerns the process by which one comes to adopt such a perspective and stand point, the process of conversion itself. As we saw, MacIntyre has stated that a 'conversion' need not be religious, as Marxists have had such experiences as well. The second concerns the way in which one then engages with the world as a Marxist, and this includes the way one engages politically with those who do or do not share one's beliefs. How does membership of a Marxist community and adherence to the beliefs of a Marxist tradition sustain practical reasoning?

Marx had very definite views on the relationship between morality and socialism. According to Marx, the 'mode of production of material life conditions the social, political, and intellectual life processes in general' (1959: 425). Thus the ideas, including the moral ideas, of a capitalist society are the ideas that its mode of production conditions, and we can 'not judge of such a period by its own consciousness' (ibid. p. 426). Although capitalism is criticized for causing 'alienation' (1844: 112–114) and as 'a system of slavery' (1875: 352), the Marxist also believes that the moral ideas of a capitalist society justifies such practices, by in particular appealing to ideas of property and free choice. As Karl Popper contended, for Marx, 'moral ideas are weapons in a class struggle', and whether or not one chose to accept Marxism was not a decision *within* morality but a decision *between* competing moral systems (1966: 203–204). You are asked to make a choice between rival, incompatible moral systems.

Indeed, G.A. Cohen notes that, at one point in his own career as a political theorist, he believed that moral reasoning could play no part in bringing about socialism, for the reason that capitalist society and capitalist ideas made such moral reasoning powerless (1995: 3). Similarly, MacIntyre speaks of liberalism and Aristotelian–Thomism as separate, competing, and incommensurable moral systems. They do not speak to each other but rather sustain practical reasoning in mutually incompatible ways. So also for Cohen, there was no point engaging in moral debate about the justifiability of socialism to the extent that everyday morality was incommensurable with socialist ideals and also justified claims and entitlements that were incompatible with socialist aspirations.

It is not only those who are committed to a totalizing ideology and system of beliefs who share this view of practical reasoning. Much the same can be said of John Mackie's interpretation and subsequent development of David Hume's account of artificial virtues. In this instance, however, it is not that there are different moral systems sustained by different traditions or revolutionary movements. It is rather that morality itself is sustained by something like what MacIntyre would call a tradition. According to Mackie, morality is an 'institution', as it does not arise from the intrinsic nature of things. Morality provides reasons to act or judge in a particular way only for those who are already within the institution in question, and there are no moral reasons to enter the institution. In everyday life, we do tend to think that morality requires certain things of us because of the 'objective, intrinsic, requirements of the nature of things', but this view, although widely held, is erroneous (Mackie 1977: 80). 'Do the desires and especially the sufferings of other people, if known to me, constitute a reason for me to do something, if I can...?' (ibid. p. 78). There are strong reasons to help others in need if they are already closely related to me, say as friends or family or colleagues. But if there is

> a further class of reasons, independent of any desire that I now have to help these other people, we are...bringing in the requirements of something like an institution: an established way of thinking, a moral tradition, demands that I show concern for the well-being of others.... (ibid. p. 79)

It could be argued that Mackie overstates the case here in arguing from Hume's account of artificial virtues to this thesis that morality is an institution. Equally plausible is the argument that there are reasons that can be offered to be moral, reasons to step inside the institution of morality: the reasons Hume gave are that morality is pleasing and useful, to ourselves and others. However, Mackie's point is that morality requires more of us than Hume's argument can make sense of, namely it requires that we take a general point of view when judging what is right and wrong and good and bad. It does not simply require that we be moved by what is useful and pleasing to ourselves and others. Crucially, there are no 'reasons' to adopt such a general and impartial point of view.

Similarly, it makes little sense to look for and expect the reasons for a religious conversion if one is not oneself also a convert. It is not that there are no reasons that can be offered for the conversion. It is simply that the reasons now acceptable to the new convert can be given only to those who have taken that step and are themselves converts. Once we have converted, we have then entered the same 'institution' in Mackie's sense, or the same moral tradition, in MacIntyre's terms. It is then and then alone that morality (as it is understood within the institution) provides reasons for us. In Graham Greene's terms, before we took that step we 'strained at a gnat', but afterwards we find ourselves able to 'swallow a camel' (1978: 107). Before the conversion, the very smallest detail of the moral system was unacceptable, but the conversion itself creates the possibility of accepting the whole system of belief:

> He was a genuine communist. He survived Stalin like the Roman Catholics survived the Borgias. ... He used to say I strained at a gnat and swallowed a camel. You know I was never a religious man ... but there were priests I sometimes met in Africa who made me believe again – for a moment – over a drink. If all priests had been like they were and I had seen them often enough, perhaps I would have swallowed the Resurrection, the Virgin birth, Lazarus, the whole works. (ibid. pp. 106–107)

So conversion makes possible an entirely new and different kind of reasoning, but it also is a bar to reasoning, to reasoning as we used to know it and to reasoning as others know it. MacIntyre's political reasoning is, on the basis of a conversion to and belief in this Catholic moral system, sustained in a unique way, and for that very reason it is a mode of reasoning that closes the door to the rest of us who have not taken the same step and have not embraced the same tradition and moral system.

An ethic based on human biology

Let us return to our question: what is the nature of political reasoning for MacIntyre as a Catholic? To answer this question we will look at his defence of the very demanding ethic of just generosity. According to some, his account of just generosity is a radical departure from the arguments in *After Virtue* and *Whose Justice? Which Rationality?* We have seen that MacIntyre has been charged with relativism, conservatism, circularity, incoherence, and an abject view of reasoning, and the root of his problems has been historicism, the thesis that all rational enquiry is context-bound. In a later work, *Dependent Rational Animals*, MacIntyre offered a naturalistic account of ethics. He endeavoured to give ethics a foundation in human nature. This has led some to conclude that MacIntyre has left historicism behind or at the very least he has diluted it beyond recognition. For that reason, we shall explore his naturalism now to see whether it provides a remedy for the problems of historicism. However, another interpretation is that, in fundamental respects, MacIntyre has not made anything like a clean break with historicism. For it is also the case that MacIntyre's naturalism is, for him, made possible by his religious faith, but also his faith gives expression to the content of his specific tradition. The process of religious conversion makes possible the kind of practical reasoning that is based on this naturalistic ethic, and therefore the Catholic tradition and the Catholic community are for MacIntyre necessary elements of such an ethic.

Although accepting an Aristotelian approach to ethics, 'the function of man' argument, in *After Virtue* MacIntyre wanted to divest Aristotle's teleology of 'his metaphysical biology' (1985: 162). MacIntyre instead conceptualized teleology in terms of a person's life narrative. In that work, the justificatory basis of rationality also was provided not by Aristotle's account of human nature but tradition-constituted enquiry. MacIntyre's more recent work, *Dependent Rational Animals*, reopens this issue. He begins by disclosing the radical change that has taken place in his thought: 'Although there is indeed good reason to repudiate important elements of Aristotle's biology, I now judge that I was in error in supposing an ethics independent of biology to be possible' (1999a: x). He now acknowledges that a plant or an animal flourishes only 'in virtue of possessing some relevant set of natural characteristics' (ibid. pp. 78–79). As he takes 'it to be a question of fact... what it is for members of this or that particular species to flourish', he is 'committed to giving what is in some sense a naturalistic account of good' (ibid. p. 78). This change of direction in MacIntyre's later work can be understood in one of two ways. The first interpretation is that, although he gives little attention to tradition and the incommensurability of traditions, nonetheless little of substance has changed. His 'naturalistic' ethic in fact gives us very little that is different from his earlier 'tradition of the virtues'. The second interpretation is that his naturalism provides a universal account of human flourishing and on that basis a universal moral doctrine.

When do we 'have reasons'?

MacIntyre has been arguing all along that value judgements, judgements of good and bad and better and best, are objective rather than subjective. He therefore rejects Hume's account of practical rationality and goodness, and defends objectivism in practical rationality and goodness.

> Good, said Aquinas, has the *ratio* of a goal (*finis*). A good moves an agent to direct her or his action towards that goal and to treat

the achievement of that goal as a good achieved...So humans are goal-directed in virtue of their recognition of goods specific to their nature to be achieved. (ibid: 23; emphasis in original)

To ascribe goods to a human is to ascribe 'reasons' for doing much that they do. If I am asked to supply a 'reason' for my action I can do so by identifying the good I am pursuing. 'What makes my statement true or false is whether my action was or was not in fact directed towards the realization of that particular good' (ibid. p. 24).

MacIntyre will also say that we can ascribe reasons for acting to the members of species who cannot employ human language to make such utterances. For instance, we can say this of dolphins: there are certain goals that dolphins pursue as goods and so, such goods give 'reasons' for dolphin actions. 'And, just as with human beings, there is a close and observable connection between the successful identification and achievement of particular goods by particular dolphins and those same dolphins flourishing in the specific dolphin mode' (ibid.).

From the observation of dolphin activity, it is possible to conclude that dolphin actions are more than a 'sequence of bodily movements' (ibid. p. 23). They are goal-directed, and 'the successful identification and classification of a great many dolphin actions commits us to an ascription to them of a purposeful pursuit of characteristic goals' (ibid.). For example, dolphins have been observed to play in a disinterested sort of way, but also to engage together in a cooperative fashion when hunting. They exercise a range of capacities in such activities: 'They include capacities for perceptual recognition, for perceptual retention, for a range of different responses to what is perceived and recognized as the same individual or kind of individual and for a range of varying emotional responses' (ibid.).

We must now address the more difficult question that these claims raise. Do non-human animals such as dolphins 'act for reasons', and how can we be sure that this is the case?

What we do need to be able to identify, if we are to ascribe reasons for action to members of such species, are a set of goods at the achievement of which the members of that species aim, a set of judgements about which actions are or are likely to be effective in achieving those goods and a set of counterfactual conditionals that enable us to connect the goal-directedness and the judgements about effectiveness (ibid. p. 25).

All these elements are present, MacIntyre contends, when we observe dolphins cooperating in the course of a hunt. It has been observed that dolphin 'scouts' search for fish on behalf of the herd, and when they detect fish the rest of the herd will change course so as to join the scouts. To determine whether the dolphins are 'acting for reasons' we need only consider the following counterfactual: the dolphins *not* changing course in response to the scouts. They would have done so, given they were engaged in a hunt, only if they had 'some other reason of comparable importance for not changing course' or they 'would have had to be physically prevented from changing course' (ibid.).

The argument is that we have reasons to do something when it is good for us, and this is the case not only for human animals but also for non-human animals. However, it is possible to respond to MacIntyre's line of argument by employing the 'open question' method. MacIntyre is stating that dolphins (and other species) have reasons for actions because they have goods they should pursue. But if MacIntyre states that the good of dolphins is D (including playing and hunting with fellow dolphins), it is still possible to respond by saying 'I know that this dolphin is pursuing D, but is a life pursuing D a good life for a dolphin?' The question being asked, and the disagreement this signifies, is not the result of conceptual confusion. For it is not clear what makes for the good of any non-human animal: is it the self-maintenance and reproduction of the individual or of the group, and is the group the species as a whole or a particular population within the species? If a dolphin dies in the process of hunting with his/her fellow dolphins, a hunt that benefits the group as it leads to a big catch and helps sustain the other members of the group, did the individual dolphin have a reason to go on the hunt? In what sense was it a good for the individual dolphin that died? Perhaps death is just one predictable consequence of hunting. If that is the case, then the connection between the hunting activity and the good of the individual dolphin becomes tenuous. There is also the consideration of dolphins held in captivity. They perform many of the playful activities that they would do in the wild, and they exercise many of their capacities in doing so. Is this a good for those dolphins as a result? Do those dolphins have reasons to stay in captivity, and also to obey their human masters/trainers in captivity?

In addition, for some species, at some times, reproduction and self-maintenance are incompatible for the individual, as reproduction involves the sacrifice of the individual. Moreover, as the experiences of animals in factory farm conditions and those used in vivisection shows, maintaining life and reproducing can go hand in hand with very low levels of animal welfare.

It is not being argued here that it is not possible to distinguish between good and bad experiences or outcomes, and to do so for humans as well as other animals. However, the point is that although it may seem that identifying 'the good' of a non-human species is a straightforward matter, in fact it is indeed an open question. This goes to the very heart of 'the function of man' argument as well. For MacIntyre has assumed that statements of fact about dolphin experiences are the first premises in an argument that concludes by stating what is 'good' for those dolphins. However, if it is still possible to ask whether what is said to be a 'good' for dolphins really is a good, then the moral conclusion does not 'follow' from the factual statements.

We return to this point again. For now, we can ask, do humans have 'objective' goods in the way that MacIntyre believes that non-human animals do? Bernard Williams has argued that 'there can be no such thing as a reason for action by a particular agent which is external to and independent of this agent's motivational set' (Williams, 1981: 105, quoted in MacIntyre, 1999a: 86). Williams does accept that 'an agent may come to be moved by considerations which do not at present move her or him', but it is only in so far as this transition occurs that it is correct to state that the agent *now* has this as a 'reason to do such and such' (ibid. pp. 86–87). In contrast, MacIntyre believes it is possible to state that as doing Z is necessary for Y, and as Y is a good for the agent X, then X has a reason to do Z even though X does not at present have Y as a goal. That is, it is possible to make objective judgements about what is 'good' for some agent, and the truth of that judgement does not rest wholly on the current aims of that agent. How can such judgements be possible, according to MacIntyre?

They are made possible by an account of human moral development derived from an account of the goods that can be attained as a member of this species. MacIntyre believes this to be the case with the virtue of temperance (along with many others, including truthfulness, justice, just generosity, openness to refutation, wisdom, and so on). We cannot say that temperance is a good for X to pursue only if and insofar as X does desire, pursue, and aim at this virtue. This would be the equivalent of saying that temperance is a virtue for X only if X finds temperance pleasant or useful. Rather, temperance is one of the virtues 'that are agreeable to and are recognized as useful by those who possess them, but that may well seem disagreeable and even harmful... to those with the corresponding vices' (ibid. p. 88).

Why is temperance a good we should pursue, even if we do not presently aim at it? MacIntyre provides a naturalistic justification for such objective goods. It is a necessary part of human flourishing that we pass from a stage of childhood to a stage of adulthood, and part of that transition involves stepping back from and analysing what one happens to desire and assessing whether there are good reasons for such desires (ibid. p. 72). But we cannot step back from our current desires in this way if we are not also temperate; hence temperance is an objective good for us as humans. If we do not learn to assess the goodness or badness of our inclinations we will never overcome childish dependence on what we happen to desire.

Some further criticisms of ethics based on human biology

1. We have already introduced the 'open question' response to MacIntyre's arguments concerning the goods of non-human animals. That response can be adapted now to address MacIntyre's account of human goods. If MacIntyre states that the good of humans is H, it is still possible to respond by saying, 'I know that this human is pursuing H, but is a life pursuing H a good life for a human?' Or, 'I see that MacIntyre is living temperately, but is a temperate life a good life for a human?' MacIntyre does not just claim that some things are goods for humans; he also is arguing that they are objectively and naturally good. In doing so he is rejecting Hume's approach to meta-ethics and moral theory. For Hume, moral sentiments are action-guiding, but reason can never by itself move us to action. Therefore, reason is inert. Moreover, morality does not consist in matters of fact. Instead it is a matter of sentiment, of disapprobation or approbation, and it is an object of feeling (not an object of thought) (Hume, T. III, 1, i).

2. John Mackie, a follower of Hume, ventures 'the argument from queerness' against the supposed objectivity of moral judgements. If there were objective values, Mackie reasons, 'they would be entities or qualities or relations of a very strange sort, utterly different from anything else in the universe' (1977: 38). These objective goods would be sought by everyone, not due to the contingent fact that this person desires it, but because it has 'to-be-pursuedness somehow built into it' (ibid. p. 40). Indeed, it is MacIntyre's argument that, even if you do not aim for temperance (and other virtues) as a goal, you do have reasons to aim for it as a goal.

3. Mackie also observes that the logic of so-called objective value judgements is suspect. There is something peculiar about any moral reasoning 'that is not contingent upon desires or purposes or chosen ends' (ibid. p. 30). What is peculiar is that, 'somewhere in the input to this argument – perhaps in one or more of the premises, perhaps in some part of the form of the argument – there will be something which cannot be objectively validated' (ibid.).

In MacIntyre's argument concerning temperance above, is there 'something which cannot be objectively validated'? Two criticisms suggest themselves.

First, perhaps one could accept that humans do have the ability to overcome a 'childlike' condition of dependence on what they happen to desire, but can one infer from this factual statement the moral conclusion that one ought to value temperance as a good? Someone may accept that the factual statement is true and the moral conclusion justified, but it does not follow that the moral conclusion was inferred from the factual statement. Instead, for the inference to be possible, it may be argued, there must first be a desire or a preference for temperance, and it is for that reason and that reason only that temperance is a good. In response, MacIntyre would need to put forward a meta-ethical argument here to establish that, when we do make value judgements, we are inferring value judgements from factual statements.

A second critique of MacIntyre is as follows: someone may accept that the factual statement is true, but reject the normative conclusion. It may be concluded that the good person should not be temperate, that temperance is not a valuable character trait. This is what the 'open question' approach allows: it is still an open question whether temperance is a good for humans. In this instance, MacIntyre needs to offer an argument in defence of his specific account of human nature but also a defence of his specific account of human flourishing, human-nature-as-it-could-be-if-it-realized-its-*telos*.

If MacIntyre is to deal with the second critique, this would involve an argument against Nietzsche, among others. Nietzsche also offers a naturalistic account of good. He does not deny the connection between character traits and human goodness, as Philippa Foot observes, but he does reject prevailing views of human motivations and also what counts as virtues. In particular he rejects Christian 'pity morality', in sharp contrast to MacIntyre's appeal to *misericordia* [pity], as we shall see in this chapter. Nietzsche calls Christianity the morality of the weak or the herd (Foot, 2001: 105). Instead of this morality of weakness, he 'represents human good in terms of individuality, spontaneity, daring, and the kind of creativity that rejects the idea of a rule of life that would be valid for others as well' (ibid. p. 106). Foot argues that what is wrong with Nietzsche's account are the facts about humanity on which he bases his evaluative judgements. For Foot, 'charity is a prime candidate as a virtue, because love and other forms of kindness are needed by every one of us when misfortune strikes, and may be a sign of strength rather than weakness in those who are sorry for us' (ibid.). However, it is not just the facts about which there is disagreement here. There is disagreement also concerning the moral conclusions inferred from those facts.

Two crucial issues have arisen here with respect to MacIntyre's later work. The first is the need for a philosophical argument in defence of his position, and this argument requires two components: a meta-ethical defence of objective value judgements, and an argument in defence of his specific conceptions of human nature, valuable character traits, and human flourishing. Are value judgements objective, and is temperance (and justice, just generosity, and so on) a virtue? The second issue is the type of argumentation and therefore the type of philosophical methodology available to MacIntyre, and here there are two possibilities. Either MacIntyre has broken new ground and his philosophy will be independent of any specific tradition, or else his enquiry is, as it was before, context-bound and tradition-constituted. The argument of this book is that MacIntyre is still wedded to historicism. In later chapters, however, naturalism will be analysed in terms of its appropriateness as a basis for political debate: it will be argued that, even if we felt confident in the defence of a universal naturalistic ethic, as such an ethic would be one among many controversial moral doctrines, it may be inappropriate as a basis for political debate.

In previous work MacIntyre concluded that Hume's argument against objectivism is not derived from an 'unrestrictedly general logical principle' (1985: 57). Instead, the argument that 'ought' cannot be inferred from 'is' was derived from a particular 'conception of moral rules and judgements' new to the eighteenth century (ibid.). We have already seen MacIntyre's argument here: what Hume and others were doing at this time was rejecting 'the function of man' argument, where ethical concepts were tied to a conception of human-nature-as-it-happens-to-be and human-nature-as-it-could-be-if-it-realized-its-*telos*. Another way to put this point is to say that, within his tradition, Hume was right to argue that 'ought' cannot be inferred from 'is', but also, such inferences can be made from within different traditions, in particular the tradition of the virtues. If MacIntyre is making this kind of argument here, his position is still an historicist one, and therefore still open to the objections noted earlier. But it has been claimed by some that MacIntyre has weakened if not completely severed his links to tradition and historicism. They believe that MacIntyre is endeavouring to offer a universal account of human flourishing and universal standards of rational justification (Breen, 2002: 186; Knight, 2007, 2000: 179).

A universal or a contextual morality?

In order to resolve this issue, let us turn to what it is for a human life to be good. Something can be good merely because it is useful. However, as an objectivist, MacIntyre believes that the goods of an activity are 'to be valued as ends worth pursuing for their own sake' (1999a: 64). What is more, as a naturalist, according to MacIntyre we use the verb 'to flourish' to refer to the unconditionally good *qua* human being (ibid.). He contends that to judge how an individual or a community is to 'order' the goods in their lives, we must 'judge unconditionally about what it is best for individuals or groups to be or to do or have not only *qua* agents engaged in this or that form of activity in this or that role or roles, but also *qua* human beings. It is these judgments that are judgments about human flourishing' (ibid. p. 67).

MacIntyre's argument is that some things are good because useful, some things are good in themselves and the goods of activities, and finally the unconditionally good *qua* human being is human flourishing. How do we flourish? MacIntyre wants to show that as humans we have the capacity to become 'independent practical reasoners', although, as animals, with animal afflictions and dependencies, we never overcome the need for the virtues associated with 'acknowledged dependence'.

An agent passes through three stages, according to MacIntyre, in becoming an independent practical reasoner. He or she must pass from a condition of 'initial directedness' towards things that are desired in an unreflective way, to a condition where he or she is able to step back from and assess whether or not there are good reasons to desire such things. Finally, an agent must pass to a stage where he or she can imagine realistic alternative futures. In moving away from the stage of 'felt wants' (ibid. p. 68), human beings 'learn to understand themselves as practical reasoners about goods' (ibid. p. 67). This is a capacity that other animals do not have (as far as we know). They cannot learn 'how to separate themselves from their desires and more especially from those desires in their primitive, infantile forms' (ibid. p. 69). Also, a dog may be said to 'believe that its master is at the door, but not that its master will come the day after tomorrow' (ibid. p. 74). In contrast, humans are able to imagine different possible futures. This involves seeing them as presenting me 'with different and alternative sets of goods to be achieved, with different possible modes of flourishing' (ibid. p. 75). The independent practical reasoner also is not just free from constraints in pursuit of what is felt to be good. He or she is also morally good, for it is only then one can be practically rational.

I return now to the two most important ways in which a thing may be good: the inherent good of an activity and the good of human flourishing. MacIntyre's discussion of this distinction may be interpreted in either of two ways. The first makes human flourishing a higher standard with which to identify and understand the goods of activities, while for the second, our ideas of human flourishing are derived from specific contexts, including practices, communities, and traditions. The former interpretation is supported by the following passage:

> What it is for human beings to flourish does of course vary from context to context, but *in every context* it is as someone exercises in a relevant way the capacities of an independent practical reasoner that her or his potentialities for flourishing in a specifically human way are developed. So if we want to understand *how it is good for humans to live*, we need to know what it is to be excellent as an independent practical reasoner, that is, what the virtues of independent practical reasoning are. (ibid. p. 77; emphasis added)

Here MacIntyre wants to say that flourishing is the same 'in every context', and this should not be surprising for in every context humans can only flourish as human beings, and the context does not change our species.

However, when MacIntyre does talk of the virtues of independent practical reasoning he gives great significance to what can happen in just these contexts.

> Independent practical reasoners contribute to the formation and sustaining of their social relationships, as infants do not, and to learn how to become an independent practical reasoner *is to learn how to cooperate with others in forming and sustaining those same relationships that make possible the achievement of common goods* by independent

practical reasoners. Such cooperative activities presuppose some degree of shared understanding of present and future possibilities (ibid. p. 74; emphasis added).

In the second quote here what it means to flourish cannot be defined independently of the context in which we pursue goods. To become an independent practical reasoner just 'is' to learn how to cooperate with others in pursuing common goods. MacIntyre also concedes that he has presupposed Aristotelian–Thomist views about flourishing and about the very nature of his enquiry into flourishing. He assumes there 'is no presuppositionless point of departure' (ibid. p. 77). But this need not be debilitating to rational enquiry, he believes. 'One mark of adequate understanding is that it explains retrospectively why enquiry well-designed to achieve it could have begun from some types of starting point, but not from others' (ibid. pp. 77–78).

Is just generosity a universal or a Catholic moral principle?

MacIntyre emphasizes the important similarities between the flourishing of humans and of non-human intelligent animals. To fully understand human flourishing we must acknowledge that humans never leave behind their animality. For these reasons, MacIntyre's account of human virtue departs from that of Aristotle and also contains important political implications. MacIntyre departs from Aristotle to the extent that MacIntyre insists the virtuous person must learn to acknowledge his or her own dependence. Aristotle in contrast assumes 'men who are manly differ from women in being unwilling to have others saddened by their grief'; and 'the magnanimous man ... dislikes any recognition of his need for aid and consolation by others' (Aristotle, NE, IX 1171b 6012, IV 1124b 9–10, referenced in MacIntyre, 1999a, p. 7). For MacIntyre, humans rely on others to become independent, and the virtuous person is able not only to give but also to receive help.

The Aristotelian virtues of justice, temperance, truthfulness, and courage are, MacIntyre now concedes, most suited to 'enabling us to become independent practical reasoners' (ibid. p. 120). However, we must also inquire into the virtues of acknowledged dependence. If we acknowledge that we are dependent on others to attain maturity and adulthood, to be socialized, and to be kept safe from many harms, and if we acknowledge that we will often be dependent again (through illness and infirmity), then we should also accept that we are duty-bound to give aid to those who are now suffering afflictions, disability, and extreme dependence. We should therefore accept the necessity of developing and exercising the virtue of just generosity. This is an insight evident in Aquinas, who claims that, in every act, we should exercise the virtues of justice, liberality (*decentia*), charity (friendship), pity (*misericordia*), and doing good (*beneficentia*).

> *Misericordia* is a grief or sorrow over someone else's distress...just insofar as one understands the other's distress as one's own. One may do this because of some pre-existing tie to the other...or because in understanding the other's distress one recognizes that it could instead have been one's own. (Aquinas, S.T. IIa-IIae, 30, 4, referenced in MacIntyre, 1999a: 125)

It is not enough to respond as just generosity requires to one's fellow community members and to no one else.

> *Misericordia* has regard to urgent and extreme need without respect of persons... And what each of us needs to know in our communal relationships is that the attention given to *our* urgent and extreme needs, the needs characteristic of disablement, will be proportional to the need and not to the relationship (MacIntyre, 1999a: 124; emphasis in original).

On the one hand, living together in a community presupposes that we each will care for those in need because and insofar as they are in need. On the other hand, the person from outside the community is put on the same footing as a community member simply by his or her great need. That person must be treated as a 'brother' or a 'neighbour'.

One important character trait is the ability to acknowledge our dependence. In particular, when I am no longer capable of independent action, I must rely on a 'proxy'. The only person who can really speak for me is someone who knows 'how I have judged my good in various situations in the past' and so the relationship 'generally has to be rooted in previously existing relationships of friendship' (ibid. p. 139). The other important character trait is the willingness to give to others. Although often we give to those from whom we have received in the past, 'often enough it is from one set of individuals that we receive and to and by another that we are called on to give' (ibid. p. 99). And although giving and receiving is a crucial feature of the family (and although the parents of disabled children are said to be the 'paragons' of the virtues of giving), parental authority is illegitimate if it does not conform to the principles of giving and receiving (ibid. p. 104). The ethic is so demanding that MacIntyre revises Marx's principle of distribution for the communist society to read as follows: 'From each according to her or his ability, to each, so far as is possible, according to her or his needs' (ibid. p. 130). (Marx's original was, 'From each according to his abilities, to each according to his needs!' (Marx, 1875: 347))

What is the type of communal environment in which such a principle can be implemented? MacIntyre calls it simply the 'local community'. However, it would be more accurate to say that it is 'the community of practices'. For MacIntyre believes that neither the modern family nor the modern nation state on their own can provide the communal environment necessary for flourishing. The family is not self-sufficient. The goods of family life are only ever realized insofar as its members also participate in various practices: in clubs, in education, in work, in politics, and so on. The nation state is 'not unimportant' (ibid. p. 142). We can meet many of the needs of local communities only 'by making use of state resources and invoking the intervention of state agencies' (ibid.). 'But it is the quality of the politics of local communities that will be crucial in defining those needs adequately and in seeing to it that they are met' (ibid.).

MacIntyre has drawn attention to the fact that human beings continue to have animal bodies and animal identities. He then argues that, as virtues are necessary for flourishing, human virtues must be such as to give due weight to our animality and the afflictions and vulnerabilities that this gives rise to. Just generosity is required of us, therefore, because as humans we pass from periods of extreme dependence to independence and back into dependence. However, is MacIntyre vulnerable to the charge of Mackie and others, namely, that 'somewhere in the input to this argument ... there will be something which cannot be objectively validated'? For instance, MacIntyre states that 'I understand another's distress as my own', and then he infers that 'I am obliged to give to the other in direct proportion to his or her need'. Does the former imply the latter, and if so why? I can acknowledge that I will be dependent on others for help, but this factual truth does not require accepting any specific moral conclusion in and of itself. For instance, one could draw the moral conclusion: therefore, everyone should be financially prudent, and save for their future, and remain financially independent, or alternatively, therefore, all should contribute to a social insurance scheme that would provide for the needs of all equally through state organized services. Either *moral* conclusion is equally justifiable given the *factual* premises regarding our neediness. MacIntyre also states that 'what each of us needs to know in our communal relationships is that attention given to our urgent needs … will be proportional to the need', and then he infers that *misericordia* 'extends beyond communal obligations'. Once again, does the former imply the latter, and if so why? As we shall see in the final chapter, some who argue for quite comprehensive welfare coverage among fellow citizens *within* a state also argue for minimal welfare responsibilities among individuals *between* states.

I am not suggesting that MacIntyre's principle of just generosity is unjustifiable, but I am saying that premises needed to make these conclusions are missing from MacIntyre's argument. Can these missing, implicit, premises be made explicit, and if so from where are they derived? We must answer this question if we are to engage in rational political debate about, for instance, provision for needy children, including those who are strangers. The evidence suggests that, for MacIntyre, such premises will be provided by a specific tradition of enquiry and a specific communal moral consensus, but this becomes problematic when political interaction involves those who do not belong to 'our' community. If the missing premises can be derived only from one specific context, then how can 'our' treatment of strangers be justified in terms acceptable to those strangers?

Reasoning in the light of 'our shared standards'

How do we engage in a rational political debate that will address and hope to resolve the moral issues we face including, among other things, the provision of aid for the most needy? What types of consideration should count as morally compelling? We have been discussing MacIntyre's historicism and Catholicism, and in particular his development of a demanding ethic of just generosity. In what way can MacIntyre enter into a political debate about the justifiability of such proposals? This question is particularly significant when we consider that MacIntyre's ethic is derived from considerations that are themselves controversial. In particular, he has assumed that such an ethic is based upon the biology of human beings and the ends or goods of creatures such as us, but also that as a Catholic the virtues needed to flourish require that we embrace just generosity.

From where do we derive the considerations and reasons we give to others in a political debate in an attempt to account for and justify ourselves and our proposals to those they affect? Many of MacIntyre's comments suggest that political debate draws on experiences we share as humans, experiences that should therefore motivate us to find considerations acceptable to all. In particular, he argues that independent practical reasoners, by virtue of their shared humanity, can learn a great deal from the dependent or afflicted or vulnerable. He takes as his example 'that kind of disablement which consists in gross disfigurement' (1999a: 136). Firstly, with respect to our desires, we can learn 'the nature and degree of the value that we have hitherto placed upon a pleasing appearance' in others and ourselves, and the extent to which these value judgements have been mistaken (ibid.). This also offers an insight into the extent to which 'we have been lacking in adequate self-knowledge in failing to understand the full range of judgements that are influenced by such feelings' (ibid. p. 137). MacIntyre is not suggesting that what we learn from the disfigured is the complete unimportance of physical appearance. A 'handsome appearance and an engaging manner are good' (ibid.), but we can be 'mistaken as to the nature and limits of their goodness' (ibid. p. 138). Thirdly, we may come to see 'examples of courage and gracefulness of spirit that can be hard-won responses to afflictions of disfigurement and disablement' (ibid.). If we do come to appreciate the importance of such 'virtues of acknowledged dependence', it is less likely that we will be unable ourselves to practice them should we undergo similar experiences.

Because of our shared humanity, the suffering of others can greatly influence us; it can speak directly to us, regardless of all those features of our lives that separate us. Nonetheless, for MacIntyre, we must agree about 'ends' if we are to debate 'means'. This follows from the Aristotelian account of practical rationality. The starting point, the first premise, of a chain of practical reasoning is something like 'Since the good and the best is such and such ... ' (ibid. p. 106). Our debate together can get off the ground only if we share this starting point, for then we can debate what is the best end to pursue in a given circumstance so as to attain the good and the best. However, I do not think that MacIntyre is simply saying that we must agree first that our goal is human flourishing, and that this goal provides standards of rationality that are independent of the standards of rationality found within specific activities and the moral consensus of specific communities.

Rational debate among fellow citizens is crucial, MacIntyre believes, just because of the importance of responsibility and accountability. But how do we account for ourselves to our fellow citizens?

> When I am called to account as a practical reasoner in this shared evaluative language, what I am invited to consider is whether what is said about me is or is not *true and justified in the light of our shared standards of truth and justification.* (ibid. p. 152; emphasis added)

MacIntyre rightly anticipates the criticism that his stand invites: 'Yet it does appear that by saying this I have already foreclosed on certain possibilities of criticism' (ibid. p. 154). The point at issue is whether he can 'give a rationally defensible account of the relationship of moral commitment to critical rational enquiry that enables us to identify and to satisfy the legitimate demands of both' (ibid. p. 156). MacIntyre's approach rules out the appeal to context-independent theoretical standards of rational justification. 'It [critical rational enquiry] is something that *we* undertake from within *our* shared mode of practice by asking, when we have good reason to do so, what the strongest and soundest objections are to this or that particular belief or concept that we have up to this point taken for granted' (ibid. p. 157; emphasis in original).

How does rational enquiry proceed? We ask whether what we have hitherto taken to be good reasons are good reasons, and whether we can accept the standards we have hitherto employed in evaluating such reasons, and what authority these standards do have and why (ibid.). MacIntyre does contend that we always argue from within our shared mode of practice. However, he assumes that such a shared practice makes rational argumentation possible. He also insists that such practices and communities are only themselves in 'good order' to the extent that their 'judgements, standards, relationships, and institutions have been periodically the subject of communal debate and enquiry and have taken their present form in part as a result of such debate and enquiry' (ibid.).

There are two ways, however, in which MacIntyre insists that rational enquiry must be limited. He rejects the notion that, if we are to do what is right, the right action must be the product of an explicit chain of deliberation. Rather, although the virtuous person will be able to offer justifications for his or her actions after the event, often it is a sign of virtue not to require such deliberation before acting. This is the case when we deliberate about what we should do when, for instance, confronted by the severe need of another. For the virtuous person, MacIntyre argues, a stranger's urgent need provides sufficient reason for her or him to go to that person's aid. Not only that, she or he 'will also be unable to conceive of such a reason as requiring or being open to further justification. To offer or even to request such a justification is itself a sign of defective virtue' (ibid. p. 158). So rational enquiry is limited here because it is a mark of virtue not to need a reason to act as the virtues require. Some things should be taken for granted as goods; they are or should be self-evident or unquestioned. But when we do offer help to a stranger: one could respond that surely we are under an obligation to account for ourselves to them and others? And if so, how do we account for ourselves and justify our actions? The second limitation to rational enquiry brings us back to Nietzsche once again. MacIntyre is concerned with the types of character traits that Nietzsche praised. Nietzsche praised hardness, the antithesis of pity (ibid. p. 163). For MacIntyre, Nietzsche was inverting the virtues of acknowledged dependence, as he praised only those who are independent of the aid provided by others. But what is so wrong with Nietzsche's approach? MacIntyre is exercised by what he sees as Nietzsche's foreclosure of genuine dialogue and debate, that is, rational enquiry within a shared mode of practice. The Nietzschean approach characterized as follows: 'I do not appeal to a standard of justification that is independent of my desires and drives...but I give expression...to whatever form the will to power may have taken in those desires and drives' (ibid. p. 165).

When we reflect together critically, MacIntyre responds, 'it must be in such a way as not to threaten...mutual recognition' (ibid. p. 161). It is only on the basis of recognition that deliberations really are 'the deliberations of the community, rather than an adversarial exercise of dialectical skill...in which the outcome of the argument may be to undermine someone's standing as a member of the community or even the whole notion of mutual recognition' (ibid.). MacIntyre believes that 'a certain range of moral commitments' must be shared so that both 'shared deliberations' and 'shared critical enquiry concerning that deliberation' become possible: 'Truthfulness about their shared practical experience, justice in respect of the opportunity that each participant receives to advance his or her arguments, and an openness to refutation are all prerequisites of critical enquiry' (ibid.).

The virtues of justice, truthfulness, and openness to refutation are prerequisites of moral debate in the political sphere. This is a debate based upon mutual respect. It is therefore informative to reflect on exactly what such mutuality and reciprocity means within MacIntyre's Catholic historicist paradigm. It does entail a commitment to moral equality, and the commitment to moral equality should be evident in the exchange of views in political debate. For it is because of the moral equality of humans that the suffering of other humans has the significance it should have for us. However, MacIntyre will combine such a commitment to moral equality with the further commitment to limit debate in the ways outlined above: some things should be taken for granted as goods (and bads), and debate and interaction must not threaten the bonds and presuppositions of our moral community. So although our moral participation in politics is motivated by the vision of a moral community of equals, we are not free to engage in politics in any way that threatens this moral community. MacIntyre has already defined a 'tradition in good working order' as one that provides a moral consensus on the hierarchical order of goods and the ultimate good. Here it transpires that, although political debate can question and probe at this consensus, at the same time the consensus must somehow be retained and preserved.

Just such a vision of moral engagement is found in the novels of Evelyn Waugh, like MacIntyre a convert to Catholicism. Here, in the *Sword of Honour* trilogy, the narrator reflects on the character Guy Crouchbank's sense of destiny and purpose:

> In the recesses of Guy's conscience there lay the belief that some-
> where, somehow, something would be required of him, that he must
> be attentive to the summons when it came. They also served who
> only stood and waited. He saw himself as one of the labourers in the
> parable who sat in the market-place waiting to be hired and were
> not called into the vineyard until late in the day. They had their
> reward on an equality with the men who toiled since dawn. One
> day he would get the chance to do some small service which only he
> could perform, for which he had been created. Even he must have
> his function in the divine plan. He did not expect a heroic destiny.
> Quantitative judgements did not apply. (Waugh, 1961: 66)

Note the way in which moral equality is in no way to be taken to imply a 'quantitative' equality, whether equality of power, of rewards, of contribution, or of standing. Rather, for Catholic social thought, all humans enjoy equal status in that they are owed equal moral concern and are equally capable of living a life of virtue. Virtue is indeed about what is difficult for humans, but it is equally difficult for us all. But this is not an equality where quantitative judgements apply: the functions of each cannot be compared and the material rewards owed to each is not at issue. In addition, this is not the equal freedom of Rawls and other liberals: the freedom to form, to rationally revise, and to pursue our conceptions of the good. It is rather an equal moral worth premised on our *not* calling into question the hierarchical ordering of goods upon which our community of mutual respect is based.

The character traits praised by MacIntyre as virtues, the traits of justice, truthfulness, and openness to refutation, are indeed strong candidates for the virtues of political debate. However, if they can be virtues only 'for us', as members of a community, then once again we face the dangers of relativism, conservatism, circularity, incoherence, and an abject view of reason. How is it possible to avoid these pitfalls and yet defend such traits as virtues?

Two different approaches could be taken, although it is the second that will be argued for here. One way is to argue that these virtues are derived from a universal moral doctrine, and are justified for that reason. This doctrine could be a naturalistic account of Aristotelian ethics shorn of MacIntyre's historicism. This may be attractive if we should first base political debate on universally valid moral truths. At the same time, this approach is unattractive if we know these moral truths will not be accepted as such by a substantial number of our fellow citizens: they will not be shared by the followers of Hume who believe value judgements are based on subjective desires; and they will not be accepted by followers of Nietzsche who praise different character traits, and so on. However, the more compelling point, morally speaking, is that these other voices in political debate (Humeans, Nietzscheans, etc.) need not accept these claims as universal moral truths, but rather that they should be free to disagree about such matters.

The alternative approach acknowledges that we are free to disagree about the truth of moral doctrines. Although the virtues listed by MacIntyre may be derived from one specific moral doctrine, they are defended on other grounds, and those grounds are equally accessible to all. That is, they are defended as virtues of the public sphere, and they are defended with public reasons. We will return to just such an approach towards the end of the next chapter. First however we must address the other strand of anti-Enlightenment thought, the approach which owes its origins to Nietzsche as well as Wittgenstein and Heidegger.

4
Agonism

Anti-Enlightenment political philosophy is a critical reaction to the Enlightenment and, specifically, the commitments to scepticism and moral equality. One way that such anti-Enlightenment thought developed can be seen in the 'historicist' work of MacIntyre, in particular the importance given to tradition. For MacIntyre, settled conviction can be provided by tradition, and settled conviction is needed for practical reasoning, that is, a consensus on the hierarchical ordering of all goods. What is more, to reason well we must learn from the wise person, the expert within the tradition, whether it is the good sportsperson or the good moral agent, and in doing so strive to emulate and even surpass their achievements. And we need to take such an approach, MacIntyre believes, because of the failings of the Enlightenment, and in particular its inability either to provide universal principles of political reason or to safeguard the moral standing of each person.

The previous chapters drew attention to a tension between MacIntyre's approach on the one hand and on the other the approach of Nietzsche and his followers. In particular, there is disagreement over the types of character traits considered virtuous and also the nature of moral argument and deliberation. MacIntyre took exception to Nietzsche's rejection of pity, but he also felt that a Nietzschean approach to deliberation and debate would be nothing more than an adversarial conflict that would dissolve the moral bonds of the community. Nonetheless, MacIntrye can agree with Nietzsche that the Enlightenment is a failure, and they can agree that, no matter how often and with what vehemence Enlightenment thinkers insist otherwise, they cannot and will not find universal moral principles and they cannot and will not resolve moral disputes and thereby guarantee social justice. However, the situation is made more complex for the following reason. Many now profess to believe that post-modernism is not so much a rejection of but a valuable addition to Enlightenment thought. The argument is that post-modernism can illuminate both the hidden will to power motivating many taken-for-granted political assumptions and also the consequent reality of violence and domination at the heart of political thought as well as political action.

The post-modernist therefore provides one further way in which to respond to the Enlightenment. But is it a rejection of, or a complimentary addition to Enlightenment thought? To begin answering that question, let us start by addressing the debate between post-modernism and one approach within the Enlightenment, liberalism. Two questions will be focused on. Can the terms of political debate be given a foundation that is universal? And do the grounds of political debate admit of a rational justification? In asking these questions we are probing the issue of whether and in what form political reasoning can be based on the Enlightenment commitments to moral equality and scepticism.

Post-modernists approach these issues in two different ways. While some deride and reject outright the broadly 'humanist' ideals of truth, liberty, and justice (see Foucault, 1984; Lyotard, 1984), this chapter will engage with those who wish to defend liberal democracy though reject what they refer to as the 'universal rationalism' of liberal theory (Mouffe, 2000; Rorty, 1989). There is no such universal rational framework waiting to be discovered or created, Chantal Mouffe claims. Politics is a contextualist task as it is pursued within a 'form of life', and also it is based on considerations that are 'contestable' and 'undecidable'. Rather than consensus she calls for 'agonism'.

Standing opposed to post-modernism, however, there are those who believe that political engagement can be based on morality-as-such and reason-as-such. The liberal version of this approach also entails the claim that the goal of democratic interaction is consensus (see Habermas, 2005; Gutmann and Thompson, 1996). There are of course disagreements within liberalism: some believe that liberalism is morally neutral between competing conceptions of the good life while others believe it should promote one way of life (i.e. an autonomous life) (see Chapter 6); and some believe that liberal political reason is based on moral truth while others instead believe it is based on only public, political considerations that do not presuppose the truth of any one moral doctrine (see Chapter 5). Nonetheless, post-modernism rejects all of the above in its critique of the 'universal rationalism' of liberal theory.

Post-modernists are calling into question the whole project of providing rational moral foundations for politics. However, the argument in this chapter will be that the post-modernist position is such that it cannot be shown to be correct or justified. As some have argued (Habermas, 1994b), post-modernists cannot avoid a 'performative contradiction' whereby the attempt to state the post-modern position contradicts the content of that statement. That is, post-modernists unavoidably assume just what they claim to reject. A further argument in this chapter is that post-modernism descends into relativism and immoralism. And although some liberals hope to find common ground with post-modernism, in particular so as better to identify the power relations shaping and distorting democratic debate, this chapter argues that liberalism and post-modernism are, in the final analysis, incompatible.

There is however reason for concern with the liberal position, in particular as it is developed by Amy Gutmann and Dennis Thompson. They call on participants within democratic debate to exercise certain virtues, namely 'reciprocity' and 'mutual respect' (Gutmann and Thompson, 1996), but they also argue that such political engagement can and should strive to promote a certain type of life, namely one that is autonomous (Gutmann, 1999). The problem arises if the promotion of one type of life leads to a contradiction for liberals: while they call for a rationally motivated moral consensus they assume in advance that we should accept one specific moral doctrine and conception of the good life. Indeed this tension or contradiction in liberal thought is grist to the post-modern mill, for it seems to confirm what post-modernists have claimed: that all forms of reasoning and all moral principles and values *are nothing more than* expressions of a specific form of life as well as its power relations and conflicts. The issue then is whether post-modernists are correct in their characterization of morals and reason, and therefore in the rejection of the Enlightenment, or alternatively, whether the principles of mutual respect and reciprocity can be disentangled from a liberal moral doctrine and a liberal form of life, and therefore whether the commitments of the Enlightenment can be disentangled from liberal morality.

The debate over 'liberalism' and 'democracy'

Mouffe accepts and defends what she calls the 'political project of modernity'. Her goal, however, is to dissociate 'liberal democracy' from the epistemological aspiration to universalism evident in the work of Kant, Rousseau, and others. She rejects the 'modernist' attempt to base democratic politics on reason, which she refers to as the 'Enlightenment project of self-foundation' (1989: 34). At the same time, Mouffe does not espouse what she calls the 'apocalyptical post-modernism' of, among others, Jacques Derrida (ibid. p. 38). It is not the case, she contends, that we 'are at the threshold of a radically new epoch, characterized by drift, dissemination, and by the uncontrollable play of significations' (ibid.). Nonetheless, Mouffe rejects 'liberal' political theory, as she describes her position as anti-rationalism and anti-universalism.

What is it that Mouffe is rejecting here? First we will briefly sketch the liberal Enlightenment position criticized by Mouffe. A political position is 'liberal' if it would guarantee civil and political rights to all adult citizens. Citizens are thought of as free and equal and for that reason as bearers of rights that guarantee this freedom and equality. Further, for the 'radical-democratic interpretation of political liberalism' (Habermas, 2005), a forum of debate must be established and maintained, and what is more, its participants must share certain value commitments that are taken to be universal in the sense of equally valid for all. The key ideas, according to Gutmann and Thompson, are 'reciprocity' and 'mutual respect'. 'The foundation of reciprocity is the capacity to seek fair terms of social cooperation for their own sake. Because the results of democratic deliberations are mutually binding, citizens should aspire to a kind of political reasoning that is mutually justifiable' (Gutmann and Thompson, 1996: 53). Political reasoning is not based simply on prudence or self-interest, a search for a *modus vivendi*, but also it is not based on a search for a general and comprehensive moral view point and conception of the good life (ibid. p. 53). People motivated by 'mutual respect' strive to find terms of social cooperation that are ethically neutral or impartial. And as Jürgen Habermas and John Rawls have argued, although it is not possible to come to a rational consensus about what is or is not 'good', it is possible to come to such a consensus about what is or is not just or 'right' (Habermas, 1994a; Rawls, 1987: 424–425). Mouffe, in contrast, rejects the liberal account of justification, justification based on reason-as-such and morality-as-such, along with its goal of consensus. Her approach to justification is addressed first.

Mouffe believes that her 'contextualist', anti-universalist, position is supported by Ludwig Wittgenstein's later work (Wittgenstein, 1953, vol 1, §241). 'For Wittgenstein to have agreement in opinions there must first be agreement on the language used and this... implies agreement in forms of life' (Mouffe, 1999: 749). The postmodernist is not rejecting rationality, she argues, but its pretension to universality. There are as many rationalities as there are 'forms of life' or 'language games'. What is more, liberal-democratic institutions 'must be seen as defining one possible "language-game" among others' (Mouffe, 2000: 64). If that is the case, how should the liberal-democrat respond to the member of a nondemocratic, or anti-democratic, 'form of life'? An anti-democratic form of life might represent the majority culture of some societies, or minority cultures within democratic societies. Mouffe assumes it is possible to call the committed participant in such a form of life 'irrational'. She agrees with Richard Rorty that to call somebody irrational 'is not to say that she is not making proper use of her mental faculties. It is only to say that she does not seem to share enough beliefs and desires with one to make conversation with her on the disputed point fruitful' (Rorty, 1997: 19, in Mouffe, 2000: 65). Therefore, I cannot reject the views of others as 'irrational' on the basis of what liberals claim to be universal requirements of rationality. However, from within my 'form of life', I can rightly judge them irrational to the extent that we do not seem to 'share enough beliefs and desires', and this would seem to hinder 'fruitful' dialogue.

Two questions need to be asked here. First, if we eschew context independent standards of rational argument, why ought we to support liberal democracy? If the postmodernist is 'promoting' and 'defending' liberal democracy, the postmodernist also must accept the responsibility of offering moral justifications for what are moral prescriptions: i.e. in effect they are saying 'You should accept liberal democratic principles'; or 'Being a liberal democrat is good'. Mouffe will not justify such policies and institutions on the basis that liberal democracy is morally superior to anti-democratic or anti-liberal forms of life. Indeed, Mouffe criticizes Rorty for assuming that we can envisage 'moral and political progress in terms of the universalization of the liberal-democratic model' (Mouffe, 2000, p. 66). But that in itself does not answer our question, for, as we shall see, in her work justification is supplanted by a separate issue of motivation.

Second, if we cannot *justify* liberal democracy on the basis of rationally binding moral considerations, how can we *motivate* others to embrace liberal democracy? This question is particularly pertinent if post-modernists assume that all reasoning is contextually specific (based as it is on language games) and not every context is a liberal-democratic language game. Although Mouffe rejects Rorty's belief in progress, she does not question one element of his vision of how liberal democracy is to become accepted and entrenched. What is required, according to Rorty, is both 'persuasion and economic progress' (Mouffe, 2000: 67). It is clear that Mouffe here discards the liberal goal of a rationally motivated and rationally justified consensus. 'Democratic values' are to be 'fostered', but it is not an issue of rational argumentation (ibid. p. 70). It is a matter of the 'constitution' of individualities and identities. It 'is a question of identification with democratic values', which occurs 'through a manifold of practices, discourses and language-games' (ibid.). However, not only does Mouffe substitute 'identification' and 'motivation' for justification, as we see below she goes on to substitute 'agonism' for a consensus-based liberal democracy.

Agonistic pluralism

Mouffe defends 'agonistic pluralism' in response to what she sees as the arbitrary exclusion of 'difference' resulting from liberal-democratic ideas and practices. There is an interesting overlap here between post-modernists such as Mouffe and historicists such as MacIntyre. As we have seen, MacIntyre too believes that liberal principles are not in fact universal. The liberal insistence that, in political philosophy, we must not make any appeal to the moral consensus of a community is, according to MacIntyre, contrary to the beliefs of many who belong to traditional groups on the 'margins' of contemporary society (1985: 252). However, MacIntyre's point is that moral and rational certainty *is* available, just not in the form that liberals suggest. In contrast, Mouffe insists that certainty *is not* and *cannot* be provided either by reason-as-such or by tradition-constituted reason. Mouffe appeals to Derrida's account of 'undecideability' here (Mouffe, 2000: 77). Undecideability remains in every decision and it 'deconstructs from within any assurance of presence, any certitude or any supposed criteriology that would assure us of the justice of a decision' (Derrida, 1992: 24, in Mouffe, 2000: 77). In politics decisions are made that determine what is to be included and what is to be excluded as 'other'. However, moral and rational principles do not require from us that we make any specific decision; the decision we make is ultimately undetermined by such principles. Therefore, 'we should never refuse bearing responsibility for our decisions' by invoking so-called general rules (Mouffe, 2000: 76). Mouffe is arguing that all so-called moral political projects, whether they are liberal or whether they are instead the politics of a local community in MacIntyre's terms, are exclusionary, and it is not the case that reason and morality somehow command these exclusions. MacIntyre also rejected the contention that moral reasoning was a matter of applying general principles. However, for MacIntyre, it is wisdom and virtue that ensure the judgement is right; for post-modernists, there is no right or correct judgement.

Therefore, one cannot call for inclusion on the basis of so-called moral considerations whether this is morality-as-such or the morality of a tradition, as undecideability deconstructs any certainty we expected or claimed. Not only that, however, Mouffe also claims that inclusion itself cannot be obtained in a democracy. Here Mouffe appeals directly to the work of Carl Schmitt (1927). She accepts Schmitt's argument that there is a tension between the 'liberal' and 'democratic' conceptions of equality (Mouffe, 2000: 39). As liberal equality is equality *qua* human being, as it excludes no one, it can only ever be an empty abstraction. For equality to have substance, a distinction must be made between those who do and those who do not participate in that equality. The account of equality that is of interest to Mouffe, therefore, is the democratic conception which, she argues, is based on a distinction between 'us' and 'them', and such distinctions are contestable 'hegemonic' constructions, she claims. Mouffe's argument here builds on her earlier work with Ernesto Laclau, when, as followers of Antonio Gramsci, they referred to themselves as 'post-Marxists' (Laclau and Mouffe, 1985). For this approach, politics is a 'process of never-ending hegemonic struggles', that is, projections of totalizing conceptions of order that always fail to correspond to what they claim to represent (Cooke, 2006: 13). As a result, 'universality', for instance the universal principle of equality, 'exists only in its incarnations in some particularity that unsuccessfully endeavours to represent it' (ibid. p. 10). If all our moral distinctions are nothing but hegemonic constructions, which also always fail in their efforts to be representative, then the project or purpose of political theory changes radically. It is no longer possible for political theorists to take at face value the concepts and terms of philosophy and politics; instead the objective is the 'deconstruction' of such concepts.

Finally, Mouffe conceptualizes different liberal-democratic societies in Wittgensteinian terms as so many different 'language-games' (Mouffe, 2000: 73). The 'democratic game' can be played in different ways, she contends, and we should 'acknowledge' and 'valorize' the 'plurality of forms of being a democratic citizen' (ibid.). She does insist that 'we need to be able to distinguish between "obeying the rule" and "going against it"' (ibid.). Nonetheless, Mouffe will not claim that liberal democracy is the one and only just society that 'should be accepted by all rational and reasonable individuals' (ibid. p. 62). It is no more than a 'political form of human coexistence, which, under certain conditions, can be deemed "just"' (ibid.). What is more, 'we have to acknowledge that there might be other just forms of society' (ibid.). That is, while she defines different democratic societies as different language-games, Mouffe is claiming that a non-democratic society represents nothing more than yet another language-game. Liberal democracies are not untouched by the play of forces in the construction and deconstruction of hegemonies; and there is no justification for assuming that non-democratic societies are inherently or at all times unjust. Nonetheless, she insists, 'such a position does not necessarily entail accepting a relativism that would justify any political system. What it requires is a plurality of legitimate answers to the question of what is the just political order' (ibid.). However, Mouffe's defence of her position and rejection of the charge of relativism are deeply problematic. This is the case as relativism is, as we have seen, compatible with accepting a 'plurality of legitimate answers' to moral questions. Her treatment of this deeply significant issue is so cursory that some detective work is needed to uncover what her position might be. Perhaps what Mouffe means to say is that she does not doubt the possibility of 'legitimate answers' as such. But accepting this point, she can still be a relativist and, as we shall see later in the chapter, there are good reasons to believe Mouffe is a relativist.

The incompatibility of post-modernism with liberalism

Mouffe believes that in political life exclusion cannot be ruled out with so-called moral and rational principles, and the distinction between 'us' and 'them' is unavoidable in a democracy, and that there might be other (non-democratic) 'just' forms of society. Given all that, how can Mouffe's approach account for the difference between liberal democracy and a society radically opposed to liberal democracy? The many historical instances of totalitarianism are relevant here, in particular the Soviet Union and the German Third Reich. In a totalitarian society democratic rights are not guaranteed, civil liberties are denied, and often there is targeted persecution of religious and/or ethnic minorities, and others such as homosexuals or political dissidents. It also may involve ethnic cleansing, forced labour, mass extermination, arbitrary arrest, and the use of torture in interrogations.

Focusing on Soviet history, Jonathan Glover writes that 'Stalinist deliberate killing was on a scale surpassed only by war' (1999: 237). Various sources estimate that over a million were executed during 1937–1938, the period of Stalin's purges and show trials, a further 2 million died in the camps, and 9.5 million were killed in the 1930s. How were all these millions of citizens put to death by their own State? Various methods were used: work on 'huge slave-labour construction projects' such as the Baltic–White Sea Canal, mass executions, the population movements and deliberate famines used to destroy the 'kulaks' in the early 1930s, the collectivization movement and the setting of impossible quotas for grain production and the forceful removal of all other food, as well as death from cold and exhaustion in the camps (ibid. pp. 238–239). Citizens' civil liberties and protections against arbitrary arrest and violence were non-existent. People 'could be arrested for nothing'; and torture was used in interrogations before confessions were extracted (ibid.).

Thanks to the personal memoirs of Primo Levi, Alexander Solzhenitsyn, Vasily Grossman, and others, we don't have to imagine the implications of totalitarian rule, in particular the experiences of a concentration camp internee. Levi's own work builds on his experiences as a prisoner in Auschwitz during the Second World War. He speaks of how easy it was to become 'forgetful of dignity and restraint':

> Imagine now a man who is deprived of everyone he loves, and at the same time of his house, his habits, his clothes, in short of everything he possesses: he will be a hollow man, reduced to suffering and needs, forgetful of dignity and restraint, for he who loses all often easily loses himself. He will be a man whose life or death can be lightly decided with no sense of human affinity, in the most fortunate of cases, on the basis of pure judgement of utility. (1958: 33)

He also makes explicit the moral implications of the concentration camp [*Lager*]. Instead of a civilized life, the human being in the concentration camp is reduced to a 'beast', but even still this is a human being (the title of Levi's memoir is 'If this is a man'), and as a human being he can refuse to consent to this treatment:

> [P]recisely because the Lager was a great machine to reduce us to beasts, we must not become beasts; that even in this place one can survive, and therefore one must want to survive, to tell the story, to bear witness; and to survive we must force ourselves to save at least the skeleton, the scaffolding, the form of civilization. We are slaves, deprived of every right, exposed to every insult, condemned to certain death, but we still possess one power, and we must defend it with all our strength for it is the last – the power to refuse our consent. (ibid. p. 47)

What can the post-modernist say about totalitarianism? What are the rational and moral resources available to the postmodernist in understanding and judging the experiences of Levi, Solzhenitsyn, Grossman, and others? To begin to answer that question, let us imagine that such totalitarian policies have been pursued consistently for 30 to 35 years, as was the case in the Soviet Union by the time of Stalin's death in 1953. It is a serious possibility that this totalitarian society may have thereby established its own 'ethos' or 'form of life' or 'language-game', as the post-modernist would characterize it. The problem with post-modernism is that a post-modernist will not, indeed cannot, judge the policies of that society to be unjustified on the basis of standards other than those of its own ethos. The practices characteristic of a form of life are, according to post-modernism, justified by the rational and ethical principles of that form of life. As the memoirs of Solzhenitsyn (1973) show, the Soviet Gulag had its own rules of conduct, its own standards of what is rational and irrational, and right and wrong, that is, its own ethos. 'Norms' were set specifying the amount of physical labour to be carried out per day by each prisoner, and all this happened in freezing temperatures, without proper nourishment or clothing, with useless work tools, and in constant fear of arbitrary violence and death. It would seem that the post-modernist must (that is, logically must) accept as 'just' in the context of the Gulag what is considered just on the basis of the Gulag's own ethos, and of course this is its great weakness. In contrast, liberals believe they can reject totalitarianism on the basis of a requirement of morality-as-such and rationality-as-such: these policies could never be derived from 'a kind of political reasoning that is mutually justifiable'. A debate designed to aid us in attaining consensus about what is 'right' could not allow us to adopt totalitarianism.

This issue is all the more sensitive, or rather damaging, for Mouffe, given that in 1933 Carl Schmitt willingly joined the German Nazi Party. For Schmitt, Hitler's success represented the end of constitutionalism and the rule of law. In their place, a 'state of emergency' (or 'state of exception') was created, which replaces universal reason with 'authoritarian' decisions and a politics based on a populist '*Volkisch* homogeneity' (Wolin, 1992: 425). The line taken by Mouffe here is that Schmitt 'is an adversary from whom we can learn, because we can draw on his insights' (Mouffe, 2000: 57). Schmitt's conceptualization is correct, she argues, as he identifies the 'paradox' of the tension between the logics of democracy and liberalism. Mouffe insists on 'the ultimate contradictory nature of the two logics', and concludes that 'no final resolution' between the two 'is ever possible' (ibid. p. 45). She nonetheless believes that this can be the 'locus of a tension that installs a very important dynamic, which is constitutive of the specificity of liberal democracy as a new political form of society' (ibid. p. 44). That is, the commitment to democracy can 'subvert the tendency towards abstract universalism inherent in liberal discourse', while reference to 'humanity' and the 'polemical use' of 'human rights' allows us to 'constantly challenge' the forms of exclusion necessary in the definition of 'the people' (ibid. pp. 44–45).

Perhaps the two final points above help explain why some believe that Mouffe's position is really not so dissimilar from the liberalism she claims to reject. Mouffe rightly judges that the totalitarian society falls outside the category of 'liberal democracy'. She also insists that we should challenge exclusion on the grounds of human rights, as she is only opposed to universalism that is 'abstract' or 'empty'. This has led some to argue that Habermas's liberalism and Mouffe's post-modernism 'are in fact mutually dependent aspects of a solution to the same problem' (Knops, 2007: 125). According to Andrew Knops, Mouffe in fact believes there should be consensus on 'at least minimal "ethico-political" principles of democracy', as well as 'a mutual respect for beliefs, and the right to defend them' (ibid. p. 116). Her account of hegemony also implies that it is 'possible to identify and condemn and act against relations of subordination and domination' (ibid.). That is, according to Knops, Mouffe is committed to a politics of consensus-building, but also, as she is offering a rational argument in its favour, she is committed to universalism as well. Knops goes on to argue that liberalism should be informed and guided by such a post-modern sensitivity to hegemony: an awareness that every effort to reach consensus is contestable. There 'is always the risk of an agreement or consensus resulting in the erroneous projection of one party's understandings onto another, constraining their meanings – it is fraught with the possibility of hegemony' (ibid. p. 125). That is, post-modernism provides Enlightenment thinkers with a radical awareness of the pervasiveness of power, an awareness that is needed in and compatible with the Enlightenment.

A different interpretation of Mouffe's work seems more plausible, however. Hers is a position that, in the end, is opposed to rational consensus as a political goal and hostile to the notion of reason-as-such and morality-as-such, and, therefore, is incompatible with liberalism. Consensus in a liberal democratic society, she claims, 'will always be... the expression of a hegemony and the crystallization of power relations. The frontier that it establishes between what is and is not legitimate is a political one, and for that reason it should remain contestable' (Mouffe, 2000: 49). Why does it follow that Mouffe's approach is incompatible with liberal theory? Mouffe is not making the quite sound point that agreements reached in practice will always fall short of the ideal of a rationally motivated consensus. Mouffe is explicit that hers is not an argument about the 'empirical' obstacles to the attainment of this ideal. Rather, she believes, the obstacles to the realization of this ideal 'are inscribed in the democratic logic itself' (ibid. p. 48). Mouffe's argument is that while liberals take mutual respect to be a requirement of reason-as-such and morality-as-such, in fact it is itself a hegemonic construction. As liberals refuse to accept this, they 'naturalize what should be conceived as a contingent and temporary hegemonic articulation of "the people" through a particular regime of inclusion-exclusion' (ibid. p. 49). Consensus on liberal democratic 'ethico-political principles' is required, Mouffe accepts. However, as 'those ethico-political principles can only exist...through many different and conflicting interpretations, such a consensus is bound to be a "conflictual consensus"' (Mouffe, 1999: 756). That is, it is not possible to make a conceptual distinction between context and power, on the one hand, and rationality and morality, on the other. For this reason, undecideability and contestation always undercut liberal pretensions to rational justification and moral rightness. It is important, therefore, to leave the space for contestation of identity 'forever open, instead of trying to fill it through the establishment of a supposedly "rational" consensus' (Mouffe, 2000: 56).

The liberal rejection of post-modernism

To recap, Knops' argument is that Mouffe does in fact offer a rational defence of her position and also she is committed to consensus-based politics. His thesis is that Mouffe is unaware of the extent to which her political philosophy is 'liberal'. In contrast, Habermas has argued that liberalism and post-modernism are incompatible, as post-modernists are guilty of a 'performative contradiction', whereby the attempt to state the post-modern position contradicts the content of that statement. That is, although post-modernists like Michel Foucault contend that knowledge and power are inextricably intertwined in a nexus, that all knowledge is local as there are no 'standards of truth claims that would transcend local agreements', and that 'the meaning of validity claims consists in their power effects' (Habermas, 1994b: 279), yet in stating just these claims the post-modernist assumes both that these claims can be rationally validated and also that there are universal rules of logic that are irreplaceable if we are to understand the argument as a refutation (Habermas, 1990: 80ff.).

There is good reason to suggest that this criticism applies to Mouffe as well. Mouffe argues that any defence of liberal democracy must be situated within a 'form of life'; any conceptualization of liberal democratic principles is 'undecideable' and provisional; the political philosopher defending liberal democracy is engaged in a non-rational task of persuasion and identification; and finally, her goal is not consensus but rather 'agonistic' relations of contestation. Despite her commitment to these theses, however, Mouffe seems to assume the truth of their antitheses when she states her position. She announces the '*impossibility* of establishing a rational consensus without exclusion', and the '*ineradicability* of power' (Mouffe, 2000: 45, emphasis added). She also defends agonism because of the '*ultimate* contradictory nature' of the logics of democracy and liberalism (ibid., emphasis added), and because there 'can *never* be total emancipation' (Mouffe, 1999: 752, emphasis added). She states these factual claims, and makes these normative prescriptions, as if they are supported by a rational justification, and as if that justification applies across the boundaries of different contexts. There is therefore a logical contradiction between the content of her statements (contestability and contextualism) and what is implicit in her making those statements: that this position should be accepted on purely rational grounds, and that her agonistic pluralism is normatively preferable to consensus-based liberalism.

There is good reason to charge Mouffe with self-contradiction, therefore. However, *pace* Knops, it does not follow that, should we make explicit what is now only implicit, we could combine her post-modernism and liberalism as two mutually supportive dimensions of the one project. This is not possible for the reason that Mouffe's position cannot be separated from relativism and immoralism, as we shall see.

First, Mouffe argues that any defence of liberal democracy must be 'context-dependent', that is, situated within a 'form of life'. Despite her explicit rejection of relativism, it would seem that, in fact, her position swings back and forth between what MacIntyre defines as 'relativism' and 'perspectivism'. For the relativist, a claim 'can be rational relative to the standards of some particular tradition, but not rational as such' (MacIntyre, 1988: 352). Mouffe seems to assume relativism when claiming, with Rorty, that we can characterize someone as 'irrational' insofar as they do not share our 'form of life', and, therefore, the degree of difference in belief between us would seem to prevent 'fruitful' dialogue. The perspectivist approach 'puts in question the possibility of making truth claims from within any one tradition' (MacIntyre, 1988: 352). For the perspectivist, there is no one truth or morality, but the many different truths and moralities of 'different, complementary perspectives' (ibid.). Similar to perspectivists, Mouffe insists that the terms of politics are always contestable hegemonic constructions and that any judgement is undermined by undecideability.

A further issue is 'immoralism'. In Philippa Foot's discussion, Nietzsche is called (and called himself) an immoralist, and his immoralism consisted in, firstly, rejecting the idea of free will as an illusion, and on that basis rejecting moral responsibility and the morality of desert. In this way it would be possible to sweep away moral blaming and the 'love of retribution' (Foot, 2001: 104). Secondly, he attacked Christian morality, in particular the virtue of charity. While he saw charity as enervating, in contrast, he represented the human good 'in terms of individuality, spontaneity, daring, and a kind of creativity that rejects the idea of a rule of life that would be valid for others as well' (ibid. p. 106). And third, 'he went so far as to deny intrinsic badness', instead arguing that it is not acts themselves that are good and bad as the nature of an act depends on 'the nature of the individual who did it' (ibid. p. 110). However, Foot sees an incoherence in Nietzsche's thought, given that he himself was concerned with what constituted a good life for a human being. In rejecting morality, he rejected the idea that there could be a 'good and evil the same for all', but he nonetheless contended that the good life was something 'that an individual had to determine for himself' (ibid. p. 122).

Is Mouffe also open to the charge of 'immoralism'? Mouffe refuses to distinguish right from wrong and good from bad. Any defence of liberal democracy, or of any other political system, is essentially contestable and provisional. At the same time, Mouffe makes her own prescriptions, but she defends basic principles and praises character traits that are in fact immoral. Just as Nietzsche praised vitality, the 'will to power', which was to establish a 'revaluation of all values' (1888: 65), Mouffe praises agonism and contestation, which are to create the terms of inclusion and exclusion between 'us' and 'them'. Mouffe does reject totalitarianism and Schmitt's populism, but not for the reason that they are hostile to fundamental moral values. Instead hers is a critique very much in line with a Nietzschean rejection of the imposition of pre-given moral categories, whatever the categories happen to be. Schmitt's '*Volkisch*' populism is unacceptable, she believes, because it takes the identities of individuals as 'given', and so Nazism is criticized on the grounds that it imposes race-based and nationality-based identities. But Mouffe offers the very same criticism of liberals who accept diversity but think of identity as pre-political or 'already given' (Mouffe, 2000: 54), and so liberalism is rejected on the grounds that it imposes respect-based and equality-based identities. Liberalism, she claims, 'will multiply confrontations over essentialist identities and non-negotiable moral values' (Mouffe, 1999: 756). It is not the content of the identities that is problematic (racist on the one hand, egalitarian on the other), nor the manner in which they are imposed (arbitrary violence on the one hand, procedures considered fair on the other), but only the fact that in each instance identity is thought of as pre-given or uncontestable.

What she is referring to is the liberal argument that mutual respect is the non-negotiable commitment of any moral agent. This, according to Mouffe, eliminates certain identities in advance because it attempts to close off the space of contestation. What liberalism excludes, however, are forms of interaction that involve a refusal or denial of mutual respect, and therefore what Mouffe wants to keep open are the possibilities of identities that are based on the denial of mutual respect.

It is not just that relativism and immoralism characterize Mouffe's politics. Relativism and immoralism are evident in Mouffe's methodology as well. That is, there is no evidence from Mouffe's work that she herself is committed to truth as a moral principle or to rational justification as such. Her approach is one of persuasion (not justification), and it is carried on within language-games (not on the basis of considerations that can be shared and/or accepted by all).

As a result, first, Mouffe cannot avoid relativism. At one point she says that by 'envisaging the issue according to a Wittgensteinian perspective, such an approach brings to the fore the inadequacy of all attempts to give a rational foundation to liberal-democratic principles by arguing that they would be chosen by individuals in idealized conditions' (Mouffe, 2000: 64). She does not explain why this position does not fall foul of relativism: she asserts that this is the case (ibid. p. 62), but never follows this up with a reasoned argument. Moreover, secondly, she does not do what is necessary to ensure her claims can be assessed for their rationality. She talks about 'the limits of giving reasons' (ibid. p. 71), and that is when 'persuasion' takes the place of reason-giving. It does seem to be the case that, if we shared Mouffe's 'Wittgensteinian perspective', we might find her pronouncements persuasive. But there are no reasons offered for us to adopt this perspective in the first place. In addition, Mouffe does not go on to show how and in what way we can rationally assess her claims, even if we were to do so only from within her post-modern, agonistic language-game. The problem is that her position does not rest simply on a chain of argument whose cogency can be assessed by her critics. Just as she believes political engagement is a matter of 'constituting identities' through 'persuasion' rather than rational argumentation as such, she approaches her readers in the same way. We are told what we will see if we share her perspective and view the world as she does, but we are never given reasons to do so, reasons whose cogency can be assessed. Argument has been replaced with aspiration, reasoning with identification. And so in the end rather than a philosophical analysis Mouffe engages in the construction of her own hegemony.

A liberal alternative?

The approach of Amy Gutmann and Dennis Thompson can be contrasted with that of Mouffe. On the one hand, Gutmann and Thompson do defend the role of reasoned argument and rational justification in politics, and on the other hand, they do so on the basis of an argument whose rational cogency we can assess. What is more, they hope to justify a liberal as opposed to a post-modern politics. However, they argue for a liberal politics by appealing to a liberal comprehensive morality. As we will discuss in much greater detail in Chapter 6, for Gutmann, in a democracy education programmes should explicitly and intentionally promote autonomy and individuality as 'a conception of the good life' and do so by appealing to autonomy and individuality as moral values (1995: 558). That is, political engagement can and should strive to promote a certain type of life, namely one that is autonomous, on the basis that we should cherish these values. This is not the only liberal Enlightenment approach to political reason, as we shall see in discussing Rawls's 'political liberalism' (Chapter 5), which it is argued does not presuppose the truth of any one comprehensive moral doctrine, not even liberalism. However, in this chapter we will focus on the attempt to provide an Enlightenment alternative to post-modernism by appealing to liberal moral values and a liberal way of life, and in Chapter 5 we look at political liberalism as an alternative Enlightenment approach again.

Gutmann and Thompson first address what cannot be included on the political agenda. Issues or aspirations are 'precluded', they argue, if they cannot be resolved through rational argumentation and debate. They highlight three elements of rational debate. First, there is the 'requirement of the moral point of view: the argument for the position must presuppose a disinterested perspective that could be adopted by any member of a society' (Gutmann and Thompson, 1990: 71). This is the requirement of fairness, but also they contend it implies ethical neutrality. That is, when we reason morally we do not simply represent the interests of ourselves and people like us but instead we offer considerations that should be acceptable to anyone regardless of their interests. Moreover, to be genuinely moral reasoning, political reasoning is not to be based on any one general and comprehensive moral philosophy and conception of the good. We are permitted to promote an autonomous way of life, but only because this allows individuals to choose *between* conceptions of the good (see Chapter 6). Second, 'any premises in the argument that depend on empirical evidence or logical inference should be in principle open to challenge by generally accepted methods of inquiry' (ibid.). That is, non-moral claims should be, in principle, rationally refutable. Finally, 'premises for which empirical evidence or logical inference is not appropriate should not be radically implausible' (ibid.). It is acceptable, for instance, to appeal to religious beliefs if and only if the appeal to those beliefs does not 'require the rejection of an extensive set of better established beliefs that are widely shared in society' (ibid.). Note that post-modernists would reject this distinction between what is and is not 'radically implausible'. Any such distinction will be simply a hegemonic construction, they would argue. What is more, post-modernists do not accept that there are universal prerequisites for moral, empirical, or logical argumentation.

The approach of Gutmann and Thompson can be employed, for instance, in a situation where fellow citizens are discussing the free provision to all citizens of state-funded, publicly provided healthcare. It is possible to assess this proposal on 'moral' grounds (as defined above): does the proposal presuppose a disinterested perspective that could be adopted by any member of a society? Also, it is possible to assess this proposal on 'non-moral' but rational grounds, whether in addition to, or in place of, these moral grounds. For instance, it may turn out that the policy, which was meant to deliver healthcare to all, as a matter of empirical fact will benefit middle-class patients far more than it does those from the working class (see Goodin and LeGrand, 1987). It is on the basis of such non-moral rational considerations that, perhaps, the policy can be rejected (or revised), if the empirical findings show that the programme or policy was not attaining the objectives that it should meet if it is to be morally justified. Finally, it is possible to argue from 'non-moral' and 'non-rational' grounds. For example, ethical socialists have argued that, as we are all soul-bearing creations of God we are owed equal respect, and, therefore, our community should ensure (among other objectives) that the health needs of each individual are met regardless of each person's ability to pay for those services (see Tawney, 1921: 185). Such a claim is not based exclusively on either a moral perspective or empirical findings. However, it is not 'implausible' to the extent that it does not require us to reject beliefs that we have good moral and non-moral rational reasons to accept.

So much for 'principles of preclusion'. 'Principles of accommodation' are needed as well so as to govern the interaction of citizens when they address the issues that are open for discussion in the political realm. According to Gutmann and Thompson, citizens of a democracy should exercise certain virtues. The virtue of 'mutual respect' is needed for

> a distinctively democratic character – the character of individuals who are morally committed, self-reflective about their commitments, discerning of the difference between respectable and merely tolerable differences of opinion, and open to the possibility of changing their minds ... if they confront unanswerable objections to their present point of view. (1990: 76)

To exercise the virtue of mutual respect, however, one must also exercise the virtues of integrity and magnanimity. Integrity requires that I be consistent in speech, and espouse moral positions because they are moral positions, not because they further my interests or promote my conception of the human good (ibid. p. 78). Magnanimity, on the other hand, requires that I acknowledge in speech that the moral position of those I disagree with is a moral position. I should not respond to it as if it were nothing but the expression of their self-interest or conception of the good (ibid. p. 79). Finally, in exercising these virtues, we will try to bring about what Gutmann and Thompson refer to as an 'economy of moral disagreement' (ibid. pp. 81–82). It is not that agreement in itself is good, regardless of what is agreed upon. Integrity and magnanimity require that we seek grounds on which we 'ought' to agree, and in that way minimize unnecessary or unjustifiable moral disagreement.

The position of Gutmann and Thompson seems to provide a way to avoid the fate of post-modernism, namely self-contradiction, immoralism, and relativism. First, they argue that claims made in politics should be open to justification or refutation by rational means, and also their claims, as political theorists, are open to justification or refutation by rational means. The content of their claim is not incompatible with what they must assume when making this claim. Secondly, according to their account of morally justified interaction, participants in a debate should be willing to have their claims tested for their rational validity and also to test the claims of their interlocutors on the same basis. This is what is entailed by the virtue of mutual respect; and, in this way, liberals avoid immoralism. For, if I make a proposal, I am stating that I believe its legitimacy depends on the possibility of my successfully showing (at least in part) that such a policy comes closer to the ideal of mutual respect than any other competing policy. And finally, deliberative democracy avoids relativism if it is the case that its account of moral virtue and moral considerations is universalizable, and also if it is the case that factual statements and logical inferences can be assessed on context-independent grounds.[1]

How can political philosophers move the debate forward after coming to this conflict between post-modernism and liberalism? Two possibilities suggest themselves, and each will be dealt with in turn: first, the position of Gutmann and Thompson – defend liberalism and reject post-modernism; second, Knops' position – defend liberalism but also acknowledge a large degree of common ground with post-modernism.

The reason for the first option is that the dispute between liberals and post-modernists seems irreconcileable. Post-modernists claim that liberalism leads to the 'essentialization' of identity and the arbitrary 'exclusion' of otherness. However, what liberals attempt to do is establish principles of rational justification that are available equally to any and all individuals. Liberals also insist that any individual can assess the legitimacy of proposed policies on rational moral grounds, and also that society should guarantee opportunities for such public debate. In contrast, post-modernists, in talking of contestation and agonism, and 'processes' of 'identification', do not guarantee respect for the separateness of each individual in public debate. The particular 'process' needed to ensure 'identification' with a set of ideas may well involve practices and procedures that do or do not respect separateness. Post-modernists have not attempted to ensure that postmodern politics is based on mutual respect. Indeed, the distinction between what is and is not respectful would be rejected by them as merely hegemonic. Further, although liberals appeal to morality-as-such and reason-as-such, they can and do accept that, in different communities, different norms can be justified. Political integration of 'citizens ensures loyalty to the common political culture', and the political culture of one society may differ significantly from that of another (Habermas, 1994a: 134). If liberals are correct here, they can reconcile whatever tension exists between 'democracy' and 'liberalism', as identified by Schmitt/Mouffe. In a political debate, liberals assess each proposal on a rational and moral basis: does it express mutual respect between moral agents? At the same time, they accept that the content of such justified policies in 'our' society will differ from those that are justified on the same universal basis in other societies (Benhabib, 2005: 761).

In contrast to this view, however, Knops and others seek out some common ground between liberalism and post-modernism (see Allen, 2003; Benhabib, 2005; Cooke, 2006; Fraser, 1999). It is hoped that liberal deliberative democracy can be renewed and strengthened by incorporating some of the aims and insights of post-modernism. As Maeve Cooke argues, in Mouffe and Laclau's account of hegemony, 'democratic political life is characterized as a never-ending process of political struggle' (Cooke, 2006: 13). This carries some important, controversial insights for liberals, she concludes. Politics involves 'projections of the fullness of the community, justice, democracy, and the like', but also, it is claimed that 'no single totalizing conception of order can escape contestation' (ibid.). Therefore, liberals should be made aware that the terms of political debate can never be ethically neutral, as they are always contestable hegemonic constructions.

However, such attempts to incorporate post-modern sensibilities or insights within liberalism seem destined to fail as, in the long run, the two positions prove to be incompatible. In practice, a choice needs to be made between liberalism and post-modernism. For instance, Amy Allen wants to avoid the extreme post-modern position whereby political theory is tied to a specific context and its contestations and struggles, what Michel Foucault refers to as a 'power/knowledge regime' or 'episteme'. Allen wants to open up Foucault's approach, so that the theorist is neither wholly inside nor wholly outside 'the episteme in question' (2003: 194). However, she goes on to conclude, 'the conception of critique... that results would of necessity be local, historically and culturally specific, and pragmatic rather than universal and ahistorical' (ibid.). Therefore, for her, the necessary, unavoidable feature of all political philosophy is its contextual specificity and the power relations of those specific contexts. The problem is that such a position remains vulnerable to the liberal critique of post-modernism. The onus is on any post-modernist to show why his or her work is not justifiably rejected on the basis of the liberal critique of relativism, immoralism, and self-contradiction.

On the other hand, Maeve Cooke's work seems to come down on the side of liberalism rather than post-modernism. Although she starts

from a desire to incorporate post-modernist insights, the logical consequence of her argument is that only *non*-post-modernist theorists
can legitimately investigate the phenomenon of hegemony, that is,
the interaction of power and knowledge. The rational basis for such
a critique, she has argued, is 'an ethical content, however residual,
which some representations can be said to capture better than others'
(Cooke, 2006: 17). It follows that it is possible to analyse and account
for any specific hegemonic construction on grounds that are not themselves reducible to any specific hegemonic construction: what she has
referred to as the 'residual ethical content'. Moreover, this residual
ethical content provides the justification for the interest we do take in
power relations and hegemony. The implication of Cooke's approach is
that while post-modernists are right to draw attention to the contestation of political terms, they lack the conceptual armoury to complete
such an analysis. If a theorist wants to be able to draw attention to
the influence of power on our deliberation and debate, and also to
identify domination and exclusion, he or she should accept the distinction between, on the one hand, reason and morality, and on the other
hand, power and context.

Liberal morality or political liberalism?

If liberalism and post-modernism are incompatible, is it possible to
establish that, morally speaking, one should be chosen rather than the
other? If such a moral argument is to be made, how is it to be justified?
If we take this as an issue for liberals to resolve, a major concern is
whether or not liberals may appeal to a specifically liberal comprehensive moral doctrine in making such an argument. While Gutmann and
Thompson do defend liberal politics on the basis that it promotes what
we know to be a morally valuable way of life, one that is autonomous, in
contrast, political liberals believe that a justification for liberal politics
should not and need not make such claims that presuppose the truth of
a comprehensive moral doctrine.

The first issue to note is that political liberals believe that ethical questions about the good life cannot be answered or resolved in the political
sphere. It is for that reason that liberal politics cannot be defended on
the basis that it will promote what we know to be a morally valuable or
good life (i.e. the life of autonomy). Comprehensive liberals are perfectionists, given they promote one way of life, but according to political liberals, perfectionists make the error of failing to distinguish the
field of ethics (judgements about what is good) from the field of justice

(judgements about what is right). Judgements about what is good are 'determined by the self-understandings and perspectival life projects of particular groups', political liberals believe (Habermas, 1994a: 122–123). In contrast, judgements of what is right are based on considerations that are 'mutually justifiable', reasons we might reasonably expect that others, as free and equal citizens, should accept. Liberalism, they argue, can guarantee rights that ensure respect for each as a moral equal in part at least because in the justification of these rights it employs only considerations that can be acceptable to anyone.

Why would 'comprehensive' liberals depart from this 'political' liberal position and start to debate the issue of the good life? One reason why they do so is based on a sociological observation regarding the origins of liberal values. If we think back to the previous two chapters, we will remember that MacIntyre rejects the liberal argument that liberal politics is justified with universal moral considerations. He tries to show that liberalism itself is the product of one specific context, namely the modern culture of subjectivism and individualism (MacIntyre, 1985: 20ff.; 1988: 97–98). After 'the function of man' argument was rejected, after we lost connection with the settled conviction of our moral traditions, in other words after virtue, then modern man and women only had their subjective desires and preferences and their individual interests to guide them. However such an insight can be employed on behalf of comprehensive liberalism. Joseph Raz offers a perfectionist, non-individualistic account of autonomy, on the basis of which he defends rights that protect autonomy. An autonomous way of life is preferable to one that lacks autonomy, in particular in a society such as ours where autonomy brings so many benefits to the autonomous person (Raz, 1986: 391). It follows that we must be explicit in promoting autonomy as a valuable way of life, and so liberals must be perfectionists. Further, Raz's purpose is to 'point to the non-individualistic elements' in rights as they are 'traditionally recognized' (Raz, 1986: 250, 252). For instance, while religious toleration is usually thought of in terms of the interests of individuals, 'that interest and the ability to serve it rested in practice on the secure existence of a public good: the existence of religious communities within which people pursued the freedom that the right guaranteed them' (ibid. p. 251). Therefore, to promote autonomy requires working towards the promotion of common or shared goods, rather than towards an individualistic agenda.

It is understandable why the 'comprehensive' rather than the 'political' variety of liberalism is chosen. Comprehensive liberalism, it could be argued, is needed for a rigorous account of virtue, but also, to conceptualize and defend general principles of democratic debate. First, they can agree with Rawls that moral considerations have generality. It is necessary so as to ensure no one can 'know how to tailor principles to his advantage' (Rawls, 1971: 131). However, it could be argued, political liberalism is problematic to the extent that it cannot distinguish general moral principles from principles that are general but immoral. For instance, although post-modernists refuse to distinguish right from wrong, they do explicitly prescribe certain general rules of thought, feeling, and action. Namely, Mouffe contends, we are to embrace contestability and contextualism. What the political liberal cannot say is that post-modernism is objectionable as a conception of the good life. In contrast, such an argument is available to comprehensive liberalism. If anything, post-modernists treat the character traits praised by MacIntyre and by comprehensive liberals as so many symptoms of an enervating sickness (see Foot, 2001: 107). We have already seen that Mouffe rejects liberalism and its goal of consensus. We are, she argues, to accept contextualism and keep the space of contestation forever open, not so as to guarantee mutual respect, but rather because it is praiseworthy to pursue and value contextualized contestation, that is, agonistic pluralism.

Political liberals also argue that virtues are required so as to be rational. For Rawls, we ought to exercise the virtues of a 'reasonable' person, as we shall see in the next chapter in more detail. Rawls defends reasonableness as a prerequisite of democratic stability, the means to ensure that each of us shows respect for every other free and equal citizen (Rawls, 1987: 432). However, the post-modernist claims that liberal democracy can be sustained only if citizens exercise a quite different set of character traits. Although both of them refer to their preferred society as 'liberal democracy', a group of agonistic contextualists can be expected to generate and perpetuate a type of society that is very different from the one arising from reasonableness and mutual respect. They also offer opposing accounts of identities and worldviews. Liberals try to foster a 'growing awareness of one's own position as being one among many others' (Benhabib, 2005: 762). The liberal hopes to encourage a 'rationalization' or 'liberalization' of worldviews themselves (ibid.). In contrast, post-modernists wish us to see ourselves as constituted by a 'form of life', and also to accept undecideability and contestability within and between such forms of life.

The disagreement between political liberals and post-modernists is not simply about the most efficient means to maintain liberal democracy, therefore. Rather, there is a dispute, which usually is only implicit, about the nature of the good life. This suggests the following question. Can liberals confront post-modern arguments only if they are willing to defend their own version of liberal democracy by appealing to the truth of an ethically controversial vision of the good life, a life of autonomy? The *comprehensive* liberal argues that certain principles are justified and certain character traits are valuable because of an underlying comprehensive moral doctrine. A politics of mutual respect is preferable because it sustains an autonomous way of life. For the comprehensive liberal, the argument against post-modernism must concern what character traits are valuable not merely because they are instrumentally useful to the maintenance of stability but rather because a liberal comprehensive moral doctrine shows them to be worthy of being cherished and loved. In sharp contrast, *political* liberals wish to remain impartial, and so they want to avoid a public debate about what is/not a truly valuable life. For instance, Rawls's ideal just society, 'a well-ordered society' or 'social union of social unions', is one in which 'the successful carrying out of just institutions is the shared final end of all the members of society, and these institutional forms are prized as good in themselves' (1997: 527). However, that entails citizens agreeing to not insist on the truth of their comprehensive doctrines, whatever they may be, and however many competing doctrines there may be.

We have seen that Mouffe's account of agonism swings back and forth between relativism and perspectivism. Her claims can be rational only 'relative to' some context, a form of life. At the same time, however, she assumes the terms of social cooperation are contestable hegemonic constructions, and so all we have are different, complementary perspectives. As liberals have argued, post-modernism is a relativistic and immoralist position. Moreover, it cannot avoid a performative contradiction. In stating the post-modernist case, the post-modernist must assume just its opposite. It has been argued here that liberalism and post-modernism are, for these reasons, incompatible.

Still at issue, however, is the way in which liberals should attempt to defend or justify a liberal politics. Either it is to be defended on the basis that it sustains what we know to be a morally valuable way of life, that is a life of autonomy, or instead that it is justified on political grounds only, without claiming that it sustains any one idea of the good life. So far we have looked at the comprehensive liberal approach, but political liberalism will be focused on in the next chapter. In fact the argument in the next chapter is that political liberalism provides the approach to political reason that best approximates the requirement to take the moral point of view in politics, and the best 'liberal' version of the Enlightenment. However, it does not follow that the content of politics must be 'liberal' in the sense understood by Rawls, and indeed it will be argued that Rawls's account of reasonableness can be defended as the best available approach to political reasoning but also that it provides a way to open up politics to issues and considerations not included by Rawls.

5
Reasonableness

If there is, as it seems, deep and pervasive disagreement about what is right and good, as well as the nature of moral judgment, how can political debate have any moral justification? How are fellow citizens to morally justify themselves and their proposals to each other in an era of moral pluralism? We have already addressed the historicist approach. According to MacIntyre, when we reason we do so from within traditions, and also those traditions are incommensurable. The plurality of moral doctrines in the modern world suggests a plurality of incompatible approaches to moral reasoning as well. The post-modernist also assumes that points of view are and will remain diverse and distinct, but while the historicist finds certainty in his/her tradition the post-modernist wishes to disrupt any supposed source of truth and objectivity, whether it is 'traditional' or otherwise.

However, as we saw, a quite different approach to political reason is available, one that carries on philosophy 'in accordance with' the Enlightenment. According to this approach, while we should rightly acknowledge the depth and the significance of moral disagreement, nonetheless the moral language of political engagement is not and should not be hopelessly disrupted by conflicting beliefs or incompatible interests. Indeed, a shared moral language, a shared moral point of view, can be found, although the question of how to adopt such a stand point is a matter of controversy. Is the moral point of view reliant on the truth of a specific moral doctrine, as comprehensive liberals argue, or is there instead a distinctively political moral point of view that does not rely on the justifiability of any one moral doctrine, as John Rawls argues, in his later work *Political Liberalism*?

Rawls believes there is a distinctively political moral point of view that does not rely on the justifiability of any one moral doctrine. And according to Rawls, in a situation of moral pluralism, citizens should be 'reasonable' (1993a: 56). In short, this means citizens should view one another as free and equal moral persons and they should offer each other fair terms of social cooperation (see Rawls, 1997: 579). Moreover, they should recognize and accept the 'consequences of the burdens of judgment', namely that differences between reasonable comprehensive doctrines have a morally innocent source, and therefore, reasonable citizens should not try to attain a rational agreement on a single comprehensive moral doctrine (see Rawls, 1993a: 55). It follows that in justifying a political conception the reasons given to others are 'reasons we might reasonably expect that they, as free and equal citizens, might also accept' (Rawls, 1997: 579). For that reason, Rawls's later work seeks to 'apply the principle of toleration to philosophy itself' (see Rawls, 1987: 435). It brackets controversial philosophical and moral issues. Rawls's conception of justice is political in the sense that it does not presuppose any general and comprehensive moral doctrine, not even a liberal doctrine of autonomy, or individuality, or social contract theory (ibid. p. 426).

Rawls presents his work as a version of 'moral constructivism'. What this entails in Rawls's view is that political philosophy has no foundation other than 'the shared notions and principles thought to be already latent' in the public political culture of modern society; and the moral point of view just is a 'suitably constructed social point of view', when the choice of principles is structured by 'the reasonable' (Rawls, 1980: 518, 570). This follows as political philosophy has a social purpose, namely to make mutually acceptable to one another our shared institutions and to do so on reasonable, public grounds.

However, Rawls also believes that reasonable citizens will not offer *perfectionist* considerations in political debate, and that this is a direct consequence of 'the fact of pluralism': a 'workable conception of justice...must allow for a diversity of conflicting, and indeed incommensurable, conceptions of the meaning, value, and purpose of human life (or..."conceptions of the good")' (ibid. pp. 424–425). For that reason, Rawls contends that political institutions should be ethically neutral or anti-perfectionist, as they should not support or promote supposedly 'higher' ends or values or specific ways of life (see Rawls, 1971: 30–33), whether they are MacIntyre's Thomist values or Gutmann's liberal way of life.

In this chapter, what will be referred to as 'Rawls's core conception of reasonableness' is defended. This rests on the following crucial moral distinction: although we may adopt a belief because of our comprehensive doctrine, nonetheless in public debate we should find political, public reasons to support our argument, and it is those reasons we should be willing to offer to our fellow citizens (see Weithman, 2005: 273).

It will also be argued that reasonableness does not presuppose a liberal comprehensive moral doctrine, despite communitarian claims to the contrary, although it does not follow that the concept of reasonableness does not presuppose some moral truths. Indeed, reasonableness seems to presuppose at the very least a commitment to moral equality. However, it will also be argued that reasonableness must not (and need not) be rigged to deliver a liberal anti-perfectionist theory of justice, although Rawls's formulation is to a substantial degree biased in this direction.

This line of argumentation is, then, quite different from the prevailing understandings of Rawls's position. First, some critics of Rawls claim that the very idea of reasonableness is unavoidably implicated in a comprehensive liberal moral doctrine: in particular, a reasonable person is just a person committed to certain liberal moral principles (see Thunder, 2006; Barnhart, 2004). It is argued in this chapter that Rawls is right to claim that, in political philosophy, we can avoid making controversial claims concerning the truth of any one comprehensive moral doctrine. In turn, Rawls's position would not be reasonable if it was based on the truths of a liberal comprehensive moral doctrine. Nonetheless, it will be argued that the willingness to account for ourselves is a key requirement of morality, and reasonableness better exemplifies this requirement than comprehensive liberal and/or historicist alternatives, but also reasonableness succeeds in this way for the reason that it expresses commitment to moral equality (see Scanlon, 2002; Fives, 2009). As even his supporters argue, Rawls must depart from constructivism at one point, as he can defend political liberalism only if he establishes that the requirement of reasonableness is itself based on moral truth (see Larmore, 1999; Estlund, 1998; Raz, 1990).

Second, it is the case that, in Rawls's formulation, reasonableness is rigged so as to deliver a liberal anti-perfectionist theory of justice, his own 'justice as fairness' (see Dryzek and Niemeyer, 2006; McCabe, 2000; Hare, 1973). However, it will be argued that, pace Rawls himself, reasonableness need not entail anti-perfectionism. While Rawls's conception of reasonableness is narrowly defined (as it is anti-perfectionist), this chapter defends a conception of reasonableness that is broadly defined. Specifically, the reasons given to others may include, but are not restricted to, perfectionist considerations.

Political not metaphysical

A theory of justice must be political not metaphysical, Rawls declares. Rawls's *Political Liberalism* is intended to be, in many ways, a departure from the arguments of the earlier *A Theory of Justice*. In the later work, he still believes that a theory of justice should be suited to the 'fact of moral pluralism', the fact that a plurality of moral doctrines will persist where individual freedom is guaranteed (1987: 425 n.7). He still contends that a theory of justice must meet the requirement of publicity, as the reasons offered in its defence must be reasons it is reasonable to expect others to accept (1980: 521). Nonetheless, Rawls now concedes that in *A Theory of Justice* he did not do enough to establish that his arguments were not derived from a liberal comprehensive moral doctrine, in particular, a moral doctrine comprised of a mixture of social contract theory and the moral philosophies of Kant and Mill and the central values of respectively autonomy and individuality (1988: 223). This is important for he now believes that a political conception is not, and cannot be, justified on the grounds of a comprehensive moral doctrine.

Rawls insists that in his later work he brackets the question of whether any one moral doctrine is true. A political conception of justice instead has a *social role*, he argues: to enable the members of a society 'to make mutually acceptable to one another' their shared institutions and to do so 'by citing what are publicly recognized as sufficient reasons, as identified by that conception' (1980: 430). The political conception is not concerned with the epistemological question of whether these premises are true. What is crucial, however, is that a political conception is to help enable fellow citizens to offer moral justifications in political debate, and also, that such moral justifications be public (ibid. p. 621; Rawls, 1987: 430). A political conception furthermore is based not on universal ideas, Rawls argues, but on notions implicit in the public political culture of a democratic society: in particular, the commitment to moral equality, which requires that we view one another as free and equal moral persons (1980: 518; see Sangiovanni, 2008). What is more, only a political conception is suited to a situation of what he calls 'reasonable pluralism' (Rawls, 1987: 421). For Rawls, reasonableness can be a quality of comprehensive moral doctrines as well as a character trait of individual citizens. So, reasonable citizens have certain commitments concerning the morally justified approach to political engagement, and at the same time they can accept or live only by one of the many different comprehensive moral doctrines informed or shaped by such commitments.

We will focus on three core elements of Rawls's concept of reasonableness: reasonable citizens view one another as free and equal moral persons, they offer each other fair terms of social cooperation, and they are willing to recognize and accept the consequences of the burdens of judgment.

If citizens recognize and accept the consequences of the burdens of judgment, they accept that disagreements between comprehensive doctrines have a morally innocent source. For that reason, they are not motivated to seek a rational consensus on one comprehensive moral doctrine (Rawls, 1997: 612, 613 n.95). Such sources of disagreement include, among others, the fact that the way we assess evidence and weigh moral and political values 'is shaped by our total experience', as well as the fact that it is difficult to make an overall assessment when there are different considerations of different force on either side of an issue (1993a: 56–57). Due to the burdens of judgment, moreover, in political debate we cannot hope to agree on definite answers to the perennial questions of moral philosophy: in particular, whether knowledge of how we are to act is directly accessible to only a few or to 'everyone who is normally reasonable and conscientious'; whether the moral order is derived from an external source or from human nature in 'combination with the requirements of living in society'; and whether or not an external motivation is needed to persuade us to accept our moral duties (ibid. pp. xxvi–xxvii). If we accept that pluralism has a morally innocent origin in the burdens of judgment, then, Rawls argues, our conception of justice must be political as it must not presuppose any one comprehensive moral doctrine (Rawls, 1997: 579). Rawls's contention is that consensus on one single moral doctrine could be maintained now only through the use of coercion, and this is unacceptable as it would not be *stable* in modern societies. Rawls's argument is not the utilitarian one that coercion is unjustified because the resulting instability would lead to dis-utilities. Coercive imposition of a moral doctrine is unjustified, rather, due to the deeply embedded intuition of moral equality, which requires us to view one another as free and equal moral persons. It is because coercion offends against this moral intuition that it would be, in Rawls's terms, unstable.

However, although Rawls's burdens of judgment thesis is offered as a justification for avoiding controversial moral issues in political debate, it is itself controversial, at least for some critics. In particular, it will not be accepted by historicists such as Alasdair MacIntyre. As we have seen, according to MacIntyre, all enquiry is context-bound. It is constituted by social and philosophical traditions, in his case the

Aristotelian–Thomist tradition. Not only that, traditions are incommensurable, so we cannot appeal to or hope to discover tradition-neutral political principles (MacIntyre, 1988: 166; see Fives, 2008). It follows that MacIntyre will not accept the burdens of judgment thesis. For MacIntyre, it is only within his Aristotelian–Thomist tradition that he has access to standards of rationality needed in political debate. Political reasoning simply would not be possible without assuming the truth of this moral doctrine. At the same time, MacIntyre has argued that Rawls's approach to politics is itself a product of one specific moral doctrine, which he refers to as emotivism. Emotivists believe that value judgments are derived from subjective feelings of approval and disapproval. As value judgments are not inferred from rational principles, they cannot be resolved by rational analysis (MacIntyre, 1985: 17). According to MacIntyre, emotivism is a moral doctrine perfectly suited to Rawls's political theory, as the latter entails that key moral issues cannot be rationally resolved in political debate. In contrast, MacIntyre believes that, when a tradition is 'in good working order', all political reasoning begins from a first premise that outlines what is good or best unqualifiedly (1988: 7, 12, 30, 222, 337; see Aristotle, NE, VI. 5, 1140^a 25). Practical reasoning begins from a conception of the good for humans, and such a conception can be rationally justified (that is, justified within the tradition). Therefore, Aristotelian–Thomists believe that they can rationally resolve these seemingly irresolvable moral debates, and they believe they can be resolved in political debate and political theory. Political theory should not and cannot remain ethically neutral between competing conceptions of the good, they insist. MacIntyre's political theory can succeed as a rational enterprise only if it presupposes an Aristotelian–Thomist account of the human good, one that gives priority to the good of the beatific vision (MacIntyre, 1988: 192). The burdens-of-judgment thesis, they claim, is not only unsuited to Aristotelian–Thomists, but there are good reasons to believe it to be a mistaken view of political morality as such.

A further dimension of the concept of reasonableness in Rawls's work is that reasonable citizens view one another as free and equal moral persons. Rawls believes that his conception of reasonableness originates from the modern Western commitment to moral equality. If we are to view one another as free and equal moral persons, political principles cannot be justified simply on the grounds of one comprehensive moral doctrine. As the free use of reason will lead to a plurality of moral doctrines, respecting the freedom and equality of each requires that we not insist on the truth of *one* of these doctrines. Furthermore, Rawls believes that the reasonable person will propose a fair distribution of benefits and burdens. The idea of 'fair terms of cooperation ... articulate an idea of reciprocity and mutuality: all who cooperate must benefit, or share in common burdens, in some appropriate fashion as judged by a suitable benchmark of comparison' (1980: 528). Reasonable citizens not only offer each other fair terms of social cooperation. They 'agree to act on those terms, even at the cost of their own interests in particular situations, provided the other citizens also accept those terms' (1997: 578).

However, once again his critics, in particular communitarians, insist that these elements of reasonableness are controversial. Rawls believes that his arguments in *A Theory of Justice* brought social contract theory to a new level of generality, and his critics argue that in fact his later work has not left behind this comprehensive moral doctrine. It is argued that he gives priority to one moral value among others, the value of consent, and this is far from uncontroversial (see Thunder, 2006: 685). Communitarians accept that morality requires our willingness to offer moral justifications to others, but they do not accept that 'publicity' is a fundamental requirement of political morality. Social contract theorists believe principles can be morally justified only if they are or could be the outcome of an agreement between free and equal persons. According to communitarians, however, the society of the social contract theorist is in fact a dis-utopia: while bureaucratic planning and organization characterize one dimension of modern life, in the sphere of judgement and debate about values there is only the 'free and arbitrary choices of individuals' (MacIntyre, 1985: 35). Therefore, in the world of social contract theory, it is only if each person has reasons *qua* self-interested utility maximizer that he or she can be said to have moral reasons to act in one way rather than another towards fellow citizens. Communitarians also offer a very different explanation of why and in it what ways we are morally obliged. For communitarians, it is because we belong to a community and share its goods, and share a common identity as members of this community with these moral commitments, that we are bound in specific ways (see Sandel, 1992: 22). Moral arguments therefore should begin from a first premise that outlines what is good or best unqualifiedly. This may be the good of a linguistic community, or the modern good of self-government, or the good of a religious community, and so on (see Taylor, 1989, 1999). Our commitment to the goods we share as members of a community provide us with moral reasons to act in one way rather than another towards fellow members of this community. Once again, it is argued that Rawls's account of reasonableness is not neutral between different moral doctrines, while at the same time it is not a correct, defensible account of political morality.

The debate between Rawls and communitarians here is in danger of becoming polarized and this may hinder rather than aid our understanding. There is a danger that we will feel compelled to conclude that reasonableness simply presupposes a liberal comprehensive morality and politics, and that we can accept reasonableness only if we also accept liberal comprehensive morality and liberal politics. However, Rawls is claiming that reasonableness does not presuppose any comprehensive moral doctrine, and there are strong grounds to accept this claim. More to the point, reasonableness is defensible precisely because and insofar as Rawls's claim here is true. However, what we shall see is that the argument cannot go in Rawls's favour all of the way. Rawls claims to be providing a way to justify a conception of justice. If this is the case it must enable us to decide *between* various competing theories of justice, that is, both liberal and non-liberal theories. It cannot perform this role if the reasonable choice of principles is rigged so as to deliver a liberal theory of justice, in particular, an anti-perfectionist ethically neutral theory, an issue we return to in this chapter.

The rational and the reasonable

According to Rawls, citizens are to make mutually acceptable to one another their shared institutions. To do so, they must exercise two complementary moral capacities: the reasonable and the rational. It is through exercising both capacities that we also attain the moral point of view.

Although he does not use the concept of reasonableness in *A Theory of Justice*, much of what is meant by it is contained in what he calls the 'requirement of publicity' (1971: 133). In that work Rawls set out to show that we choose principles of justice behind a veil of ignorance, where we do not know what our interests are, but do know we will have some interests that we will wish to promote. We can then reason in a way that is 'mutually disinterested' (ibid. p. 128). We know that we would prefer more rather than less of the all-purpose goods needed by anyone to pursue any conception of the good, which he refers to as primary goods. However, Rawls also believed that our choice of principles based on mutually disinterested reasoning is limited by what he called the requirements of moral justification. For our purposes here, it is sufficient to focus on the fact that Rawls believed any proposed principles must satisfy the requirement of publicity. Not only must all 'understand and follow a principle', this fact itself must be 'widely known' (ibid. p. 133, pp. 453–454; see Rawls, 1980: 521). In his later work, Rawls not only gives public reason a more explicit role. He also makes publicity a more demanding requirement. What publicity now requires is not just that reasons in support of a principle be such that they could be made public and accepted by all. As Charles Larmore observes, 'We honour public reason when we bring our own reason into accord with the reason of others...The conception of justice by which we live is then a conception we endorse, not for the different reasons we may each discover, and not simply for reasons we may happen to share, but instead *for reasons that count for us because we can affirm them together*' (Larmore, 2003: 368; emphasis added). It is because the reasons are shared that they can count for us: they can be reasons that confer moral legitimacy.

How do we reason well in politics? In the original position we choose principles on the basis of what Rawls refers to as rational autonomy. We are rationally autonomous when our higher-order interests in the realization and exercise of our two moral powers govern our deliberation and conduct. Moral persons, according to Rawls's definition, have two moral powers: they have a sense of justice, and they have 'the capacity to form, to revise, and rationally to pursue a conception of the good' (1980: 525). They are equal in that they have an equal right to reflect on and determine first principles of justice. They are free as 'they think of themselves not as inevitably tied to the pursuit of the particular ends they have at any given time, but rather as capable of revising and changing those ends on reasonable and rational grounds' (ibid. pp. 521–522). Although in the original position we do not know the content of our conception of the good, it is assumed that we are 'developed moral persons' and therefore have 'a determinate set of final ends, a particular conception of the good' (ibid. p. 525). We therefore also have a third higher-order interest in protecting and advancing our conception of the good, whatever it may be (ibid.). Further, the parties' preferences for primary goods are rational as they are 'necessary as social conditions and all-purpose means to enable human beings to realize and exercise their moral powers and to pursue their final ends' (ibid. p. 526).

For Rawls, the moral point of view is attained behind a veil of ignorance, where, as rationally autonomous persons, we each strive to exercise our two moral powers and advance our conception of the good, whatever it may be. Nonetheless, Rawls accepts that exercising rational autonomy, by itself, is not sufficient to establish the moral point of view.

He distinguishes the rational from the reasonable, and concludes that, in the original position, the reasonable presupposes and subordinates the rational (ibid. p. 530). 'The reasonable is incorporated into the background setup of the original position which frames the discussions of the parties and situates them symmetrically' (ibid. p. 529). The reasonable subordinates the rational because it limits absolutely 'the final ends that can be pursued' (ibid. p. 530). Rational autonomy does not predominate in Rawls's account of justification, therefore, as he gives priority to reasonableness and public reason. This is relevant to the question of whether Rawls's position simply presupposes a social contract moral doctrine. Rawls had used the veil of ignorance as a device to represent what social contract theorists referred to as the hypothetical initial situation, the thought experiment for the choosing of principles of justice (1971: 11, 136–137). Although the later work gives greater significance than the earlier work did to the reasonable, in both the early and late work Rawls is employing the intuitions and even the architecture of social contract theory.

Not a comprehensive liberal moral doctrine?

Is it the case that reasonableness does not presuppose a comprehensive liberal moral doctrine? Reasonable people can attain an overlapping consensus, Rawls believes, because they recognize and accept the consequences of the burdens of judgment. An overlapping consensus 'includes all the opposing philosophical and religious doctrines likely to persist and to gain adherents in a more or less just constitutional democratic society' (Rawls, 1985: 225–226; 1988: 421). However, it has been suggested by Dryzek and Niemeyer, Rawls represents the situation as though a consensus can be attained only by those committed to a comprehensive liberal moral doctrine. Rawls's model case of an overlapping consensus involves support for the principles of equal liberty by the following: those whose religious doctrine and account of free faith lead to their accepting a principle of toleration; those who affirm the political conception on the basis of a comprehensive liberal doctrine, such as that of Kant or Mill; and finally a pluralist view, where the political conception of justice is combined with a loose network of non-political values and convictions (see Rawls, 1993a: 145; Scheffler, 1994: 8, 11). This model case is problematic, Dryzek and Niemeyer argue, if all of those involved sign up to the overlapping consensus because they are committed to a liberal moral doctrine: 'Lockean protestants, secular Lockeans, Kantians, and Millians are all species of liberal, and consent to the liberal principle of religious toleration for essentially liberal individualist reasons' (2006: 636).

In addition, Rawls's critics have argued that, at different times, he offers both a 'thin' and a 'thick' account of the reasonable, and the latter is unacceptable as it presupposes a comprehensive liberal moral doctrine. According to this critique, the 'thin' conception of reasonableness requires only that persons be sufficiently competent reasoners and sufficiently responsive to the demands of justice or the interests of others; but Rawls's 'thick' conception requires in addition a willingness to propose fair terms of cooperation and to abide by them provided others do, and also to recognize and accept the consequences of the burdens of judgment (Thunder, 2006: 683). David Thunder believes that proponents of comprehensive doctrines who are reasonable in the thin sense could argue that the burdens-of-judgment requirement is not reasonable in the thin sense. In particular, neo-Aristotelians or Catholics can be 'sufficiently competent reasoners and sufficiently responsive to the demands of justice or the interests of others', but they will not accept that they should put to one side commitments tied up with their comprehensive doctrine, for instance, their commitment to 'goods associated with a social environment structured by shared expectations of non-destructive behaviour' (ibid. p. 686). It is possible, Thunder argues, to be a competent reasoner and to respect the interests of others, *and also* appeal to comprehensive moral principles in political debate. Thunder also believes that Rawls's burdens-of-judgment requirement itself is derived from a comprehensive liberal moral doctrine. As Rawls insists that political values are legitimate only if they could be accepted by all, Thunder contends, then Rawls's account of reasonableness is simply a disguised version of social contract theory. That is, it prioritizes one value, consent, over non-liberal values such as 'the moral ecology of society, unborn life, or the stability of family life' (ibid. p. 685). Principles are deemed satisfactory by Rawls, the argument goes, if and only if they could be accepted (i.e. consented to) by anyone. For his opponents, we should simply accept the truth of some values, such as the sanctity of human life, and our confidence in their truth comes from our comprehensive moral doctrine.

However, another line of thought observes that Rawls actually brackets certain controversial issues from consideration, and so he compartmentalizes the political and non-political. His is a position quite different from that of liberals who give priority to liberal values, such as the values of autonomy, the separateness of persons, or toleration. The latter believe that those belonging to communities, with their own comprehensive doctrines, should themselves give priority to liberal values; and a liberal political society will be stable only insofar as people's private beliefs become more liberalized (see Chabot, 1997: 325). In contrast, Rawls does not insist that all those who sign up to an overlapping consensus must also accept a comprehensive liberal moral doctrine. Nonetheless, Rawls does believe that a political conception will have and should have 'transformative effects' on reasonable comprehensive doctrines (see Barnhart, 2004: 261). It is for this reason that, to be reasonable, one's political commitments must be a central feature of one's comprehensive moral doctrine. Nonetheless, it does not follow that commitment to a political conception must also entail commitment to a comprehensive liberal moral doctrine. A reasonable doctrine is one that is compatible with whatever conception of justice is accepted in an overlapping consensus, but also, it is compatible with reasonableness itself, with public reasoning and the civic virtues of a democratic citizen. The central issue is that a person cannot be reasonable if his or her comprehensive doctrine is incompatible with reasonableness.

To be reasonable, we must recognize and accept the consequences of the burdens of judgment. This does not imply that we are free to regard non-liberal beliefs and values as false or invalid or flawed. Indeed, Rawls explicitly puts to one side the question of their truth or falsity. However, it is precisely in doing this that, his critics argue, Rawls implicitly trivializes comprehensive non-liberal moral beliefs and also indirectly privileges comprehensive liberal moral beliefs. For non-liberals believe that they can establish that their doctrine is true, and that it is for this reason that they should employ these ideas in crucial political debates (ibid. p. 265; see MacIntyre, 1988: 345ff.).

Rawls does have a response for the non-liberal, and it is a powerful argument and one that is crucial to his whole approach. Rawls argues that, in our deliberations, it is possible to employ a comprehensive doctrine and yet at the same time accept the burdens of judgment. That is, we can argue from a comprehensive doctrine, but this is permissible only so long as the following *proviso* is respected: 'that, in due course, we give properly public reasons to support the principles and policies our comprehensive doctrine is said to support' (Rawls, 1997: 584). In this way he hopes to rebut the charge that he trivializes comprehensive non-liberal moral doctrines, but also insist that the moral point of view cannot be equated with the viewpoint of any one comprehensive moral doctrine. In other words, for Rawls, a political conception is 'complete' as, when values conflict, decisions about the weight of different values are 'decidable according to a reasonable political conception', and not according to a comprehensive moral doctrine (Freeman, 2000: 410). It just might be that a non-liberal moral value is more reasonable than a liberal moral value in a given debate, but this conclusion cannot be accepted for the reason that it is a non-liberal moral value (whatever non-liberal moral doctrine is involved).

Those who reject this approach, MacIntyre and communitarians in particular, are faced with real difficulty concerning moral justification. It would be forgivable to assume MacIntyre and others believe that they need not account for themselves to others, those who happen to belong to some other tradition, with terms that should be acceptable to those others. It is the reasonable citizen who accepts the requirement to offer moral justifications when necessary. Not only that, the concept of reasonableness is highly defensible as an approach to moral justification because at its core is the idea of moral equality. It states that in morally justifying ourselves to others we view those others as free and equal moral persons. This is what is meant when Rawls says that reasonableness 'involves a readiness to politically address others of different persuasions in terms of public reasons' (ibid. p. 401). MacIntyre and communitarians are open to criticism insofar as they do not and cannot clearly show that they, in moral reasoning, view others as free and equal moral persons.

The reasonable citizen seeks out an overlapping consensus. In such a consensus, although people may affirm the same principles of justice each from his own point of view, nonetheless those committed to this conception must also regard it *as* a political conception (see Rawls, 1993a: 134). Some critics believe that requiring citizens to regard a legitimate conception *as* a political conception is mistaken, as legitimate principles can be defended in other ways. For example, some may be committed to a legitimate conception on the basis of a comprehensive liberal moral doctrine, at whose core is the ideal of ethical autonomy; while others may reject comprehensive liberal morality yet agree that this conception of justice does regulate society's basic structure, and therefore, it is the final court of appeal in ordering conflicting claims (Scheffler, 1994: 14, 18). The people in both cases are excluded from Rawls's overlapping consensus, it is argued, as they do not affirm the legitimate principles *as* a political conception. Once again, however, this line of argument does not do great damage to the core conception of reasonableness. It may seem that sincerity and good faith require that the reasons we give to others should be the reasons that have moved us, which may often be reasons derived from our comprehensive moral doctrine (see Weithman, 2005: 273). This is not the case, however. For if we are initially moved to reach a conclusion by reasons that may alienate others, and if we sincerely believe that public reasons do also support our conclusion, then in political debate we should be willing to offer those public reasons (ibid. p. 272). Rawls's argument is that, if you respect your interlocutor as a fellow citizen, then in your argument you should offer reasons that any citizen can reasonably be expected to accept. Therefore, although the people in the two examples above accept legitimate principles of justice, they are open to blame for the reason that they refuse to offer justificatory reasons that any citizen should find acceptable.

Bracketing moral truth

It still needs to be shown that Rawls can justify this requirement of reasonableness itself. He does not believe that the moral point of view can be, never mind must be, based on moral truth. We should bracket the truth or falsity of the principles involved, he argues. Nonetheless, even other political liberals have questioned this standpoint. It has been argued that, if political liberalism is to lead to legitimate political power, it must establish the truth of its authorizing doctrine. It requires 'a mooring – a single point of contact with the moral truth' (Estlund, 1998: 272, 254). Rawls's thesis is that a political conception must be acceptable to a certain range of citizens, namely 'people-being-reasonable'. However, as Rawls does not establish the moral truth of the requirement of reasonableness, nothing stands in our way of concluding that the relevant range of citizens are redheads, or Branch Davidians (ibid. p. 257, 259, 261), or indeed Roman Catholics. Thomists such as MacIntyre could agree among themselves that they should choose principles *as* Catholics. Although Rawls would not accept that this is legitimate moral deliberation for politics, it is argued by his critics that he cannot establish the moral truth of this claim. Rawls can insist that the relevant range of citizens is people-being-reasonable, but as a constructivist he can only argue that this claim should be accepted on the basis of our shared ideas and our fundamental intuitive ideas.

For Joseph Raz, Rawls's political philosophy can be intelligible only if its reliance on certain truths is acknowledged: 'It recognizes that social unity and stability based on consensus ... are valuable goals of sufficient importance to make them and them alone the foundations of a theory of justice for our societies' (Raz, 1990: 14). Similarly, according to Charles Larmore, to be coherent, Rawls would have to argue that reasonableness is based on a morally true principle, and for Larmore that principle is respect for persons (1999: 602). The appeal of this critique of Rawls may lie in the need to avoid relativism. It might be argued that, as Rawls bases political theory on nothing but the intuitions and institutions of Western society and Post-Enlightenment culture, its findings can only have validity in a relative sense.

Possibly the simplest solution to this dispute is found through the following distinction: Rawls is correct to insist that a reasonable conception does not rely on the justifiability of any one comprehensive moral doctrine, but nonetheless it does and should rely on certain moral truths, and those moral truths can be shared by many if not all moral doctrines, and therefore they may be uncontroversial. In this way Rawls's core conception of reasonableness can be coherent. To be coherent, a political theory cannot both claim that moral truth must be put to one side and also claim that certain key premises of its arguments should be accepted because they are morally true. However, it is coherent to say that a political conception must not rely on the justifiability of any one moral doctrine but may rely on certain moral truths shared by most if not all moral doctrines. What moral truths are presupposed by Rawls's account of political reason? Not only is Rawls committed to a moral point of view, for him it involves viewing others as free and equal. Not only does he presuppose that a distinctively moral point of view can be attained but also that it requires commitment to moral equality: taking the moral point of view just is a willingness to offer others reasons they should be able to accept.

An important consideration here is the distinction between justification *in* morality and the justification *of* morality. It may well be possible to offer rational justifications *of* morality, but it is also likely that such justifications will be highly contentious. We need only look at the competing justifications given by Kantians, utilitarians, Thomists, and Aristotelians to see that this is so: for example, it is variously argued, we should be moral because rationality demands it, or because it is necessary for utility, or because it is required by our *telos*. However, it is also the case that justification *in* morality is a common feature of all comprehensive moral doctrines. For instance, the contractarian Thomas Scanlon argues that the content of morality includes 'principles that no one could reasonably reject, *insofar as they were moved to find principles that others who share this aim also could not reasonably reject*' (Scanlon, 2002: 518–519; emphasis in original). The Aristotelian–Thomist Alasdair MacIntyre also talks of the importance of a life narrative, as a means to give 'an intelligible account' of ourselves and to be 'held to account' (MacIntyre, 1985: 222).

It can be argued that Rawls's political conception is concerned with justification *in* morality, and he insists that in politics justifications have the quality of publicity. He need not establish that the requirement of publicity should be accepted because it is necessary for the *telos* of human life or rationality or utility, and so on. He need only show that it is a better approximation than its competitors of justification *in* morality. The argument in its favour is that, on the one hand, morality requires us to treat others as free and equal moral persons and that, on the other, to reject the requirement of publicity in political debate is incompatible with the commitment to view others as free and equal moral persons.

Not a liberal politics?

So far a qualified defence has been given of 'Rawls's core conception of reasonableness'. The core conception has three elements: reasonable citizens view one another as free and equal moral persons; they offer each other fair terms of social cooperation; and they recognize and accept the consequences of the burdens of judgment. The concept of reasonableness represents the moral requirement to justify ourselves to others. The argument so far is that there is nothing in the requirement of reasonableness that trivializes comprehensive moral doctrines, and reasonableness is not implicitly based on a comprehensive liberal moral doctrine. However, it still needs to be seen whether reasonableness is implicated in, or biased towards, a liberal anti-perfectionist politics.

At times, Rawls writes as if only a liberal theory of justice could be accepted as a political conception. He uses the terms 'political' and 'liberal' interchangeably, and refers to a 'family of reasonable political conceptions', and 'competing liberalisms' (1997: 581–583). He also believes that all political conceptions are variations of his own theory, justice as fairness: they guarantee a list of certain basic rights that are placed in an order of priority and 'adequate all-purpose means to make effective use of...freedoms' (ibid. pp. 581–582). He even claims that 'The way the reasonable is represented in the original position leads to the two principles of justice', his own theory, justice as fairness (1980: 530). It is not wholly surprising then that even some of Rawls's supporters believe that '[t]o be reasonable ultimately is to have a settled disposition to reason and act from the requirements of a *liberal* political conception of justice' (Freeman, 2000: 400; emphasis in original). Nor is it wholly surprising that Rawls's critics, whose philosophical and moral commitments range between utilitarianism, republicanism, perfectionism, and libertarianism, all believe that his account of the justification of principles is rigged so as to deliver a liberal theory of justice (see Hare, 1973: 149; Dryzek and Niemeyer, 2006: 636; McCabe, 2000: 315; Nozick, 1974).

It will be argued here that, although it is the case that the reasonable person must bracket comprehensive moral doctrines, it does not follow that the reasonable person also must bracket perfectionist ideas of the good. Nonetheless, Rawls often writes as if this is *not* the case and for that reason is open to the charge that he has rigged his account of reasonableness to justify a liberal anti-perfectionist politics.

Here we can distinguish between a 'narrow' and a 'broad' conception of reasonableness. Rawls is employing a 'narrow' conception of reasonableness, as he argues that the reasonable person must be ethically neutral and therefore cannot employ perfectionist considerations. A 'broad' version of reasonableness allows reasonable people to appeal to various kinds of considerations, including but not of course limited to perfectionist ideas. It will be argued here that nothing in the core conception of reasonableness forbids use of perfectionist ideas, so long as the reasons given in their defence are public, and therefore it itself need not be rigged so as to deliver a liberal theory of justice.

Ideas of goodness play a crucial role for Rawls himself in his justification of the choice of principles. A 'political conception must draw upon various ideas of the good', he contends, but ideas of the good can be employed only if they 'are, or can be, shared by citizens regarded as free and equal; and ... do not presuppose any particular fully (or partially) comprehensive doctrine' (Rawls, 1985: 253). That is, the reasonable person must employ ideas of goodness and these ideas can be reasonable. However, Rawls goes on to argue that ideas of goodness can be used only if this is compatible with a rejection of perfectionism. The purpose of primary goods, for instance, is *not* to represent 'what, from within anyone's comprehensive doctrine, can be taken as ultimately important' (ibid. p. 258, pp. 255–256). Instead, primary goods are defined with respect to the similar structure evident in all permissible comprehensive conceptions of the good.

Therefore, Rawls's account of ideas of the good can be presented as follows: a political conception must draw upon various ideas of the good, and ideas of the good can be employed only if they are, or can be, shared by citizens regarded as free and equal, and do not presuppose any particular fully or partially comprehensive doctrine, and do not represent what can be taken as ultimately important.

Rawls's argument here invites one serious objection, namely, that he is conflating the burdens of judgment requirement with anti-perfectionism. He is assuming that, if we recognize and accept the consequences of the burdens of judgment, we must reject perfectionism as well: he is assuming that ideas that represent what can be taken as ultimately important always rely on the justifiability of some one comprehensive moral doctrine. This issue can be addressed by looking at the way Rawls himself employs ideas of the good.

What Rawls calls 'goodness as rationality', or 'the thin theory of the good', is dealt with at length in *A Theory of Justice*, but it retains its centrality in his later works as well. He argues that it is a basic idea from which, in conjunction with the political idea of the person, 'other ideas of the good may be elaborated' (ibid. p. 254; see Rawls, 1993a: 176–178). Not only that, it 'provides part of a framework serving two main roles: first, it helps us to identify a workable list of primary goods; and second, relying on an index of these goods, it enables us both to specify the motivation of the parties in the original position and to explain that motivation as rational' (Rawls, 1988: 254–255). According to his account of goodness as rationality, a rational plan 'allows for the encouragement and satisfaction of all the aims and interests' included in some other plan and 'for the encouragement and satisfaction of some further aim and interest in addition' (Rawls, 1971: 413). He believes that individuals should regard themselves as normatively prior to their conceptions of the good, and they should remain ethically neutral concerning the relative merit of different aims they may or may not adopt in the future (1980: 544). According to some, Rawls is proposing a conception of the good that is subjective, or emotivist: something is good insofar as it is felt to be good, or desired, or preferred (see Barnhart, 2004: 264; Sandel, 1992: 18). Nonetheless, Rawls's account of goodness as rationality is such that it leaves open the possibility of non-subjective standards of evaluation. Rawls argues that a plan of life is rational if it is one of the plans 'consistent with the principles of rational choice' and also 'would be chosen ... with full deliberative rationality, that is, with full awareness of the relevant facts and a careful consideration of the consequences' (1971: 408). Moreover, subjective desires and preferences do not determine what is of value, as Rawls believes he can account for our ability to 'assess the rationality of a person's desires': 'The aim of deliberation is to find that plan of life which best organizes our activities and influences the formation of our subsequent wants so that our aims and interests can be fruitfully combined into one scheme of conduct' (ibid. p. 407, 410).

Rawls is saying that a person may make a value judgment that something is good for her, and in doing so accurately and sincerely follow his or her subjective desires, and yet at the same time be mistaken with respect to full deliberative rationality and a rational plan of life. Nonetheless, as his argument develops, he will not say that there is either a rational or a moral requirement to accept rational deliberation as part of one's life. 'There is nothing irrational in an aversion to deliberation in itself provided that one is prepared to accept the consequences', he argues (ibid. p. 418). It would follow that one can live a good life, that is, a rational life, without living in accordance with rationality as goodness. 'Nevertheless', he continues, 'a person is being irrational if his unwillingness to think about what is the best (or a satisfactory) thing to do leads him into misadventures that on consideration he would concede that he should have taken thought to avoid' (ibid.). However, this is a problematic passage. If it is possible to lead a good life without being committed to goodness as rationality, why should there be any force in Rawls's argument that it is irrational not to take into consideration what the effects of a rationally planned life would have been? He has said that full deliberative rationality should influence the formation of our wants, yet he also writes as if rationality is one among many different life goals that we may or may not desire, and that it is good only insofar as it is desired, and there is no rational requirement to do so.

Rawls's account of ideas of the good also includes what he calls the Aristotelian Principle. Once again, this concept is dealt with in depth in *A Theory of Justice*, but still plays a central role in later work. The Aristotelian Principle is crucial for Rawls's whole approach as it, along with his account of goodness as rationality, is to help account for 'the list of primary goods' (ibid. p. 434). It states that 'other things equal, human beings enjoy the exercise of their realized capacities (their innate or trained abilities), and this enjoyment increases the more the capacity is realized, or the greater its complexity' (ibid. p. 426, 428). For Rawls, 'someone who can do both generally prefers playing chess to playing checkers', because the 'simpler things he enjoyed before are no longer sufficiently interesting or attractive' (ibid. p. 434). Rawls's comments recall John Stuart Mill's belief that those who have experienced both prefer the higher to the lower pleasure; and they resemble those of perfectionists such as Charles Taylor, who talks of judging actual desires against 'strong evaluations' or higher-order values (see Mill, 1861: 139; Taylor, 1989: 20). Is Rawls saying that some goals and preferences are better than others, and that this can be known on the basis of the Aristotelian Principle? The Aristotelian Principle also features in Rawls's account of the inherent value of a politically just community. A well-ordered society is a 'social union of social unions': 'the successful carrying out of just institutions is the shared final end of all the members of society' and 'these institutional forms are prized as good in themselves' (Rawls, 1971: 527; see Rawls, 1988: 269; Rawls, 1993a: 207). The well-ordered society is a 'larger plan', a plan that 'provides a framework for these many associations and sets up the most complex and diverse activity of all', and for that reason it 'must be experienced as a good' (Rawls, 1971: 528; see Rawls, 1993a: 207). Indeed, the 'collective activity of justice is the preeminent form of human flourishing' (Rawls, 1971: 529). This line of argument has led some to conclude that Rawls is a republican, as he is willing to argue that political activity among fellow citizens is the highest good to be attained (see de Francisco, 2006; Vatter, 2008: 254). However, as was the case with his treatment of goodness as rationality, Rawls continues as if the Aristotelian Principle was one goal among others, and that it is of value only insofar as it is desired and preferred. He accepts that the principle may 'not be true of some persons', for instance, the person 'whose only pleasure is to count blades of grass' (1971: 432–433). Rawls concludes that 'surely a rational plan for him will centre around this activity [counting blades of grass]' (ibid.). It would follow that any person may freely jettison the Aristotelian Principle and plan their lives so as to ensure they do *not* develop their abilities, and that such a plan of life is rational and good for that person.

Our purpose at this point is not to evaluate the merit of Rawls's account of goodness as rationality and the Aristotelian Principle. What is relevant is that Rawls's use of these ideas is unsatisfactory. Although Rawls uses these ideas to show that the choice of primary goods in the original position is rational, it could be said that he will not attempt to establish that these ideas are reasonable. His position is therefore under-defended. Perhaps Rawls feels he must proceed in this way so as to remain 'neutral' about such ideas. It has already been argued that, for Rawls, ideas concerning what is ultimately important are derived from within comprehensive moral doctrines, and therefore, the use of such ideas in political deliberation is excluded on the basis of the burdens-of-judgment requirement. However, as we have already seen, ideas derived from a comprehensive moral doctrine can be employed in political debate so long as we respect the *proviso* that at some stage we offer public reasons in their support. Therefore, Rawls's insistence that political debate must be ethically neutral is not required by reasonableness. Indeed, as there are no logical grounds for this stance, this gives further support to the charge that Rawls has rigged his formulation of reasonableness to deliver a liberal politics. To put the same point another way, Rawls cannot justify his summary exclusion of non-liberal ethical ideas from political debate. For if we derive ideas of the good from other doctrines, whether Romantic ideas of self-expression, Marxist ideas of conscious life activity, Aristotelian ideas of political virtue, and so on, it cannot be decided in advance whether or not public political reasons can be found in their support.

It may be objected that, nonetheless, perfectionist ideas in particular are not reasonable, as their use in the justification of basic political principles opens the way to 'sectarian' politics. Politics is sectarian when citizens do not agree to treat their fellow citizens as free and equal moral persons, do not offer fair terms of social cooperation, and also strive to attain agreement on a single comprehensive moral doctrine. It is this which Rawls is concerned to avoid, and indeed Rawls's objection to perfectionism is, in part, an objection to a monistic account of value. He rejects the belief that any *one thing* can be the 'privileged locus of the good life', although he does argue that political participation is a good for persons individually and a shared good of persons in a democracy, and also that the collective activity of justice is the preeminent form of human flourishing (Rawls, 1988: 273, 270–271; Cf. Rawls, 1971: 528). However, Rawls does not address the possibility that the state may operate on the basis of a pluralist version of perfectionism (Raz, 1986: 395ff.; Cf. MacIntyre, 1988: 337). For the pluralist perfectionist, although there is no single good that is higher than all others, or a single good against which all other goods are to be ranked, it is still the case that some values are objectively worthwhile and should be promoted. Moreover, for the perfectionist, not every element of politics need be based on perfectionist considerations. We can distinguish between a 'strict' and a 'moderate' principle of perfection. For the strict principle, 'the cultivation of human excellence is the sole criterion regulating the basic structure of society', whereas for the moderate principle, 'claims of excellence figure as considerations to be balanced among others in regulating the basic structure' (McCabe, 2000: 312–313). Included among these other non-perfectionist principles should be some that are ethically neutral. For instance, it could be argued that non-interference with the freely pursued lives of others is one basic requirement of the moral point of view, as Rawls would agree.

If we can argue in a reasonable fashion that some ways of life, character traits, and goods have special value, and do so with 'public' reasons, nonetheless, a further argument is required to establish that the state should promote the pursuit of those goods (Cf. Deveaux, 2000: 476). That is, an argument is needed to make the transition from 'moral perfectionism' to 'state perfectionism'. One important consideration is that, if the state is pressed into the pursuit of goods, it does not follow that the state may justifiably coerce individuals to pursue specific goods and do so for their own sake. That is, 'state perfectionism' need not entail 'state paternalism'. The state may, for instance, ensure that worthwhile working arrangements are provided (see Breen, 2007; Keat, 2009). It does not follow that any person may be coerced to enter into such working relations and to do so for their own sake (see Clarke, 2006: 117). Therefore, perfectionism and reasonableness need not be incompatible. On the one hand, perfectionism need not be incompatible with certain reasonable liberal commitments, in particular, pluralism, ethical neutrality in many crucial areas, and non-paternalism. On the other hand, however, if we are to be reasonable then we must not base perfectionism on a comprehensive doctrine, including a comprehensive liberal moral doctrine.

The first conclusion of this chapter is a qualified defence of what has been referred to as 'Rawls's core conception of reasonableness'. Rawls is successful in his endeavour to ensure political reason does not rely on the justifiability of one comprehensive moral doctrine. His core conception of reasonableness is an attempt to represent the moral requirement to justify ourselves *in* political debate. The argument in its favour is that morality requires us to treat others as free and equal moral persons and that rejecting publicity in political debate is incompatible with that moral requirement. Nonetheless, this argument rests on a distinction, between moral truth as such and the justifiability of a comprehensive moral doctrine, a distinction that Rawls himself does not make.

The second conclusion of this chapter is however critical of Rawls: there are no sufficiently strong grounds to accept that perfectionist considerations are and must be unreasonable. There is no reason to assume that perfectionist ideas are not or cannot be shared by citizens regarded as free and equal, or that perfectionist ideas must rely on the justifiability of a particular comprehensive moral doctrine. Therefore, it is possible to defend the core conception of reasonableness without presupposing a comprehensive liberal moral doctrine but also without it being rigged to deliver a liberal anti-perfectionist theory of justice. This conclusion has implications beyond Rawlsian political philosophy. For, as a consequence, in political philosophy the space between liberals and others is reduced, and greater room is created for mutual dialogue. This is the case as liberals and non-liberals can engage in a reasonable debate and that debate can include, but is not restricted to, perfectionist considerations. This is the case in particular with regard to the debate on civic education, and the question of what values it may promote and how such a programme of civic education could be justified.

6
Civic Education for Democracy

What kinds of consideration are appropriate in politics, and what values should inform and shape political life? In answering these questions it has been argued that the reasons offered in political debate should be public, or reasonable, and that politics should be informed by such public values as the commitment to view others as free and equal moral persons and to offer fair terms of social cooperation. Crucially, in promoting and defending values and ideas, public reasons are to be offered in their defence, reasons it is reasonable to expect others to accept. So far, debate and disagreement have been observed between those adopting such a political conception on the one hand and on the other those who believe political debate should be based on comprehensive moral doctrines, including liberals defending the values of autonomy and liberty, along with communitarians defending the shared values of a community or tradition. This debate will be returned to now when considering the topic of civic education.

Civic education for democracy is of increasing interest to political philosophers, in particular those concerned with the moral and political status of children (see Freeman, 1997, Archard, 2004). A number of difficult-to-resolve debates converge on this issue. This is the case firstly as civic education is a concern with education for good citizenship but there is no single shared view of what a good citizen should do or should be disposed to do (see Hess, 2004: 258, Westheimer and Kahne, 2004). The debate over the definition of the good citizen also informs a disagreement about the values of civic education. There is controversy here over whether values should be promoted at all, as any attempt to do so may face the charge of indoctrination (Hess, 2004, p. 258). Even those who accept that civic education should promote values do not have a shared view on which values to promote, as there is disagreement for instance over whether civic education should promote only secular values, or the values of a liberal democratic culture, or only the values of the specific culture or nation or ethnic group concerned (see Kymlicka, 2003, Archard, 2003).

Any attempt to promote values through civic education must address two questions. First, given the plurality of ethical norms, systems, and theories, which values can and should be promoted? For some, citizenship 'should be about trying to work out and communicate a common set of values', whereas, in contrast, communitarians and multi-culturalists believe that the values promoted should be relevant to 'the resolution of disputes locally and in contexts in which their resolution makes a difference' (Halliday, 1999: 48; see MacIntyre, 1985: 252). Second, if civic education is to be non-coercive, to whom should arguments be addressed? Any attempt to promote values in civic education will affect the interests of citizens generally, the parents of the young people involved, and the young people themselves. Although parents are thought to have rights to teach values to their children, there are limits to just how far this process of value promotion may go, and those limits are set in large part by the interests of their children as well as the interests of other citizens (Brighouse and Swift, 2006, O'Neill, 1989).

In this chapter a conception of civic education is defended that is political in a Rawlsian sense. It will be argued that civic education should promote the values of reasonableness, mutual respect, and fairness, but also, and in contrast to comprehensive liberalism, it is argued that only public, political reasons count in attempting to justify the content of civic education (Cf. Gutmann, 1995, 1999). However, contra Rawls, the content of civic education may legitimately be broader than this, including but not restricted to the liberal values of autonomy, integrity, and magnanimity (see Gutmann and Thompson, 1996) and the communitarian values of truthfulness and generosity (see MacIntyre, 1999a). At the same time, if civic education is seen merely as a means to shape and form future citizens, then the promotion of values in civic education will be a coercive imposition on young people. If the promotion of values is to be non-coercive it must be defended with reasons that young people should be able to accept (see Archard, 2004, Harris, 1996). Neither comprehensive nor political liberals have succeeded in doing so up to now.

An autonomous way of life?

The debate over these questions between comprehensive liberals and political liberals is the theoretical point of departure for this chapter, starting with Amy Gutmann's comprehensive liberalism. Comprehensive liberals appeal directly and explicitly to liberal moral principles and a liberal (i.e. autonomous) way of life. They believe that the justification of political proposals need not be independent of the values of liberal morality and also that civic education programmes should promote an autonomous way of life (Gutmann, 1995; Raz, 1986, 1990). However, although Amy Gutmann's liberalism is of the comprehensive variety, she agrees with some political liberals on the content of civic education. That is, she concurs with those political liberals who believe that civic education should teach mutual respect, while criticizing comprehensive liberals who reject the teaching of mutual respect.

Mutual respect is defined here as 'reciprocal positive regard' among citizens who pursue ways of life consistent with the basic liberties and opportunities of others (Gutmann, 1995: 561). The goals of civic education that Gutmann espouses are taken in large part from Rawls's work. Education, according to Rawls, should 'encourage the political virtues so that they want to honor the fair terms of social cooperation in their relations with the rest of society' (1993a: 199). The political virtues include 'toleration and mutual respect, and a sense of fairness and civility' (ibid. p. 122). Civic education furthermore should teach all children 'such things as knowledge of their constitutional and civic rights ... to ensure that their continued membership [in their parents' religious or cultural group] is not based simply on ignorance of their basic rights or fear of punishment for offences that do not exist' (ibid. p. 199). Such political knowledge gives the individual the very real ability to exit the group, should there be reason to do so (Brighouse, 1998: 730). Therefore, in sum, civic education should teach toleration, mutual respect, fairness, civility, and political knowledge.

Political liberals who support the teaching of mutual respect do so for purely civic, public reasons. In contrast, for Gutmann, mutual respect should be taught for the non-political reasons provided by commitment to the values of autonomy and individuality, while a programme of civic education should also explicitly and intentionally promote autonomy and individuality as 'a conception of the good life' (1995: 558). The first part of Gutmann's argument is that to develop individuality and autonomy requires substantial understanding of other ways of life, which in turn requires the teaching of mutual respect (ibid. p. 561). There is a distinction between understanding, respecting, and accepting unfamiliar ways of life, according to Gutmann, and the purpose of civic education is to help distinguish them, and to teach the first two (understanding and respecting) and not to teach the third (accepting). Moreover, Gutmann contends, there is an overlap between the skills and virtues of democratic citizenship and those of individuality. On the one hand, teaching mutual respect 'can aid students in understanding and evaluating both the political choices available to them as citizens and the various lives that are potentially open to them as individuals' (ibid. p. 563). On the other hand, teaching mutual respect also teaches the importance of people being free to live the life they choose: for example, the practice of exposing children to different religious beliefs is politically relevant not so that government should regulate religion but 'because citizens need to think about why religious belief should not be regulated' (ibid. p. 573).

Therefore, first, if civic education should promote autonomy it must be done through the teaching of mutual respect. However, a further argument is needed to establish that autonomy should be promoted at all. Gutmann accepts that the 'good of children includes not just freedom of choice, but also identification with and participation in the good of their family and the politics of their society' (1999: 43). Her approach is non-neutral in the sense that it accepts civic education will and should promote a way of life: i.e. autonomy. However, there is a very real possibility that the promotion of autonomy will come into conflict with a family or a community's promotion of its own values and goals insofar as promoting autonomy encourages the freedom to decide to leave the group or to reject its values (see Crowder, 2006: 423). The question at issue then is how to resolve any disputes that do arise concerning the competing goals of autonomy on the one hand and group identification and participation on the other. Gutmann goes some way towards an appeal to moral truth when discussing what she calls 'the value of moral freedom': 'All societies of self-reflective beings must admit the moral value of enabling their members to discern the difference between good and bad ways of life' (1999: 43). At other points, however, she only makes the pragmatic claim that freedom of a particular sort is 'most suitable' to a society such as ours: 'Rational deliberation remains the form of freedom most suitable to a democratic society in which adults must be free to deliberate and disagree but constrained to secure the grounds for deliberation and disagreement among children' (1999: 45; see Raz, 1986: 391). She goes so far as to say that independent philosophical accounts of autonomy 'are not sufficiently strong or determinate enough to override the actual disagreements among citizens' (1999, p. 64). Nonetheless, she concludes that a democratically agreed programme of civic education must not be 'repressive': although families and communities are permitted to 'shape but not totally to determine their children's future choices' (ibid. p. 46), adults must be 'prevented from using their present deliberative freedom to undermine the future deliberative freedom of children' (ibid. p. 45). It is understandable that Gutmann at first refrains from relying on an argument from moral truth, given that hers is an argument directed towards those who she believes will reject her liberal comprehensive moral doctrine. Nonetheless, ultimately she falls back on just such moral certainty by insisting that the requirement to refrain from coercing others provides the proper limit to pluralism.

Therefore, Gutmann's argument ultimately rests on a presupposition of the truth of a liberal moral doctrine. It is also the case that many fellow liberals will find these proposals controversial. Comprehensive liberals agree that the purpose of civic education should be to promote autonomy. However, liberals may fear that state-enforced or publicly controlled civic education cannot promote autonomy but will instead lead to some form of coercive indoctrination. In responding to such fears, Gutmann contends that, with reference to US education, publicly controlled schools can promote autonomy if they are sufficiently decentralized and 'constrained not to indoctrinate or discriminate against minorities' (1995: 563). As we have already seen, Gutmann also contends that the teaching of mutual respect is necessary so as to promote autonomy. Once again there are many liberals who will object. They will argue that, although children should be taught the value of toleration, teaching children to respect others violates their freedom (ibid. p. 559). This is Mill's point that others are free to lead lives we find repugnant and we in turn are free to avoid their company, to 'stand aloof from a person...that displeases us' (1859: 146). Requiring us not to coerce others does not violate our freedom; but requiring us to have a positive view of others is a potential threat to liberty. Gutmann's response is to argue that, if we value autonomy, we must also accept the teaching of mutual respect as the necessary means to attain that goal:

A state makes choice possible by teaching its future citizens respect for opposing points of view and ways of life. It makes choice meaningful by equipping children with the intellectual skills necessary to evaluate ways of life different from that of their parents. (1999: 30)

To teach 'rational deliberation among ways of life' requires the teaching of 'mutual respect' as well (ibid. p. 31). Therefore, Gutmann believes that teaching mutual respect will also teach the values of autonomy and individuality, and that teaching autonomy and individuality can aid students in making choices about the various lives open to them. However, the list of values required for democratic participation, in Gutmann's view, actually is longer than this.

As we saw in Chapter 4, she and Denis Thompson argued that the virtue of mutual respect is needed for 'a distinctively democratic character – the character of individuals who are ... open to the possibility of changing their minds ... if they confront unanswerable objections to their present point of view' (1990: 76). To exercise the virtue of mutual respect, however, one must also exercise the virtues of integrity and magnaminity. Integrity requires that one be consistent in speech, and espouse moral positions because they are moral positions, not merely because they further one's interests or promote one's conception of the human good (ibid. p. 78). Magnanimity, on the other hand, requires that one acknowledges in speech that the moral position of those one disagrees with is a moral position. One should not respond to it as if it were nothing but the expression of their self-interest or conception of the good life (ibid. p. 79).

Gutmann is therefore proposing that democratic participation requires a quite lengthy list of potentially controversial values and virtues. For that reason, the justification of Gutmann's proposals for civic education is all the more significant, in particular given the opposition within liberalism already noted. However, a quite serious methodological and moral issue arises here. Strictly speaking, Gutmann's argument addresses only the interests of adults and also the interests of the future adults the current generation of young people will one day be. It is in this spirit she observes that, although teaching mutual respect does not prevent parents from fostering deep religious convictions in their children, it limits the authority parents can claim over their children's public education (1995: 577). This is the case, she believes, as mutual respect involves 'teaching *future* citizens to evaluate different political perspectives that are often associated with different ways of life' (ibid.; emphasis added). Her argument is that the authority of parents is limited by the fact that one's 'child is at once a *future* adult and a *future* citizen' (ibid. p. 576; emphasis added). Therefore, in justifying teaching mutual respect Gutmann offers arguments to the parents of the present generation of young people and also to the adults those young people will one day be, but no argument is offered to young people themselves.

This is problematic to the extent that in justifying ourselves we must consider how our proposed actions will affect others and in regard to civic education young people will be affected, and also that we must address ourselves to those capable of understanding moral arguments themselves. We return to this methodological and moral issue again.

Reasonable citizens?

Comprehensive liberals are arguing that a programme of civic education should teach mutual respect but also in doing so it should presuppose the truth of a liberal moral doctrine. Political liberals can agree with the first objective but will reject the second. As Stephen Macedo has illustrated, political liberals find fault with Gutmann and other comprehensive liberals on the following basis. As comprehensive liberals insist on 'the importance of critical thinking in all departments of life', and as they make such an assertion concerning religious belief and practice (and any other domain where choices are made between ways of life), it follows that such comprehensive liberals 'premise political authority on the contention that critical thinking is the best way to attain religious truth' (Macedo, 1995: 473). That is, it is because critical thinking is the correct route or approach to moral choices generally that comprehensive liberals believe it to be the correct way in which to make specifically political choices. Macedo's alternative approach is explicitly indebted to Rawls's political liberalism. First, Macedo states that, given the difficult matters of judgement involved with respect to religious truth, or moral truth more generally, in political debate it should be acknowledged that people can reasonably disagree about such issues (Rawls, 1987, p. 435). Second, as fellow citizens, our basic motive should be the desire to respect reasonable people, and therefore the reasons given to others are 'reasons we might reasonably expect that they, as free and equal citizens, might also accept' (Rawls, 1997: 579). The rejection of comprehensive liberalism rests on the following distinction, Macedo believes. The crux of the matter is the legitimate grounds of coercion, not the legitimate basis of moral belief (Macedo, 1995: 475).

Macedo believes that political liberalism is neutral in one sense but accepts it is not and should not be neutral in another. It is neutral in the sense of 'not relying on the justifiability of any particular comprehensive ideal or view of the whole truth' (ibid. p. 477). In contrast, according to Macedo, comprehensive liberals *do* rely on such a comprehensive ideal or view of the whole truth. On the other hand, he accepts that the goods of 'freedom, peace, and prosperity', goods promoted by political liberalism, will not be valued equally by people of different faiths. However, even more to the point,

> promoting core liberal political values – such as the importance of a critical attitude toward contending political claims – seems certain to have the effect of promoting critical thinking in general. Liberal political virtues and attitudes will spill over into other spheres of life. Even a suitably circumscribed political liberalism is not really all that circumscribed: it will in various ways promote a way of life as a whole. (ibid.)

Political liberalism will promote 'critical thinking in general', and this will 'spill over into other spheres of life', and as a result it will 'promote a way of life as a whole'. However, this is a way of life not totally dissimilar from the autonomous individuality explicitly promoted by Gutmann. The only difference it seems is between the explicit and intentional promotion of a way of life by comprehensive liberals and the political liberal approach which leads only indirectly (but unavoidably and unapologetically) to the promotion of this way of life.

As we have already seen in Chapter 5, comprehensive liberals believe that political liberals in fact cannot, and do not, avoid reliance on or appeal to moral truth (see Raz, 1990: 14; Estlund, 1998: 272, 254). Rawls's response to such criticism was that there is no way to gain agreement in politics on the truth of one single comprehensive moral doctrine, other than by means of coercion, and it is this reason alone that leads to the bracketing of the truth or otherwise of comprehensive liberal morality (Rawls, 1987: 435). However, political liberals must address a further argument made by their comprehensive liberal rivals, for the latter insist that using and appealing to comprehensive moral values in political debate need not lead to the coercive imposition of those values. Instead, it can better encourage rational persuasion. Rather than bracketing them, we should invite our deepest disagreements on to the political stage, as this will lead to a more profound diversity of political viewpoints, deeper forms of mutual respect, and also a more robust political life (see Raz, 1990; Macedo, 1995: 491–492).

It is however important not to overstate the role played in comprehensive liberalism by a comprehensive liberal moral doctrine. It was clear from Gutmann's own position that, although she believed civic education should promote an autonomous way of life, she concluded that it is through democratic debate that the content of civic education programmes should be fixed. It is also the case that Rawls for his own part accepts that comprehensive moral principles can play a role in political debate, and this is possible without violating the requirement of publicity. He believes we can argue from a comprehensive doctrine if 'in due course, we give properly public reasons to support the principles and policies our comprehensive doctrine is said to support' (Rawls, 1997: 584). Therefore, there is considerable agreement here between comprehensive and political liberals. Neither political nor comprehensive liberals assume that political principles are justified solely by appealing to a liberal conception of the good, while at the same time both accept that moral doctrines can be introduced in political debate. What is more, political liberals propose a system of civic education the outcome of which is expected to be the promotion of an autonomous way of life. Once again, the differences between these two versions of liberalism may seem insignificant.

Nonetheless, a clear and important distinction can be made between them. It is political liberals who provide a way in which to offer arguments in politics that are suited to politics and yet at the same time meet the requirements of morality: that we offer public reasons in support of the principles we propose, and we do so also for principles our comprehensive doctrine is said to support. Macedo therefore has good reason to claim, as he does, that political liberalism is better able to attract the trustful allegiance of people with opposing but still reasonable conceptions of the good (1995: 493). He does then go on to claim that political liberalism is better able to attract trustful allegiance for the specific reason that it bars 'coercive perfectionism in principle' (ibid.). However, it is not at all clear that political liberalism, as it stands, bars coercive perfectionism in principle, and this is the case for two reasons.

First, political liberals accept that the promotion of autonomy in non-political spheres is an indirect but inevitable consequence of teaching mutual respect. While the rationale for political liberalism is that moral justification in politics requires publicity, political liberals are not offering public justifications for the foreseeable consequences of civic education, the promotion of an autonomous way of life. Indeed, they had tried to keep the issue off the agenda altogether claiming that, as a matter of principle, political liberalism does not promote comprehensive moral values.

Second, Macedo, in justifying a programme of civic education that promotes the value of mutual respect, does not address his argument to those who would be receiving this education, the young people themselves, and this is a further reason to doubt that political liberalism, as it stands, bars coercive perfectionism in principle. Macedo believes families do not have a moral right to opt out of reasonable measures designed to educate children towards very basic liberal virtues even if 'those measures make it harder for parents to pass along their particular religious beliefs' (ibid. p. 485). The reason why 'religious fundamentalists' do not have 'a right to shield their children from the fact of reasonable pluralism' is that children are not mere extensions of their parents (ibid.). An 'awareness of alternative ways of life is a prerequisite not only of citizenship but of being able to make the most basic life choices' (ibid. p. 486). However, we saw above that Gutmann addressed her arguments only to adults and took into consideration only the interests of adults. Similarly, Macedo's argument takes into account only the interests of future adults and the current generation of adults. This is the case as the ultimate justification for the promotion of mutual respect is as follows: 'Each of us can reasonably be asked to surrender some control over our own children for the sake of reasonable common efforts to ensure that all *future citizens* learn the minimal prerequisites of citizenship' (ibid. pp. 485–486; emphasis added).

Public reasons for ethical values

A political conception of civic education has been defended here, although the defence has been a qualified one. It has been argued that it is correct to bracket the truth of a comprehensive moral doctrine in political debate and also that a political conception should attract allegiance from reasonable citizens. It also follows that the values required in civic education must at the very least include reasonableness, mutual respect, and fairness, as Rawls has claimed. However, political liberals have been criticized here for the reason that they accept civic education will promote an autonomous way of life but they do not offer public reasons in its defence. That autonomy is to be promoted is not itself the issue. Indeed, there are strong grounds to conclude that civic education should promote autonomy, and other values as well. What is crucial is that if this is to be the case then some justification must be offered, and specifically, the proper content of civic education should be determined only by offering public reasons in support of such proposals.

It is illustrative to look again at Rawls's position. He has argued that civic education should teach toleration, mutual respect, fairness, and the value of civility, along with the political knowledge necessary to know one's rights and duties as a citizen and thus have the wherewithal to 'exit' the group should one wish. The underlying value that should be promoted, however, is reasonableness. It requires us to recognize and accept the consequences of the burdens of judgement. We should therefore accept that differences between reasonable moral doctrines have a morally innocent source and that in politics we should not strive for a consensus on a single comprehensive moral doctrine; as such a consensus could be attained only through coercion. We should also be willing to respect others as moral equals, and therefore also to offer moral justifications for proposals and actions using considerations that others in principle should be capable of accepting. This is the willingness to offer public reasons for our proposals, reasons whose force in political debate does not simply derive from a comprehensive moral doctrine.

Rawls's approach can be illustrated by looking at what it requires of someone like MacIntyre, namely a citizen who sees himself foremost as the member of a community and tradition with its own (Catholic) comprehensive moral doctrine. In Rawls's approach, MacIntyre is entitled to make proposals in political debate that are informed by Catholic values and also by historicist moral theory, for example, in arguing both that there should be civic education programmes that are based on Catholic teachings but also that values (for instance, both the 'political' and the 'theological' virtues) should be promoted along the lines of the apprentice model already discussed where the young person is encouraged to follow the example of the 'expert', the 'good person' of the community. However, Rawls also expects that, at some point, properly public reasons must be offered for such a position. It is not sufficient to base one's argument either on the fact that those with Catholic faith will accept Catholic values, or the historicist claim that all reasoning is tradition-constituted. This would not be sufficient because it is just such claims that we do not agree about, and will not agree on without the use of coercive force.

Liberals of course do worry about the consequences of a thoroughgoing communitarian politics. Liberals can accept that families and communities should promote social values, but also that children must be taught critical reasoning so that in the future they will be free to make informed decisions, including the decision to 'exit' the group and reject its values (see Gutmann, 1999, Crowder, 2006). Promoting autonomy is different from promoting other values, liberals assert, as it is autonomy that enables the individual to make choices *between* ways of life, whereas social values are tied up with and presuppose specific ways of life. Nonetheless, Gutmann has willingly conceded that hers is not a morally neutral approach, as it promotes a way of life. However, if teaching autonomy will affect the 'ends' chosen by individuals (see

Callan, 2002: 123), with respect to that point it does not differ from the teaching of social values. Liberal civic education programmes, if they are successful, will produce 'liberal' individuals in the sense that they will approach life in a particular way, namely autonomously. Communitarians go on to argue that, as liberals wish to promote an autonomous way of life, what liberal politics does promote is a set of ends that is incompatible with communitarian ends. In a liberal public sphere, they argue, it is no longer legitimate even to discuss shared or common goods as it is only the wants or desires of (autonomous) individuals that are considered relevant or appropriate (see Sandel, 1984: 22, MacIntyre, 1988: 337).

There are two crucial characteristics of the liberal-communitarian debate above. The first is that, as it stands, there seems to be no way to resolve the disagreement. They cannot agree on the liberal contention that autonomy should always be promoted and that doing so is very different from the promotion of social values. However, the second crucial characteristic of the argument is that neither side is offering public, political reasons. Liberals are arguing from a moral commitment to promote an autonomous way of life and/or from an individualistic ontology. Communitarians are arguing from very different premises but they too are derived from controversial moral doctrines and philosophical commitments. Either the communitarian is arguing from a commitment to one specific way of life (for instance, in Charles Taylor's work, the shared values of the French-speaking Quebecois (1992)) or from a social ontology and/or a communitarian moral theory (for instance, Taylor's notion of a background of moral sources (1989)).

What is instead required is an argument based ultimately on public reasons. That is, in giving reasons to others, citizens must view one another as free and equal moral persons; they must offer fair terms of social cooperation; and finally, they must recognize and accept the consequences of the burdens of judgement. *What public reasons can be given for the promotion of autonomy in civic education?* The argument could be that, if the participants in a civic education programme are to be treated as free and equal moral persons, participants must be willing to offer moral justifications but also they must be willing and able to understand and analyse the justifications offered to them. This is possible only if critical abilities are fostered and encouraged. It is for this reason that civic education is thought to be permissible only if it includes elements that direct the critical scrutiny of children and young people to the very values they are taught (Brighouse, 1998: 719; see Coleman, 2002: 176; see Brighouse, 1998: 732). Hence, in principle public reasons are available to support the promotion of autonomy.

However, the same form of argument, at least in principle, is available to those who wish to promote social values in civic education, for example generosity. As we saw in Chapter 3, generosity requires that at times we go beyond what justice requires of us, and instead respond to the neediness of the needy person (MacIntyre, 1999a). The 'political' defence of generosity could include the observation that, as generosity requires that we give to others according to their needs, rather than their past contribution, it involves viewing others first and foremost as moral equals. Generosity is something owed to all because of this shared moral status. Moreover, in giving to the needy stranger we put to one side our moral doctrine in the sense that differences in moral doctrine are irrelevant to the relationships of giving and receiving. We are called on to help the needy person irrespective of the tradition or community to which he or she belongs to or identifies with.

Furthermore, communitarians could argue that each community should have its own civic education programme, that is, the programme of a local community or a sub-community, and it would seem that a public, political argument could be made in defence of such proposals. For instance, it could be argued that Catholics should be free to provide education to their children that is infused with a Catholic ethos, including civic education. However, for this to be justifiable, in accordance with 'Rawls's core conception of reasonableness', it must be the case that the 'Catholic' civic education programme will itself promote the values and virtues that Rawls has described. That is, although the Catholic school may promote specific religious values and beliefs, this can be acceptable only if it also promotes the values of reasonableness, and therefore, it must also promote mutual respect, civility, and fairness, along with knowledge of one's civil and political rights. We have also seen that such a 'reasonable' approach will also promote autonomy as an indirect consequence. So although the communitarian may make a public, political argument in defence of community-based civic education programmes, in effect the communitarian has to argue for civic education programmes that promote not only public values but also critical scrutiny and autonomy.

However, a note of caution is required. It is highly informative that communitarians have not made public, political arguments in defence of the promotion of social values. It suggests that, as it stands, a communitarian programme of civic education would not be compatible with taking a political approach to moral values. For instance, MacIntyre assumes that apprentices in a practice first learn the standards of excellence of that practice from those in authority, and then strive to emulate and surpass those standards and those achievements of excellence (1988: 30). The crucial thing is that the truth of these values is taken as a given. Therefore, not only must the arguments in defence of social values change if there is to be any likelihood of engaging non-communitarians in the debate, but also only a political approach to the promotion of social values in civic education would be attractive to non-communitarians.

Non-coercive promotion of values

Political liberals in their attempt to justify a programme of civic education have encountered one significant problem. They will promote 'critical thinking in general' and 'a way of life as a whole', but they have failed to offer public, political reasons in support of these values. However, there is a further problem with the justification of civic education by political liberals, a problem that was also evident in Gutmann's comprehensive liberalism. They seem unable to establish that theirs is a civic education programme that will not be 'coercive', as they are unwilling to address their arguments to the young people who will be the participants in civic education.

Any proposals for civic education at some stage must deal with the moral and political status of children and young people. Arguments should be addressed only to those who have what is assumed to be the capacity needed to understand justifications, to judge the merits of arguments made, and to offer their own justifications in return. For that reason we must ask: do young people have sufficient moral capacity for arguments to be directed to them concerning matters that directly affect them? Do young people have a unique moral status in this sense?

For Robert Noggle, whereas adults are 'moral agents' children are 'moral patients' capable only of what he calls 'simple agency' (2002: 100; see Brighouse, 1998: 737). Children are capable of the deliberate, intentional, and rational pursuit of goals. However, they lack 'temporal extension', the ability to take into consideration their long-term interests; also they do not have a sense of justice; and nor finally do they have a conception of the good and therefore the ability to act according to the dictates of prudence and personal commitments (Noggle, 2002: 101). Children lack the capacity for the kind of moral agency that allows adults to interact with other moral agents on equal terms, Noggle claims. The 'moral community requires and presupposes a willingness to give and accept moral considerations as reasons for action', and that its 'members understand, value, and have at least some motivation to act upon, the norms of moral decency' (ibid. p. 110). To the extent the child or young person is incapable of such moral agency, it is the role of parents or guardians, acting as a bridge between the child and community, to facilitate the child's meeting these requirements (ibid. p. 111; see Freeman, 1997: 37, Brennan, 2002: 60). It is for these reasons that, in debates on civic education, arguments are offered to adults, including the parents who now act as a 'bridge' between the young person and the community.

Gutmann explains the special status of young people with the observation that, although schools can help young people move from a 'morality of authority' to a 'morality of association', '[v]ery few sixteen year olds (or adults) ever embrace the morality of principle[sic]' (1999: 60). Here her argument follows very much Rawls's own account in *A Theory of Justice* of psychological and moral development (Rawls, 1971: 462–479). First, the 'morality of authority' involves following rules because they have been issued by authority figures (e.g. parents and teachers). Those rules must be clearly enunciated and the authority figures must be worthy of love and trust, but crucially the child is thought to lack the notion of justification itself at this point. Second, the 'morality of association' involves accepting rules 'because they are appropriate to fulfilling the roles that individuals play within various associations' (Gutmann, 1999: 60). Although the content of morality can be demanding, including the requirements of justice, at this stage we are motivated by feelings of friendship and fellowship. Finally, the 'morality of principles' involves post-conventional moral reasoning, where the acceptance of rules is founded on each individual's own capacity to construct and comprehend the general principles from which the rules derive (see Coleman, 2002: 167–168). Gutmann believes that adolescents by and large are only capable of the morality of association, expressed in the cooperative virtues of empathy, trust, benevolence, and fairness, and it is these that can and should be taught in schools (1999: 61). Similarly, others have argued that a preoccupation with autonomy is suited to an 'associational view of human relations', where society is based on consent and each member has equal rights (Arneil, 2002: 82). In contrast, the child's membership in the family is not based on consent, and duties of adults to children cannot be reduced to, or limited to, protecting the rights of their children (see O'Neill, 1989).

A distinction is being made between moral agents and moral patients, or full moral agency and simple agency (see Archard, 2004). However, while this distinction may have application to the real world when comparing adults and young children, it becomes questionable when comparing adults and adolescents. Advocates of children's rights have claimed that many adults do not live up to this ideal of moral agency while many young people can and do. If adults do not live up to the ideal of moral agency then there no longer is justification for assuming young people incapable of the moral agency adults are said to exercise. However, advocates of children's rights often have not clearly specified the point at which a child becomes capable of moral agency and therefore have unwisely claimed that *all* children should have *all* of the rights that adults have (see Harris, 1996). An alternative approach is to accept that young children do not have the capacity for full moral agency, but also to look at the way in which moral agency can be quite highly developed in adolescence, and then investigate the implications for political theory and political practice of this developmental process.

There are however two very different implications that can be drawn from the claim that many adolescents have the same or similar capacity for moral agency as many adults. Some infer that the conventional standards of moral agency are too demanding, both for adults and adolescents. In contrast, this chapter will argue for retaining these high standards. Joe Coleman has contended that adults by and large do not develop the capacities for moral agency as they are set out in Rawls's work: i.e. the morality of principles (Coleman, 2002: 167). The implication of Coleman's argument is that adolescents and adults do have an equal moral status, but this is an equality judged by quite modest standards: i.e. standards appropriate to the morality of association. However, more needs to be said about the capacities for rationality and a sense of justice. The empirical claim that many or even most adults *do not* on a daily basis exercise the capacities for rationality or for a sense of justice to the highest possible level is not sufficient to conclude that the morality of principles is inappropriate. For it may be that most adults rarely attain the standards of the morality of principles and yet at the same time that these are reasonable benchmarks, or ideals, or requirements for adults, and for that reason the morality of principles *should be* the guiding force shaping the political system, including guaranteeing specific rights and requiring the performance of certain duties. In other words, it may be possible to offer public, political reasons in defence of such principles, even though most of us most of the time do not live up to them. The benefit of such an approach is that the requirements of morality are not watered down to lower standards or less demanding requirements. This is one way in which to retain high standards or ideals in respect of political morality, and therefore also in respect of the content of civic education. However, this does not by itself tell us whether adolescents should be obliged to take civic education classes and whether they should be more or less participant-oriented. It could be argued that, if these high ideals are reasonable for those adults who do not always live up to them, then surely they are appropriate for young people as well. If that is the case, and if we are unwilling to oblige adults to take civic education classes, how can we justify such an obligation to young people? However, it is possible to respond by pointing out that, even if the interests of children and adults are given equal consideration, it does not follow they have the same or identical interests. Equality of concern for interests does not entail uniformity of interests. Moreover, it can then be possible to put an argument to adolescents defending civic education programmes that are within limits participant-oriented, an argument directed towards their interests as adolescents. Gutmann has pointed out that a more participant-oriented education programme is in many respects more compatible with democracy, as it 'builds upon the students' interests and elicits their commitment to learning' (1999: 90). However, she has also rightly warned that this commitment 'should be overridden when disorder and arrogance are so great as to threaten the very enterprise of education within schools' (ibid.).

An argument, based purely on public reasons, needs to be addressed to young people (as well as to adults) along the following lines: youth is a stage of human development characterized by *relative* incompetence, dependence, and vulnerability. It is not that young people have no moral capacities, but that those capacities are in the process of development. As a result, the interests of young people are to a large extent unique. In particular, young people have a higher-order interest in education as a necessary element of development. They also have interests in an education for citizenship more specifically. Partly this is an interest in their future lives: an interest in becoming an adult with certain attributes. However, it is also an interest in their current experience: an interest in being treated in ways that show respect for their moral equality. Taking both sets of interests together, it is plausible to make an argument to adolescents in particular that they have interests in civic education and also in a participant-oriented approach. This is the case as civic education strives to foster values beneficial to the future adult but also participant-oriented civic education treats the participants as ends in themselves.

We have looked at what values if any should be promoted in civic education and also how the promotion of values can be non-coercive. It was argued that civic education should promote the values of reasonableness, mutual respect, and fairness, but also that at some point public, political reasons should be used in any attempt to justify the content of civic education. It was argued as well that the content of civic education may legitimately be broader than this. It is possible to offer public, political reasons to justify promoting the values of autonomy, integrity, and magnanimity, as well as the 'social' values of truthfulness and generosity, among others.

However, civic education programmes themselves must live up to the requirements of a political approach. Therefore, it is not acceptable for civic education programmes to indoctrinate students with the values in question, and this supports calls for a more participant-oriented approach to civic education, in particular with respect to adolescents. The fundamental issue is that civic education must not approach the current generation of young people as if they were merely the means to bring about the future adults and future citizens they will hopefully one day be. Such an approach will be a coercive imposition of values on young people. If instead the promotion of values is to be non-coercive it must be defended with reasons that both young people and adults should be able to accept.

7
Global Distributive Justice

The previous chapter explored one way in which ideas about public reasoning and reasonableness, ideas adapted from the arguments of Rawls, can be applied to one practical issue, namely civic education programmes for young people. This chapter is again an exploration of the practical application and significance of those ideas, as it addresses the question of our moral obligations to the distant poor. The previous chapter also resulted in a more nuanced and critical understanding of what we have called 'Rawls's core conception of reasonableness'. Similarly, in this chapter, we will depart somewhat from Rawls's own arguments, although it is hoped that in doing so we remain true to the concept of reasonableness.

Global poverty is morally significant, and it gives rise to moral responsibilities, but the precise nature of those responsibilities is a matter of some controversy. According to one line of thought, represented in Rawls's *The Law of Peoples* (1993b, 1999), while poverty within a democratic society is a matter of distributive justice, the poverty of non-citizens in non-democratic societies is a matter of human rights but it falls outside the scope of distributive justice. Although Rawls does believe that citizens of wealthy democratic societies have a duty to 'assist' what he refers to as 'decent hierarchical societies' faced with 'unfavorable conditions' so that they can guarantee the human rights of their members, he does not believe it possible to establish that the poor of such societies have rights of distributive justice, or that the non-poor (in their own or other societies) have obligations of distributive justice towards them (Rawls, 1993b: 558).

Rawls believes that this conclusion regarding the content of global justice is required by his approach to political reasoning. Reasonableness requires that, when we engage in political reasoning, we do not insist on the truth of our moral doctrine, for the reason that individuals, by freely using their own powers of reason, will inevitably disagree about controversial philosophical and moral issues (1987: 425 n.7). Rawls also contends that a political conception is presented in terms of not universal ideas but the 'fundamental intuitive ideas' of the culture in question (Rawls, 1980: 518, 570). Thus, in working out a political conception for a 'closed and self-contained democratic society', we do appeal to the idea of moral equality, as it is a fundamental intuitive idea of post-Enlightenment, Western, liberal-democratic culture. However, this intuitive idea is not available, Rawls claims, when constructing a 'Law of Peoples' that will include 'decent hierarchical societies' and so, 'not all of them can reasonably be expected to accept any particular liberal principle of distributive justice' (1993b: 558).

In Joshua Cohen's terms, Rawls's thesis is that minimalism regarding the content of human rights ('substantive minimalism') is required by minimalism regarding the considerations that may rightly be offered to others ('justificatory minimalism') (Cohen, 2004: 192). In this chapter, however, it is argued that a tension is apparent in Rawls's conception of political reason and by extension his account of global politics. Political reason requires 'reasonable' citizens to view one another as free and equal, offer each other fair terms of social cooperation, and recognize and accept the consequences of the burdens of judgement (Rawls, 1993a; 1997). However, Rawls assumes both that the representatives of a decent hierarchical society *can* agree to a reasonable 'Law of Peoples' at the level of a 'Society of Peoples', and yet at the domestic level the members of a hierarchical society are merely 'decent' and therefore are *not* required to view one another as free and equal. At the same time, representatives of democratic societies *are* expected to treat decent hierarchical societies as equally independent societies and yet they are *not* required to treat the members of such hierarchical societies as moral equals. The reason for this apparent inconsistency is as follows. There is a tension in Rawls's thought between on the one hand, a commitment to moral equality and the assumption that this is required by a political conception, and on the other hand, a commitment to pluralism and the assumption that a political conception draws only on the intuitive ideas of the culture(s) in question and that non-democratic cultures do not share the intuitive commitment to moral equality.

The argument of this chapter is that Rawls is guilty of contradiction when addressing decent hierarchical societies. It will not be argued that the commitment to moral equality can be discovered within the cultures of non-liberal societies, the so-called argument from constructivism. Nor will it be argued that because global society has a basic structure Rawls's difference principle should apply at that level, the so-called argument from a mutually advantageous system of cooperation. Instead, the argument of this chapter is that the requirement to view one another as free and equal moral persons is a requirement of political morality *per se*. In offering moral justifications in politics, whether domestic or global, we must view others as free and equal and offer each other fair terms of social cooperation. One implication is that Enlightenment ideas are not restricted to Western societies. A further implication of this critique moreover is that minimalism concerning justification should be a qualified minimalism. As we saw in Chapter 5, reasonableness should be seen to presuppose a commitment to moral truth in the sense that it requires commitment to moral equality. Qualifying minimalism in this way does not however violate the requirements of reasonableness. It is simply that consistency requires we cannot treat one and the same person or society as merely decent for some purposes and yet fully reasonable for others.

The justification and content of human rights

Obligations to the distant needy are increasingly thought of in terms of the human rights of the poor. In discussing human rights, in particular the socio-economic rights of the global poor, as we saw two related issues arise. First, some have argued that the content of human rights is or should be minimal. 'Substantive minimalism' entails both the list of human rights and the responsibilities of non-citizens are restricted or limited (see Ignatieff, 2001; Rawls, 1999; Scanlon, 1998). The alternative approach lengthens the list of rights that can be claimed and/ or expands the responsibilities of non-citizens (see Beitz, 2001a, 2001b, 2004; Cohen, 2004; Hinsch, 2001; Pogge, 2004, 2005, 2008; Wenar, 2001). The second issue concerns the justification of human rights. Again there is a distinction between those who do or do not adopt minimalism. 'Justificatory minimalism' entails that any moral arguments about or for human rights must be minimal in the sense that morally speaking they require agreement on very little (see Beitz, 2001a, 2001b, 2004; Cohen 2004; Pogge, 2004, 2005, 2008; Rawls, 1999, Scanlon, 1998). Others in contrast believe that moral arguments must be substantive or 'thick', in the sense that they must be derived from more significant and admittedly controversial moral commitments (see Campbell, 2007: Huseby, 2008; James, 2007; Singer, 1993, 2002, 2004).

Two closely related questions suggest themselves. First, are there good reasons to adopt minimalism with respect to justification, and second, does justificatory minimalism entail or require substantive minimalism?

As we have seen, Rawls provides what is perhaps the most significant answer to the first of these questions. Because of what he calls 'the fact of pluralism', to ensure that moral doctrines are not coercively imposed, in political debate the requirement of 'publicity' must be satisfied. We should only offer reasons it is reasonable to expect others to accept, which is to say reasons that could be made public (Rawls, 1997: 579).

In regard to the content of justice, Rawls adopts a non-minimal approach at the level of the democratic society, which we return to later in this chapter, but he insists on substantive minimalism at the global level. He believes that such minimalism concerning the content of human rights is required by justificatory minimalism. Rawls's contention is that we cannot expect members of what he calls 'decent hierarchical societies' to accept 'liberal' principles of distributive justice without violating the requirements of publicity (1993b: 558). It follows that we cannot insist that the poverty of members of decent hierarchical societies is a distributive injustice as defined by a liberal theory of justice and therefore that the poor have rights of distributive justice as a result. This conclusion follows, Rawls believes, from the observation that liberal principles are premised on a commitment to moral equality, and it is not reasonable to expect the members of non-democratic societies to accept this commitment.

Thomas Scanlon has defended a similarly minimalist approach to the content of human rights on the grounds that this is required by a 'reasonable' moral debate (1998: 191; 224–225). Rawls and Scanlon are not objecting to human rights for the global poor, unlike those who reject such rights on the grounds they could never be enforced and/or claimed (Ignatieff, 2001: 57; O'Neill, 1996). Rawls and Scanlon accept the global poor have rights against poverty. What they reject is the idea that principles of distributive justice suited to a democratic society can be extended to the whole of humanity (see de Vita, 2007).

If substantive minimalism is perceived to be required by justificatory minimalism can substantive non-minimalism be defended only with the simultaneous rejection of justificatory minimalism? That is, must we jettison 'Rawls's core conception of reasonableness' so as to defend a more demanding global ethic? Peter Singer's defence of far-reaching duties to assist the global poor is of interest precisely because it is based on utilitarian moral theory and therefore it does not limit itself to minimalism in justification. There is no significant moral distinction between acts and omissions, according to Singer, on the basis of utilitarian moral theory, as moral significance is derived from the consequences of our acts and omissions. Therefore, there is very little moral significance in the difference between, on the one hand, not acting so as to prevent poverty when we have the capacity to do so 'without sacrificing anything of comparable moral significance', and on the other hand, causing poverty by harmful actions (Singer, 1993: 231). He also argues that having the capacity to prevent poverty is sufficient reason to justify the duty to do so (see Campbell, 2007: 64). If we have the capacity to prevent poverty but omit to do so, then we are morally responsible for the poverty we could have removed.

Singer's argument is based on and part of a utilitarian moral theory. For utilitarians, actions are right insofar as they promote utility, or interests, and when we deliberate about what we should do, we should give 'equal consideration' to the 'like interests' of all (Singer, 1993: 21). However, some interests have far greater significance than others, including interests that severe poverty will in all likelihood infringe. These 'important human interests' include avoiding pain, developing our abilities, satisfying our basic needs for food and shelter, enjoying friendly and loving relations, and being free to pursue our chosen projects without unnecessary interference (ibid. p. 23).

Singer's proposals are not uncontroversial. Some may question whether the best way to promote utility is, as he insists, to give priority to the needs of the most deprived, rather than say those who would make most efficient use of resources. If we are duty bound to promote utility, maybe the most deprived will be very inefficient at doing so. Others may question if actions are made right (or wrong) by their likely consequences, rather than by their conformity to general rules of action. Some actions may have good consequences but may also be perceived to be morally wrong in their own right. Presumably Singer considers his proposals to be justifiable to others for the reason that the interests of everyone have been taken into consideration. However, utilitarians do not consider the justifiability of their proposals as a primary consideration. As we shall see in the next section, utilitarians sometimes distinguish between an everyday level of moral thinking and a higher level of moral thinking where our everyday principles have a justification that most of us can be unaware of. In contrast, for those who defend the idea of reasonableness, in Scanlon's terms, 'an act is right if and only if it can be justified to others' (1998: 189). If Singer's conclusions cannot 'be justified to others' the actions they require cannot be right. What Rawls's later work attempts to show is that political theory cannot both proceed from a comprehensive moral doctrine (such as utilitarianism) and at the same time satisfy the requirements of moral justification in politics. If publicity is necessary for moral justification in politics that in itself would be significant grounds to question Singer's utilitarianism.

A closed and self-contained democratic society

Morality requires us to willingly justify or account for ourselves with reasons that have a uniquely moral quality. According to Rawls and others, however, to justify ourselves we must only employ reasons it is reasonable to expect other persons to accept. This is referred to as the requirement of publicity, and for Rawls it is especially relevant to the justification of principles of justice. Principles of justice must enable the members of a society 'to make mutually acceptable to one another' their shared institutions and to do so 'by citing what are publicly recognized as sufficient reasons, as identified by that conception' (Rawls, 1980: 517). Rawls's thesis is that, in political debate (as opposed to moral deliberation and discussion outside politics) principles can be legitimate only if they are also 'political' (or 'public' or 'reasonable').

Three core elements of the concept of reasonableness have already been discussed in Chapter 5. They are that reasonable citizens view 'one another as free and equal in a system of social cooperation over generations', they offer each other fair terms of social cooperation, and third, 'recognize and accept the consequences of the burdens of judgement...' (Rawls 1997: 578, 613, 612 n.95). Crucially, as we shall see later in this chapter, Rawls stresses that the requirements of reasonableness are relevant when citizens of a 'closed and self-contained democratic society' deliberate over principles of justice (1993b: 532). A reasonable public debate seeks agreement on principles of justice, and the particular theory defended by Rawls is 'justice as fairness'. It ensures a fair distribution of what he refers to as primary social goods. On the one hand, this requires guaranteeing equal civil and political liberties for all and fair equal opportunity in the distribution of offices and powers. On the other hand, his Difference Principle requires that any inequalities in income and wealth must be to the benefit of the least advantaged (Rawls, 1971: 302). Crucially, therefore, a just distribution is also one that prioritizes the interests (in terms of income and wealth) of the least advantaged. The Difference Principle states that 'the higher expectations of those better situated are just if and only if they work as part of a scheme which improves the expectations of the least advantaged members of society' (ibid. p. 75). In effect, it is a government-guaranteed 'social minimum' or 'a certain level of well-being' (ibid. p. 275, p. 276).

The strengths of a political conception can best be seen by exploring precisely why, according to Rawls, a non-political conception is problematic. For instance, Singer's argument from capacity deserves criticism precisely because in some instances, perhaps often, his central commitments and premises cannot be made public. Critics of Singer have noted that his proposals are so stringent that only 'moral saints' could do what he believes is right and, in consequence, his position is self-defeating. The utilitarian believes that an act is right in proportion as it tends to promote happiness. However, to the extent that we are motivated to prevent those very bad things from happening that we are capable of preventing, which is what Singer requires of us, we will be unable to do all those other things that do in fact promote happiness, that is, acting on the basis of our self-interest and what gives us pleasure (Wolf, 1982: 428; see James, 2007).

Singer concedes that 'making morality so demanding threatens to bring the whole of morality into disrepute' (Singer, 2004: 28). His proposed solution is that in public we should advocate a less demanding ethic than in private we know to be right and justified (ibid. p. 17; see Hare, 1981). It is not the ideals of utilitarianism that are wrong, Singer's argument goes, but rather the wearing of utilitarian ideals on one's sleeve, insofar as doing so does not promote happiness: instead it might 'inhibit other's ability to enjoy themselves' (Wolf, 1982: 428). However, distinguishing what one believes to be right from what one believes one should state publicly to be right, in this way, has been criticized as 'hypocritical and condescending' (ibid.). The utilitarian is motivated by equality in the sense that the objective is to give equal consideration to the like interests of each, but Singer's approach to public debate suggests utilitarians are not motivated by a commitment to moral equality in regard to public deliberation over the merits of their proposals.

There is a misleadingly superficial similarity between Rawls's account of public reasoning and Singer's version of the utilitarian two-level theory. As we know, according to Rawls, in public debate we may argue from a comprehensive doctrine, such as Kantian moral philosophy for example, but this is permissible only as long as the following proviso is respected: 'that, in due course, we give properly public reasons to support the principles and policies our comprehensive doctrine is said to support' (1997: 584). Rawls is saying that while we may be motivated to hold a belief by a comprehensive moral doctrine, in political debate we should give different considerations in support of those beliefs, namely public reasons. Therefore, like Singer, Rawls believes that the reasons we offer to others may rightly differ from the reasons that motivated us in the first place to reach the conclusion we have reached. But Rawls's point is *not* that we should conceal from others what we take to be the right thing to do and why we think it is right, which is the implication of Singer's position. Rather, according to Rawls, we should be explicit about what we think is the right thing to do and why it is right, but the reasons offered in its defence must be such that they can be made public.

Reasons for substantive minimalism

An injustice is an inequality not to the benefit of the least well off, Rawls has argued, but he also concludes that the Difference Principle is valid only within a closed and self-contained democratic society. His rationale for this distinction is that principles of justice constructed for a 'closed and self-contained democratic society' are very different to those constructed for what he calls the Society of Peoples. There are a number of related reasons for Rawls's adoption of such a minimalist position concerning the content of global politics, beginning with the burdens of judgement argument.

(1) The burdens of judgement argument

Reasonable citizens 'recognize and accept the consequences of the burdens of judgement', Rawls argues (1997: 613, 612 n. 95). For that reason they do not hold out for agreement on one comprehensive moral doctrine, but they also agree to bracket controversial philosophical and moral issues in political debate. Turning to public debate at the global level, Rawls believes that liberal, 'Western' societies (i.e. societies shaped by Enlightenment ideas) should not require non-liberal societies to accept the fundamental moral principles of liberal societies. This is the case as, Rawls believes, within a hierarchical society the members 'are viewed as decent and rational, as well as responsible', but this 'does not require acceptance of the liberal idea that persons are citizens first and have equal basic rights as equal citizens' (1999: 66). It is the case that in a global political debate, representatives of liberal, Western societies are asked to treat hierarchical representatives as equals, just as hierarchical representatives are asked to view liberal representatives as equals. However, Rawls does not agree that 'treating societies equally depends on their treating their members equally' (ibid.). The commitment to view others as free and equal is a fundamental intuitive idea of Western societies, and it cannot be assumed that representatives of hierarchical societies will accept such ideas. Nonetheless, Rawls is confident that 'decent hierarchical societies' can and should engage reasonably with liberal societies. That is, they can and should 'accept the symmetrical (equal) situation of the original position as fair' (1999: 69). Representatives of decent hierarchical societies are expected to treat liberal representatives as their moral equals, which implies it is reasonable to expect them to accept such a commitment.

Rawls wants to ensure that global political discourse does not involve simply the imposition of one culture's set of beliefs on another, alien culture. This is part of his concern to ensure the fact of pluralism is accepted by all. At the same time he is forced by the logic of his own argument to ascribe to decent hierarchical societies commitments that seem to be at odds with his assumption that the different cultures involved, liberal and hierarchical, are marked by a radical incommensurability in respect of just those beliefs and commitments. It seems he must assume that the commitment to moral equality is applicable to the hierarchical society while at the same time insisting such commitments cannot be expected of them. More generally, there is potentially a serious tension in the argument that moral considerations are valid only if they are discovered as fundamental intuitive ideas of the culture(s) in question and also that we can judge whether or not such cultures are reasonable. In Rawls's work, there is an acute danger that his efforts to ensure respect for plurality will come into direct conflict with the means by which respect is to be ensured, namely through reasonable, public debate. Rawls must therefore show how this tension can be resolved.

(2) Constructivism

Rawls's constructivism entails firstly that a political conception of justice is not and cannot be based on universal ideas. Rather it is based on notions implicit in the public political culture of a specific society (Rawls, 1980: 518). Further, a constructivist conception of justice is not concerned with the epistemological question of whether these premises are true. Instead it has a 'social role', to enable the members of a society 'to make mutually acceptable to one another' their shared institutions and to do so 'by citing what are publicly recognized as sufficient reasons, as identified by that conception' (ibid. p. 517).

Principles of justice also are constructed in stages or steps, and 'rational parties adopt principles of justice for each kind of subject as it arises' (1993b: 532). The first of these 'subjects' to arise is the 'basic structure of a closed and self-contained democratic society' (ibid.). When extended beyond this to the Society of Peoples, the principles and conceptions of practical reason on which it rests must be 'suitably adjusted' and the principles must be 'endorsed on due reflection by the reasonable agents to whom the corresponding principles apply' (ibid. pp. 532–533).

The extension of ideas of justice to new subjects is to occur in two stages. The first stage is to move from a closed and self-contained democratic society to a Society of Peoples comprising all liberal societies only.

> In such a Law of Peoples, peoples are free and independent, are equal and parties to their own agreements, have the right to self-defence but no right to war, are to observe treaties and undertakings, are to observe restrictions on the conduct of war, and are to honour human rights. (ibid. p. 540)

In choosing principles of justice, moreover, the 'veil of ignorance' is employed as 'a device of representation' (ibid. p. 538). The veil of ignorance, or original position, is appropriate as it represents the parties 'fairly'; it represents them as 'rational'; and it represents them as deciding between available principles for 'appropriate reasons' (ibid.).

The second stage in the construction of principles of justice is to extend them to what Rawls calls 'well-ordered hierarchical societies'. Rawls believes that once again the veil of ignorance is the appropriate device for representatives of a 'well-ordered hierarchical society', and behind the veil of ignorance they would chose the same Law of Peoples that representatives of liberal societies have chosen above. Rawls believes a hierarchical society is 'well-ordered' if, first, it is peaceful and not expansionist (ibid. p. 545); second, its system of law must be such as to impose obligations on all within its territory and there must be 'a sincere and not unreasonable belief' on the part of its judges and officials that the law is indeed guided by a common good conception of justice; and finally,

> its conception of the common good of justice secures for all persons at least certain minimum rights to means of subsistence and security

(the right to life), to liberty (freedom from slavery, serfdom, and forced occupations) and (personal) property, as well as to formal equality as expressed by the rules of natural justice. (ibid. pp. 546–547)

It follows that even hierarchical societies can be included in a Society of Peoples. This is the case as 'basic human rights express a minimum standard of well-ordered political institutions for all peoples who belong as members in good standing, to a just political Society of Peoples' (ibid. p. 552). The resulting Law of Peoples is not peculiarly liberal, Rawls contends, as it does not require that each person be viewed as a free and equal citizen. It simply requires that 'persons be responsible and cooperating members of society who can recognize and act in accordance with their moral duties and obligations' (ibid.).

The potential tension in Rawls's thought highlighted above concerned the commitment to reasonableness on the one hand and the commitment to moral pluralism on the other. His constructivist approach to political theory promises to provide a way in which reasonable agreement can be attained between liberal and decent hierarchical societies. However, one cause for concern is the assumption that a person (representative) can be or should be reasonable when deliberating on a Law of Peoples, but also the same person (representative) cannot be expected to be reasonable when deliberating on domestic principles of justice. Rawls expresses this position by stating that the original position argument 'is used twice for liberal societies (once at the domestic level and once at the Law of Peoples level), but only once, at the second level, for decent hierarchical societies' (1999: 70). Once again there is reason to fear that Rawls is operating a double standard. A further concern is the modesty, or conservatism, of these proposals, specifically how little is owed to the global poor. Rather than extending the Difference Principle to the global poor, they are granted 'minimum rights to means of subsistence and security (the right to life)'.

(3)   The political culture argument

Rawls places significant limits on what he considers is owed to the global poor, as we have seen. This is partly due to the way in which he conceives of the nature and causes of global poverty. Rawls refers to situations where decent hierarchical societies are unable to become well-ordered due to 'unfavorable conditions' (Rawls, 1993b: 558). The conditions are 'unfavourable' when a society lacks political and cultural traditions, human capital and know-how, and material and technological resources. In such situations, 'each society now burdened by

unfavourable conditions should be raised to, or assisted towards, conditions that make a well-ordered society possible' (ibid.). Moreover, Rawls
believes that the reason why such societies experience 'unfavourable
conditions' is 'often not the lack of natural resources', but rather is
likely to be 'oppressive government and corrupt elite; the subjection
of women abetted by unreasonable religion, with the resulting over-
population relative to what the economy of the society can decently
sustain' (ibid.). It follows the obligation of wealthier societies includes
'an emphasis on human rights...backed up by other kinds of assistance,
to moderate, albeit slowly, oppressive government, the corruption of
elites, and the subjection of women' (ibid. p. 560).

Rawls accepts that natural resources are distributed unequally
between peoples and a people's level of resources is arbitrary from a
moral point of view in that it cannot count as a reason for retaining the
benefits that such resources subsequently generate. However, as he also
believes that it is a people's culture rather than their level of natural
resources that is 'the crucial element in how a country fairs', then the
arbitrariness of natural resources 'causes no difficulty' (1999: 117).
What Rawls refers to as the 'duty of assistance' is not a duty to bring
about a particular level of resources in poorer societies. Instead, the
duty is to assist such societies in overcoming 'unfavorable conditions' and becoming well-ordered hierarchical societies, in particular
by requiring that they respect basic rights and reduce corruption and
oppression. This duty of assistance is distinct from and does not in any
way imply or require a theory of distributive justice.

(4) Considerations for the difference principle do not apply

The responsibilities of the wealthy to the global poor go only as far
as a 'duty of assistance', Rawls has argued. While within a democratic
society, certain considerations support the adoption of the Difference
Principle, Rawls offers three reasons why these considerations are *not*
relevant at the level of the Society of Peoples.

First, within a democratic society, the gap between rich and poor
cannot be wider than the criterion of reciprocity allows, so that the
least advantaged 'have sufficient all-purpose means to make intelligent
and effective use of their freedoms and to lead reasonable and worthwhile lives' (Rawls, 1999: 114). In contrast, in the Society of Peoples, the
duty of assistance is satisfied when 'all peoples' have a 'working liberal
or decent government' (ibid.). There is no reason to go further than
this so as to 'narrow the gap between the average wealth of different
peoples' (ibid.).

Second, within a democratic society, the gap between rich and poor should be narrowed if such a gap leads to feelings of inferiority and wounds the self-respect of the least well-off. However, at the level of the Society of Peoples, once the duty of assistance is satisfied, 'and each people has their own liberal or decent government', then there is no justification for such feelings of inferiority and therefore no call for redistribution (ibid.).

Finally, third, within a democratic society, the gap between rich and poor should be narrowed so as to ensure fairness in the political process and also fair equality of opportunity. Fairness 'among peoples', in contrast, requires each 'preserve the independence of their own society and its equality in relation to others' (ibid. p. 115). What this will require is 'standards of fairness for trade' as well as 'certain provisions for mutual assistance' (ibid.) but once again it does not require a narrowing of the gap in wealth between peoples.

For Rawls, the duty of assistance has a 'target', beyond which the duty no longer holds, and that target is the 'political autonomy of free and equal liberal and decent peoples' (ibid. p. 118). The duties of the wealthy come to an end when other societies are 'fully just and stable for the right reasons' (ibid. p. 119). Rawls contrasts this with the 'cosmopolitan view', the ultimate concern of which being the well-being of individuals (ibid. p. 120).

(5)   Argument from the basic structure

Rawls has argued that considerations counting in favour of the Difference Principle at the level of a democratic society do not have such implications at the level of the Society of Peoples. One explanation for his adopting this position is his 'constructivist' argument that moral principles are worked out for a particular 'subject', and principles of justice are worked out in the first instance for the 'basic structure' of a closed and self-contained democratic society (1980: 518). The basic structure of a society is made up of its major institutions. It is of central importance for a theory of justice as it has two features: it not only divides up the benefits and burdens of social cooperation, but also the institutions themselves are coercive. As Wenar observes, Rawls presumes that 'coercive political power is only legitimate when exercised in accordance with ideas that all who are coerced can reasonably accept' (Wenar, 2001: 84; Rawls, 1993a: 136–137). At the level of the closed and self-contained democratic society, Rawls argues, the basic structure can be justified only if it is a fair scheme of cooperation among citizens regarded as free and equal (Wenar, 2001: 84).

Before Rawls's publication of *The Law of Peoples* essay in 1993 (later expanded and published in book form in 1999), others had attempted to construe how his ideas, developed mainly in *A Theory of Justice*, apply at the level of global politics. They began from the observation that global society has a basic structure, as it is coercive and also divides up the benefits and burdens of global social cooperation, and therefore it too will be justified only if it is a fair scheme of cooperation among (global) citizens regarded as free and equal (see Beitz, 2001a, 2001b, 2004; Pogge, 2004, 2005, 2008). When Rawls did publish his own arguments on this issue he did not draw this conclusion, as has been seen, and this is the case in large part because of the way in which he conceptualized the basic structure at the global level. On the one hand, Rawls concluded that it is a basic structure populated by 'peoples' rather than individual 'persons'. He therefore rejected the cosmopolitan approach whose concern is first and foremost with individuals rather than societies. On the other hand, Rawls concluded that the interests of peoples are different from those of individual persons to the extent they do not support the employment of a theory of global distributive justice. We turn to this latter issue now.

(6) Peoples not persons, and their interests

Rawls decides to conceptualize issues of global poverty in terms of relations between peoples whereas issues of poverty within a democratic society are conceptualized in terms of relations between free and equal individual citizens or persons. He argues that the global public political culture, and its documents and treaties, mainly 'concern how domestic governments should treat their citizens' and also that on the global political stage it is peoples rather than persons who are the main actors (Wenar, 2001: 87). This explains why Rawls is not a cosmopolitan, namely that he is concerned with peoples rather than persons. However, his non-egalitarian approach to global politics is explained by his view of the fundamental interests of peoples and individual persons. Peoples, he believes, 'have interests in protecting their territorial integrity, securing the safety of their citizens, maintaining their independent and just social institutions, and sustaining their self-respect as peoples' (Wenar, 2001: 88; Rawls, 1999: 24, 34). What is markedly absent from the interests of peoples, on Rawls's view, is the interests that individual persons do have, namely interests in greater resources.

In *A Theory of Justice* Rawls had argued that primary social goods are 'human goods'. Primary goods have 'the properties that it is rational for someone with a rational plan of life to want', and also they 'satisfy this condition for persons generally' (1971: 399). Not having enough primary social goods to pursue whatever goals we want to pursue is such a terrible prospect that it is only rational to choose principles of justice that would guarantee that this would not happen (to us or anyone else) (ibid. p. 154). Rawls's thesis involves the claim that this 'human' and 'rational' want is not relevant when representatives enter the original position and deliberate concerning the Law of Peoples.

Rawls also uses two examples purported to illustrate why a global principle of distributive justice would have 'unacceptable' results (1999: 117–119). In each example two hypothetical societies are presented, and in each case to begin with the societies are well-ordered and equally prosperous.

In the first example, one of the societies chooses to industrialize and also increases its savings, while the other chooses 'a more pastoral and leisurely society' (ibid. p. 117). After a period of time the former becomes twice as wealthy as the latter. Despite the change in fortunes, according to Rawls, there is no reason for the duty of assistance to apply, as both societies were already well-ordered. Moreover, Rawls also rejects the use of what he refers to as a 'global egalitarian principle without target' as it would require a flow of wealth from one society to another as long as one is more wealthy (ibid.).

The second example again has two well-ordered societies, each 'granting elements of equal justice to women' (ibid.). However, a policy of fair equal opportunity for women is actively pursued in one society only, leading over time to zero population growth and as a result increased levels of wealth in that society. In the second society, in contrast, the population continues to grow leading to lower levels of economic growth. However, once again, as each society was well-ordered to begin with, their people are free and responsible and able to make their own decisions, and therefore neither the duty of assistance nor a 'global egalitarian principle without target' would be justified.

According to Hinsch, Rawls's argument relies on the highly questionable assumption that in each example above the two societies are not already, at the outset, joined together in one mutually advantageous system of cooperation. For this reason Rawls believes that 'incentive effects' are absent, and therefore, if the Difference Principle were applied it would lead to an egalitarian redistribution of funds until both societies are at equal levels of wealth (Hinsch, 2001: 71). Rawls does assume that when considering what is owed to those with whom we share a mutually advantageous system of cooperation, then the individual's 'obligations' are relevant. In contrast, when considering what is owed to the distant needy, the 'duty' of assistance can be seen as an extension of what Rawls refers to as the 'natural duty to support and further just institutions' (Hinsch, 2001: 66). For Rawls, unlike obligations, 'natural duties apply regardless of the voluntary actions of individuals and irrespective of institutional ties between them' and while the Difference Principle regulates the actions of institutions, natural duties regulate the actions of individuals (ibid.).

The two examples used by Rawls to illustrate why the Difference Principle should not be applied at the global level also throw more light on the presuppositions and underlying assumptions motivating his argument. For Rawls, the Difference Principle is suitable for a society where individuals are viewed as free and equal citizens; it is to be applied to the basic structure of a society whose coercive institutions distribute benefits and burdens to its members; it is suitable to individuals with a fundamental interest in receiving more rather than less primary social goods; and it is suitable to a society that is a mutually advantageous system of cooperation.

The duty of assistance, in contrast, is suitable when a liberal people is interacting with people for whom the commitment to moral equality is not present at the level of domestic justice but is present at the level of the Society of Peoples; it is suitable when decent hierarchical societies are burdened with unfavourable conditions; it is suitable where cultural reasons explain why a society is so burdened; and it is suitable where there is not a system of cooperation in place between the peoples concerned.

A political conception of global distributive justice

The central issue in the discussion above is whether justificatory minimalism requires substantive minimalism at the global level, as Rawls assumes. Of the possible lines of argument in defence of a more substantive political conception of human rights, three are addressed below. The first is a constructivist argument from the cultural commitments of each society; the second is an argument from the existence of a basic structure at the global level; and the final argument is from the requirements of moral justification *per se*. Each will be addressed in turn, but it is the third of these that is, it seems, the most robust.

(1)   The constructivist argument for global distributive justice

The first line of argument is that, if a political conception of the Law of Peoples draws only on the resources of the specific culture(s) in question, the commitment to view others as free and equal must be a cultural commitment of each of the societies making up the Society of Peoples. Therefore, the commitment to moral equality must be a cultural commitment of so-called decent hierarchical societies. Although such an approach would be compatible with constructivism, it is of course not Rawls's actual argument. Rawls will not insist that, in the Society of Peoples, all individuals must be viewed as free and equal. The reason he does not do so is that, in his view, individuals are not viewed in this way within decent hierarchical societies. Any principles of justice that require all individuals to be viewed as free and equal would be 'rejected as peculiarly liberal or special to our Western tradition' (Rawls, 1993b: 552). At the same time, however, human rights are guaranteed in a decent hierarchical society, although '[a]dmittedly it ensures those rights to persons as members of estates and corporations and not as citizens' (ibid. p. 553).

One way in which to develop the constructivist argument for global distributive justice is as follows. Rawls insists that decent hierarchical societies must be assisted to change so that they overcome political corruption and the oppression that results from 'unreasonable religion'. Presumably, so as to avoid the kind of imposition of values he criticizes, Rawls believes that it is from *within* the cultures of these societies that these imperatives for reform are derived. Granted in such a society the individual is in the first instance viewed as a bearer of specific roles and as a member of various groups, as such a society is a 'decent consultation hierarchy' in Rawls's terms (1999: 71). In contrast, in the Enlightenment tradition of Western culture, in the first instance the individual is viewed as a separate person and has significance independently of his/ her roles and associations. Nonetheless, if the hierarchical society is committed to the view that oppression of individuals is wrong, it can be argued there must also be a moral commitment to view the oppressed person as free and equal. If the oppressed person is not viewed in this way, why would the oppression be morally significant? One possible answer is that oppression may be seen as an abuse of power and responsibility on the part of the oppressor and for that reason morally wrong, even without a commitment to view the oppressed as free and equal. However, if we ought to respond to oppression by promoting individual rights, as Rawls claims, does it not follow that oppression is morally wrong in part because the oppressed should instead be viewed as moral equals and it is for this reason that oppression is a violation of individual rights? Again this conclusion need not follow. It is possible to think of rightful claims as claims that can be made by an individual in virtue of his/her role, as opposed to claims that can be made by any individual regardless of their roles, and just as roles can be hierarchically ordered so too can rights lead to unequal but just treatment. The first attempt to develop a constructivist argument for global distributive justice seems to come to an end here. However, a second version of such an argument focuses on the participation of representatives from decent hierarchical societies in the deliberative process from which a reasonable Law of Peoples is to emerge. As we have already seen, Rawls is confident that decent hierarchical societies can and should engage reasonably with liberal societies. They can and should 'accept the symmetrical (equal) situation of the original position as fair' (1999: 69). Representatives of decent hierarchical societies are expected to treat liberal representatives as their moral equals, which implies it is reasonable to expect them to accept such a commitment. The line of argument above is that, a commitment to view others as free and equal must be discoverable in the culture of the decent hierarchical society, if it is also the case that their representatives can engage reasonably in global politics. Note that no appeal has been made to moral principles known to be true independent of the culture of the people concerned. The political conception has used nothing other than the resources said to be already present in the culture of the decent hierarchical society, as well as the Western society.

If this second line of argument is taken, it would follow that the political conception is discovered at the point where the different moral doctrines 'overlap'. It is the point of intersection of different moral systems, or the lowest common denominator shared by all. One or other of these approaches has been adopted elsewhere concerning the morality of global politics (see Cohen, 2004; Walzer, 1994; Etzioni, 2004). Such an approach is however problematic in the first instance as it may leave one a hostage to fortune. As it relies on the discovery of specific commitments in the cultures in question, it is reliant on empirical observation, and it may turn out that such commitments are not observed. If there is a failure to observe such commitments then there are no resources to fall back on in the evaluation or judgement of the society in question, and this brings us to a second weakness of such an approach. It is questionable as it seems unable to provide the basis or resources needed to adopt a critical attitude on the content of a culture, its intuitions, practices, and institutions. Instead, it takes this cultural content as the only valid basis of moral critique, and thus is inherently conservative in the sense that all moral judgement must be internal and interpretative.

(2)   Argument from the basic structure of global society

An alternative way in which to provide a Rawlsian basis for global distributive justice centres on the significance Rawls gives to the basic structure. The line of argument here is that, if Rawls was successful in showing that the Difference Principle was justified as applying to the basic structure of a democratic society, it can and should be applied to the basic structure of the global society. The argument is based both on the Rawlsian idea that principles of justice are designed for the basic structure of a society and also on the claim that there is a basic structure at the global level. Alvaro de Vita argues that global society has all the features of a basic structure. As is the case within a democratic society, at the global level 'huge distributive inequalities could and do arise in society's basic institutional arrangements from individual transactions and acts that, in themselves … were morally unobjectionable', and also these institutions have a 'pervasive influence' on the lives of individuals living under them (de Vita, 2007: 126). The basic structure of global society profoundly influences people's lives, therefore, but does not yet do so in a way that satisfies the 'conditions for reciprocity'. For that to be remedied a mutually advantageous system of cooperation is required, where 'all parties stand prospectively to benefit from the scheme' (ibid. p. 127).

Thomas Pogge's argument for socio-economic human rights is based similarly on the premise that global society is a system of interaction and as such it needs to be regulated by principles of justice. He argues that societies and their individual members do interact with and influence the lives of other societies and their members, and concludes that the global poor have socio-economic rights that are justified as 'compensation' for 'harm' caused within this global system. His argument is that global poverty has been caused by the global non-poor and also that this is a harm (Pogge, 2005: 1). Pogge is concerned with what can be claimed against institutions or on behalf of institutions, including nation states but also global economic and political institutions (Pogge, 2008: 63–64). This is an important point as his thesis requires determining what proportion of poverty has been caused by global institutions, in particular the global market, and what proportion has been caused instead by national agencies, in particular corrupt or inefficient nation states, and on that basis deciding who is responsible for what harm caused to whom (Pogge, 2008: 118ff; see Huseby 2008: 7ff.). Those that have caused poverty, and therefore harmed the poor, should compensate the poor for these harmful actions.

Global poverty is an injustice because it is a harm inflicted on the poor and justice requires compensation for this harm, according to Pogge. Whereas Rawls was concerned with what is owed to 'peoples' rather than individual persons and assumed that peoples did not have an 'interest' in a greater share of primary goods, Pogge is concerned with the rightful claims of individuals within a global society. The rationale for Pogge's argument is that, if individuals within a decent hierarchical society have been harmed, say both by their own inefficient and corrupt national government and also by rapacious and exploitative global institutions, then justice requires that those individuals be compensated.

Pogge's argument is however problematic primarily for the reason that 'harm' and 'poverty' are two separate phenomena and the latter need not imply the former. Harm has been defined elsewhere as 'thwarting, defeating, or setting back some party's interests' (Beauchamp and Childress, 2009: 152). However, some poverty will have resulted from natural disasters rather than harmful actions, and therefore if Pogge is to be consistent, such poverty should not give rise to duties of justice (see Mieth 2008: 31). Poverty also can have resulted from 'in themselves innocent individual acts whose unforeseeable cumulative effects result in economic harms' (Campbell, 2007: 62). Pogge's approach makes the eradication of poverty 'dependent on how the poverty came about' and also 'on establishing who or what is to blame' (ibid. p. 63). However, if the original cause of deprivation was not harmful human actions, then, on Pogge's account, that poverty does not by itself generate duties of justice for the wealthy. What Pogge cannot say from within his paradigm is that, regardless of the cause of poverty, the poor have socio-economic rights.

Moreover, it is very difficult to identify, within the complex systems of interactions in a global society, the causal relation that can account for a person's poverty (Huseby 2008: 7ff.). Morally speaking, it is also questionable whether it is those who have caused harm who are obliged to remedy the harm, as others may have greater capacity to do so and as a result a more demanding obligation (see Campbell, 2007; Singer, 2004). However, the more fundamental issue concerns drawing moral conclusions from empirical observations. The fact that individuals *can* be observed to interact does not by itself justify a moral conclusion concerning what each person *owes* to others (see Nozick, 1974). For instance, Rawls can accept that democratic societies do interact with decent hierarchical societies, but he does not accept that as a result inequalities are justified only if they benefit the least advantaged members of both societies. What is required therefore is an account of what moral considerations and what kind of moral reasoning justify principles of distributive justice for the global level.

(3)   Reasonableness as a requirement of political morality

This brings us to the third line of argument in defence of global distributive justice. The argument here is that if the requirements of reasonableness are applied consistently to all political actors on the global stage, then global poverty must be seen as an issue of distributive justice. And the requirements of reasonableness should be applied consistently first so as to avoid the charge of operating a double standard and also second so as to avoid a conflict between the commitments of pluralism and reasonableness.

In politics, Rawls has argued, we must be willing to justify our proposals to others and to do so by offering reasons it is reasonable to expect others to accept. His own rationale for a political conception as worked out for a closed and self-contained democratic society sets a very high bar on moral justification. At this level, citizens must be willing to view one another as free and equal and offer each other fair terms of social cooperation. At the level of the Society of Peoples, however, two developments can be observed in Rawls's thought, neither of which is compatible with the other. On the one hand, he assumes that deliberation on a Law of Peoples can and should be reasonable, and that this is possible because the representatives of a hierarchical society can accept the reciprocity of the original position and the representatives of Western societies can adopt this reciprocal perspective in regard to their hierarchical counterparts. On the other hand, he assumes it is unreasonable to expect members of a hierarchical society to view each other as free and equal, or to be viewed as free and equal by members of Western societies, and therefore unreasonable for the principle of reciprocity to apply to the domestic politics of the hierarchical society or to any dealings between individuals of the hierarchical society and individuals from other societies.

There are two ways to interpret what has happened in Rawls's work in moving from the scenario of the closed and self-contained democratic society to the Society of Peoples. The first interpretation is that what is offered at the level of the Society of Peoples is not a political conception, as it does not include the requirement to view one another as free and equal. However, this would mean that the terms of cooperation at this level would be nothing more than a *modus vivendi*, which is an agreement based solely on perceived self-interest, and would therefore be subject to the instability of any such agreement based on shifting self-interest that Rawls explicitly wishes to avoid (1993: 147). This interpretation will not do therefore as Rawls sees himself as offering a moral justification at the level of the Society of Peoples.

The second interpretation is that Rawls is guilty of operating a double standard. For no good reason, the argument goes, he has applied a less demanding standard to the level of the Society of Peoples. To avoid the charge of double standards, the political conception at the level of the Society of Peoples would have to demand that we view one another as free and equal for the simple reason that this is the standard applied at the level of the closed and self-contained democratic society. The virtue of this line of argument is that we retain a political conception at the level of the Society of Peoples (thereby avoiding a *modus vivendi*), but also to make the political conception as demanding at the level of the Society of Peoples as it is at the level of a closed and self-contained democratic society.

However, it is not precisely the case that Rawls operates a double standard in this way. As we have seen, he does require representatives of decent hierarchical societies to be reasonable, and also that representatives of Western societies be reasonable in return. Instead the issue is one of contradiction on Rawls's part. Rawls's position seems to be that reasonableness is the appropriate standard of political reasoning at the global level when establishing agreement around global norms, including those that require us to respect plurality, but because of the need to respect plurality reasonableness is not the appropriate standard of political reasoning when individual persons from a hierarchical society are involved. There is therefore a contradiction between the commitment to pluralism on the one hand and the moral basis for such a commitment, namely reasonableness. The alternative approach is to apply reasonableness consistently, and limit pluralism appropriately. The logic for adopting this latter approach is that, first, all parties are in fact assumed to be capable of being reasonable, which is an assumption that Rawls makes, and second, there is no other approach to moral reasoning that is appropriate to the political sphere, which is Rawls's argument. We do not need to establish that reasonableness has universal foundations, but also we do not need to establish that reasonableness can be discovered as part of each specific culture and its heritage.

Finally, if we are obliged to offer fair terms of social cooperation to those we view as free and equal, and if we must view non-citizens as free and equal, it follows we must offer fair terms of social cooperation to the global poor. If it is unreasonable to expect citizens of one's own society to accept a pattern of distribution whereby the least well-off become poorer over time as the wealthy become wealthier, it is also unreasonable to expect the global poor to accept such a pattern of distribution.

8
Conclusions

Can and should political philosophy be carried on 'in the manner of' the Enlightenment? In this book we examined the Enlightenment commitments to scepticism and moral equality, and the idea that morality-as-such and reason-as-such should be pre-eminent in our political reasoning. In contrast, for one school of thought, historicism, the Enlightenment was a failure because it encouraged the false belief that reason and morality are not constituted by tradition. For MacIntyre, reason and morality must be re-connected with the 'settled convictions' of a community where there is a consensus on the hierarchical ordering of goods. MacIntyre's rejection of the Enlightenment commitments to moral equality and scepticism is illustrated by his small-scale (non-State) communitarianism and his historicist epistemology and moral theory.

It was argued that MacIntyre's could be a conservative, insular politics hostile to pluralism and individual freedom. A further argument was that, to avoid incoherence, MacIntyre must make a choice. He could choose to accept that we can arrive at standards of rationality that are independent of any specific traditions, and therefore standards that can be used in a critical rather than an insular fashion, but this would entail rejecting historicism. The only alternative is to retain historicism but accept that he cannot avoid the charge of relativism, that for his position truth is relative to specific traditions and therefore that he cannot provide a narrative of rational progress.

Although MacIntyre's own religious conversion, and subsequent reappraisal of Thomism is seen by some as a significant departure from his earlier work, it was argued here that MacIntyre's thought is still open to the same criticisms, namely both political conservatism and relativism and incoherence in epistemology and ethics. Perhaps

MacIntyre's ethical goals can be pursued within a democratic politics, but his attempt to engage politically was problematic due to the relativistic implications of his position. What is the alternative? One approach is to formulate a non-relative account of human flourishing, to base ethics on human biology and human nature. This was rejected as a *political* strategy, for not only would consent on one such account of human flourishing be unlikely, morally speaking it would never be required of us. We are free not to agree on the meaning of life, a freedom that follows from our status as moral equals and also the commitment to scepticism.

We next turned to the post-modern rejection of the Enlightenment, and what Mouffe calls the 'universal rationalism' of liberal theory. In Chapter 4 we saw that, for Mouffe, politics is a contextualist task as it is pursued within a 'form of life', and also it is based on considerations that are 'contestable' and 'undecidable'. Rather than consensus she calls for 'agonism'. However, Mouffe's account of agonism swings back and forth between relativism and perspectivism. Her claims can be rational only 'relative to' some context, a form of life. At the same time, however, she assumes the terms of social cooperation are contestable hegemonic constructions, and so all we have are different, complementary perspectives. As liberals have argued, post-modernism is a relativistic and immoralist position. Moreover, it cannot avoid a performative contradiction. In stating the post-modernist case, the post-modernist must assume just its opposite. Also, it is not possible to join liberalism with post-modernism, so that liberal moral commitments are somehow strengthened by post-modern insights concerning the all-pervasiveness of power. A choice needs to be made. Either it is accepted that we are guided and limited by morality-as-such and reason-as-such, or else we believe no distinction can be made between reason and morality on the one hand and power and context on the other.

How can political theory acknowledge the plurality of moral viewpoints without at the same time conflating reason with such plurality? How can political theory accept the validity of competing moral doctrines and yet morally and rationally account for that in a manner that is not merely relative? Can political theory avoid incoherence and self-contradiction as well as relativism?

We argued that Rawls's work can be seen as a reformulation and defence of Enlightenment commitments. A qualified defence of 'Rawls's core conception of reasonableness' was made on that basis. It was argued that Rawls is successful in his endeavour to describe political reasoning that does not rely on the justifiability of one comprehensive moral doctrine. His core conception of reasonableness is an attempt to represent the moral requirement to justify ourselves *in* political debate. So, while MacIntyre accepted the necessity of giving an account of ourselves and being held to account, it was the manner in which we were to give such an account that was found wanting. It is one thing to accept that we must be willing to justify ourselves, it is another to accept that the reasons we provide must count as reasons to those we address. It is this that Rawls insists upon, and in doing so expresses the Enlightenment commitments to moral equality and scepticism. Scepticism requires the willingness to justify ourselves to others, and the commitment to moral equality requires that in politics we do so with public reasons.

However, in contrast to Rawls himself, it was argued as well there are no sufficiently strong grounds to accept that perfectionist considerations are and must be unreasonable. Rawls wants to limit unnecessary disagreement and also facilitate moral agreement, and this is to be done through a type of political debate where public reasons must be offered at some stage. However, there is no reason in the first instance why this would require us to forego appeal to perfectionist considerations about human flourishing, about the virtues and happiness (in the sense of a worthwhile life). This is important from a pragmatic point of view as citizens can and do come to political debate informed by ideals of human flourishing and ideals of social organization, whether they are libertarian, socialist, ecological, feminist, and so on. There is no reason to assume that such perfectionist ideas are not or cannot be shared by citizens regarded as free and equal, or that perfectionist ideas must rely on the justifiability of a particular comprehensive moral doctrine. To paraphrase Rawls slightly, what is crucial is to insist that at some point we be willing to provide public reasons in support of such conclusions, and although we may find this a difficult discipline to adopt, that does not mean it will be impossible for us to do. Indeed, consideration can legitimately be given to such perfectionist ideas in the debate over civic education, and the question of what values it may promote and how such a programme of civic education could be justified.

Can and should political philosophy be carried on 'in the manner of' the Enlightenment? This question has been answered through an engagement with Rawls's work, an engagement 'in the manner of' the Enlightenment. The first type of engagement was purely theoretical, but in the final two chapters two practical applications of Rawls's ideas have been discussed. While Chapter 6 explored the issue of civic education programmes for young people, the final chapter addressed the question of our moral obligations to the distant poor. In both cases we moved towards a more nuanced and critical understanding of 'Rawls's core conception of reasonableness'. While departing some distance from Rawls's own arguments, in doing so it is hoped that we remained true to the meaning of reasonableness. In turn, this is offered as an illustration of the core thesis of this book, for this is political philosophy carried on 'in the manner of' the Enlightenment. The twin commitments of scepticism and moral equality have been the resources used to critically engage with both the philosophy of Rawls (as well as others from different approaches) and also the pressing moral issues of civic education and global poverty.

We looked at what values if any should be promoted in civic education and also how the promotion of values can be non-coercive. It was argued that civic education should promote the values of reasonableness, mutual respect, and fairness, but also that at some point public, political reasons should be used in any attempt to justify the content of civic education. Up to that point we had not deviated from Rawls's own arguments. It was argued as well that the content of civic education may legitimately be broader than this. It is possible to offer public, political reasons to justify promoting the values of autonomy, integrity, and magnanimity, as well as the 'social' values of truthfulness and generosity, among others. That is, it may be possible to justify the promotion of some of the values espoused by comprehensive liberals and indeed by historicists like MacIntyre, but only if public reasons can be offered in their defence.

The first part of Chapter 6 proceeded in the conventional manner of addressing what the content of civic education should be. The second half was different as it questioned whom those arguments should be addressed to. Civic education programmes themselves must live up to the requirements of a political approach. Therefore, it is not acceptable for civic education programmes to indoctrinate students with the values in question, and this supports calls for a more participant-oriented approach to civic education, in particular with respect to adolescents. A related issue is that civic education must not approach the current generation of young people as if they were merely the means to bring about the future adults and future citizens they will hopefully one day be. Such an approach will be a coercive imposition of values on young people. If instead the promotion of values is to be non-coercive it must be defended with reasons that young people should be able to accept.

The focus of Chapter 7 was our obligations to the distant poor. In particular, we asked whether minimalism regarding the content of human rights ('substantive minimalism') is required by minimalism regarding the considerations that may rightly be offered to others ('justificatory minimalism'). Although Rawls gave an affirmative answer to this question, the rationale of his own position on both justice and political reason calls that conclusion into question. So as to avoid contradiction in the engagement between 'liberal' and 'decent hierarchical' societies, it has been argued here, it is not possible to conclude that the poverty of non-citizens is not a matter of distributive justice. What Chapter 7 has tried to do is show that morality requires us to engage with non-citizens as moral equals and offer them fair terms of cooperation. If we do accept that we should engage 'politically' in this way with non-citizens then we are forced to accept that the extreme poverty of non-citizens is a matter of distributive justice for us. No solution to global inequality automatically follows, however, but this is no different than the situation regarding national inequality. In both instances it is a matter of moral, public debate what should be done, but crucially what the argument does is bring non-citizens in to the debate as equal participants.

Notes

1 Introduction – Political Reason after the Enlightenment

1. In saying that philosophy can be *after* the Enlightenment in this way we are using the term 'after' in a manner more usually associated with art history. It is often said the work of one artist is 'in the manner of' a previous master. Perhaps the most well known example concerns the influence of seventeenth-, eighteenth-, and nineteenth-century Spanish artists on nineteenth-century French work: many of Manet's works were 'after' Velasquez in this sense, and the same is said of Delacroix in relation to the works of Goya. The use of the term is not intended as a critique. So Manet did not slavishly follow or imitate the work of Velasquez; in fact the styles are different in important respects. Nonetheless there is obvious and acknowledged inspiration, as the Spanish masters made possible fresh and original and daring departures by their French followers (see Tinterow *et al.*, 2003).
2. Citations of Aristotle's *The Nicomachean Ethics* are presented as follows: book number, followed by Part number, page number, either 'a' or 'b' page, and line number.
3. References to Hume's work will normally be given in parenthesis and they will follow the form of the example below: *A Treatise of Human Nature*: T followed by Book, Part, Section, and page number from the Penguin edition, for example, the form T 2.1.7: 348.
4. References to Hume's *An Enquiry Concerning the Principles of Morals* will be given as follows: EPM: followed by Section, Part, and page number from the Hackett edition.

4 Agonism

1. It is the case that theory will inform the observation of the material world even in the natural sciences. Nonetheless, we need not accept Kuhn's account of scientific paradigms. We can still acknowledge that any person could repeat my observation of an empirical phenomenon, even if it is the case that that observation will be interpreted differently in different theoretical contexts (Kuhn, 1957).

Bibliography

Allen, A. 'MacIntyre's Traditionalism', *Journal of Value Inquiry*, vol. 31, no. 4, (1997): 511–525.

Allen, A. 'Foucault and Enlightenment: A Critical Reappraisal', *Constellations*, vol. 10, no. 2 (2003): 180–198.

Aquinas, T. *Summa Theologiae* [ST] (Cambridge: Cambridge University Press, 2006).

Archard, D. 'Citizenship Education and Multiculturalism', pp. 89–102, in Andrew Lockyer, Bernard Crick, John Annetto (eds), *Education for Democratic Citizenship: Issues of Theory and Practice* (Aldershot: Ashgate, 2003).

Archard, D. *Children: Rights and Childhood*, second edition (London: Routledge, 2004).

Aristotle, *The Nicomachean Ethics*, trans. D. Ross, revised by J. L. Ackrill and J. O. Urmson (Oxford: Oxford University Press).

Aristotle, *Politics*, trans. E. Barker, revised by R. F. Stalley (Oxford: Oxford University Press, 1995).

Arneil, B. 'Becoming versus Being: A Critical Analysis of the Child in Liberal Theory', pp. 70–94, in David Archard and Colin M. Macleod (eds), *The Moral and Political Status of Children* (Oxford: Oxford University Press, 2002).

Austen, J. [1818] *Persuasion* (London: Penguin, 1998).

Bakhurst, D. 'Ethical Particularism in Context', pp. 157–177, in Brad Hooker and Margaret Olivia Little (eds), *Moral Particularism* (Oxford: Oxford University Press, 2003).

Barnhart, M.G. 'An Overlapping Consensus: A Critique of Two Approaches', *Review of Politics*, vol. 66, no. 2 (2004): 257–283.

Beauchamp, T.L. and J.F. Childress, *Principles of Biomedical Ethics* (New York: Oxford University Press, 2009).

Beitz, C. 'Human Rights as a Common Concern', *American Political Science Review*, vol. 95, no. 2 (2001a): 269–282.

Beitz, C. 'Does Global Inequality Matter?' *Metaphilosophy*, vol. 32, no. 1/2 (2001b): 95–112.

Beitz, C. 'Human Rights and the Law of Peoples', pp. 193–214, in Deen K. Chatterjee (ed.) *The Ethics of Assistance: Morality and the Distant Needy* (Cambridge: Cambridge University Press, 2004).

Benhabib, S. 'Beyond Interventionism and Indifference: Culture, Deliberation and Pluralism', *Philosophy and Social Criticism*, vol. 31, no. 7 (2005): 753–771.

Bentham, J. [1780] *An Introduction to the Principles of Morals and Legislation* (Dover Publications, 2009).

Breen, K. 'Alasdair MacIntyre and the Hope for a Politics of Virtuous Acknowledged dependence', *Contemporary Political Theory*, vol. 1 (2002): 181–201.

Breen, K. 'The State, Compartmentalization and the Turn to the Local Community: A Critique of the Political Thought of Alasdair MacIntyre', The European Legacy, vol. 10, no. 5 (2005): 485–501.

Breen, K. 'Work and Emancipatory Practice: Towards a Recovery of Human Beings' Productive Capacities', *Res Publica*, vol. 14, no.1 (2007): 381–414.

Brennan, S. 'Children's Choices or Children's Interests: Which do their Rights Protect?' pp. 53–69, in David Archard and Colin M. Macleod (eds), *The Moral and Political Status of Children* (Oxford: Oxford University Press, 2002).

Brighouse, H. 'Civic Education and Liberal Legitimacy', *Ethics*, vol. 108, no. 4 (1998): 719–745.

Brighouse, H. and A. Swift, 'Parents' Rights and the Value of the Family', *Ethics*, vol. 117 (2006): 80–106.

Burke, E. [1790] *Reflections on the Revolution in France* (London: Penguin, 1986).

Callan, E. 'Autonomy, Child-Rearing, and Good Lives', pp. 118–141, in David Archard and Colin M. Macleod (eds), *The Moral and Political Status of Children* (Oxford: Oxford University Press, 2002).

Campbell, T. 'Poverty as a Violation of Human Rights: Inhumanity Or Injustice?' pp. 55–74, in Thomas Pogge (ed.), *Freedom from Poverty as a Human Right* (Paris: Unesco; Oxford: Oxford University Press, 2007).

Chabot, D. 'At Odds with Themselves: David Hume's Skeptical Citizens', *Polity*, vol. 29, no. 3 (1997): 323–343.

Clarke, S. 'Debate: State Paternalism, Neutrality and Perfectionism', *Journal of Political Philosophy*, vol. 14, no. 1 (2006): 111–121.

Cohen, G.A. *Self-ownership, Freedom, and Equality* (Cambridge: Cambridge University Press, 1995).

Cohen, G.A. *If You're An Egalitarian, How Come You're So Rich?* (Cambridge, MA: Harvard University Press, 2000).

Cohen, J. 'Minimalism about Human Rights: The Most We Can Hope For?' *Journal of Political Philosophy*, vol. 12, no. 2 (2004): 190–213.

Coleman, J. 'Answering Susan: Liberalism, Civic Education, and the Status of Younger Persons', pp. 160–180, in David Archard and Colin M. Macleod (eds), *The Moral and Political Status of Children* (Oxford: Oxford University Press, 2002).

Cooke, M. 'Resurrecting the Rationality of Ideology Critique: Reflections on Laclau on Ideology', *Constellations*, vol. 13, no. 1 (2006): 4–20.

Crisp, R. 'Particularizing Particularism', pp. 23–47, in Hooker and Little (eds), *Moral Particularism* (Oxford: Oxford University Press, 2003).

Crowder, G. 'Value Pluralism and Communitarianism', *Contemporary Political Theory*, vol. 5 (2006): 405–427.

Davidson, D. [1974] 'On the Very Idea of a Conceptual Scheme', in *Inquiries into Truth and Interpretation* (Oxford: Clarendon Press, 1984)

De Francisco, A. 'A Republican Interpretation of the Late Rawls', *Journal of Political Philosophy*, vol. 14, no. 3 (2006): 270–288.

Derrida, J. 'Force of Law: The "Mystical Foundation of Authority"', pp. 3–67, in D. Cornell, M. Rosenfeld, and D. G. Carlson. (eds), *Democratization and the Possibility of Justice* (New York: 1992).

Deveaux, M. 'Cultural Pluralism from Liberal Perfectionist Premises', *Polity*, vol. 32, no. 4 (2000): 473–497.

De Vita, A. 'Inequality and Poverty in Global Perspective', pp. 103–132, in Thomas Pogge (ed.) *Freedom from Poverty as a Human Right* (Paris: Unesco; Oxford: Oxford University Press, 2007).

Dryzek, J.S. and Simon Niemeyer, 'Reconciling Pluralism and Consensus as Political Ideals', *American Journal of Political Science*, vol. 50, no. 3 (2006): 634–649.

Dworkin, R. *A Matter of Principle* (Oxford: Clarendon, 1985).

Estlund, D. 'The Insularity of the Reasonable: Why Political Liberalism Must Admit the Truth', *Ethics*, vol. 108 (1998): 252–275.

Etzioni, A. 'The Emerging Global Normative Synthesis', *The Journal of Political Philosophy*, vol. 12, no. 2 (2004): 214–244.

Fives, A. 'Virtue, Justice, and the Human Good: Non-Relative Communitarian Ethics and the Life of Religious Commitment', *Contemporary Politics*, vol. 11, no. 2–3 (2005): 117–131.

Fives, A. 'Aristotle's Ethics and Contemporary Political Theory', *21st Century Society*, vol. 1, no. 2 (2006): 201–220.

Fives, A. *Political and Philosophical Debates in Welfare* (Houndmills: Palgrave Macmillan, 2008a).

Fives, A. 'Human Flourishing: the Grounds of Moral Judgment', *Journal of Value Inquiry*, vol. 42, no. 2 (2008b): 167–186.

Fives, A. 'Reasonable, Agonistic, or Good? The Character of a Democrat', *Philosophy & Social Criticism*, vol. 35, No. 8 (2009): 961–983.

Fives, A. 'Reasonableness, Pluralism, and Liberal Moral Doctrines', *The Journal of Value Inquiry*, vol. 44, no. 3 (2010): 321–339.

Fives, A. 'Non-Coercive Promotion of Values in Civic Education for Democracy', *Philosophy and Social Criticism* (2012, In press).

Foot, P. *Virtues and Vices* (Oxford: Blackwell, 1978).

Foot, P. *Natural Goodness* (Oxford: Clarendon, 2001).

Foucault, M. [1971] 'Nietzsche, Genealogy, History', pp. 76–100, in P. Rabinow (ed.) *The Foucault Reader* (New York: Pantheon Books, 1984).

Foucault, M. [1984] 'What Is Enlightenment?' pp. 32–50, in P. Rabinow (ed.) *The Foucault Reader* (New York: Pantheon Books, 1984).

Fraser, N. 'Social Justice in the Age of Identity Politics', pp. 25–52, in L. Ray and A. Sayer (eds) *Culture and Economy after the Cultural Turn* (London: Sage, 1999).

Freeman, M. *The Moral Status of Children: Essays on the Rights of the Child* (The Hague: Martinus Nijhoff, 1997).

Freeman, S. 'Deliberative Democracy: A Sympathetic Comment', *Philosophy and Public Affairs*, vol. 29, no. 4 (2000): 371–418.

Gadamer, H.-G. [1975] *Truth and Method*, second edition, trans. Joel Weinsheimer & Donald G. Marshall (London: Sheed and Ward, 1989).

Geuss, R. *History and Illusion in Politics* (Cambridge: Cambridge University Press, 2001).

Glover, J. *Humanity: A Moral History of the Twentieth Century* (London: Pimlico, 1999).

Goodin, R.E. and J. LeGrand, *Not Only the Poor: The Middle Classes and the Welfare State* (London: Unwin Hyman, 1987).

Greene, G. [1978] *The Human Factor* (Penguin, 1980).

Griffin, J. 'Do Children Have Rights?' pp. 19–30, in David Archard and Colin M. Macleod (eds), *The Moral and Political Status of Children* (Oxford: Oxford University Press, 2002).

Grossman, V. [1964] *Everything Flows*, trans. Robert and Elizabeth Chandler, with Anna Aslanyan (London: Vintage, 2011).

Gutmann, A. 'Undemocratic Education', pp. 71–88, in Nancy Rosenblum (ed.), *Liberalism and the Moral Life* (Cambridge: Harvard University Press, 1989).

Gutmann, A. 'Civic Education and Social Diversity', *Ethics*, vol. 105, no. 3 (1995): 557–579.

Gutmann, A. *Democratic Education*, second edition (Princeton: Princeton University Press, 1999).

Gutmann, A. and D. Thompson, 'Moral Conflict and Political Consensus', *Ethics*, vol. 101, no. 1 (1990): 64–88.

Gutmann, A. and D. Thompson, *Democracy and Disagreement* (London: Belknap Press, 1996).

Habermas, J. *Moral Consciousness and Communicative Action*, trans. C. Lenhardt and S. Weber Nicholsen (Cambridge: Polity Press, 1990).

Habermas, J. 'Struggles for Recognition in the Democratic Constitutional State', pp. 107–48, in A. Gutmann (ed.) *Multiculturalism: Examining the Politics of Recognition* (Princeton, NJ: Princeton University Press, 1994a).

Habermas, J. *The Philosophical Discourse of Modernity*, trans. F. Lawrence (Cambridge: Polity Press, 1994b).

Habermas, J. 'Equal Treatment of Cultures and the Limits of Postmodern Liberalism', *Journal of Political Philosophy*, vol. 13, no. 1 (2005): 1–28.

Haldane, J. 'MacIntyre's Thomist Revival: What Next?' pp. 91–107, in John Horton and Susan Mendus (eds), *After MacIntyre: Critical Perspectives on the Work of Alasdair MacIntyre* (Cambridge: Polity Press, 1994).

Halliday, J. 'Political Liberalism and Citizenship Education: Towards a Better Curriculum Reform', *British Journal of Educational Studies*, vol. 47, no. 1 (1999): 43–55.

Hardin, R. 'Deliberation: Method, Not Theory', pp. 103–119, in Stephen Macedo (ed.), *Deliberative Democracy: Essays on Democracy and Disagreement* (Oxford: Oxford University Press, 1999).

Hardin, R. *David Hume: Moral and Political Theorist* (Oxford: Oxford University Press, 2007).

Hare, R.M. 'Review of Rawls' Theory of Justice I', *Philosophical Quarterly*, vol. 23, no. 91 (1973): 144–155.

Hare, R.M. *Moral Thinking: Its Levels, Method, and Point* (Oxford: Clarendon Press, 1981).

Harris, H. 'Liberating Children', pp. 135–146, in M. Leahy & Dan Cohn-Sherbok (eds), *The Liberation Debate: Rights at Issue* (London: Routledge, 1996).

Harsanyi, J. [1977] 'Morality and the Theory of Rational Behaviour', pp. 39–62, in Amartya Sen and Bernard Williams (eds) *Utilitarianism and Beyond* (Cambridge: Cambridge University Press, 1982).

Heidegger, M., [1927] *Being and Time*, trans. Max Niemeyer Verlag (Oxford: Blackwell, 1962).

Herdt, J.A. 'Alasdair MacIntyre's "Rationality of Traditions" and Tradition-Transcendental Standards of Justification', *Journal of Religion*, vol. 78, no. 4 (1998): 524–546.

Hess, D.E. 'Controversies about Controversial Issues in Democratic Education', *Political Science and Politics*, vol. 37, no. 2 (2004): 257–261.

Hibbs, T. 'MacIntyre, Aquinas, and Politics', *Review of Politics*, vol. 66 (2004): 357–383.

Hinsch, W. 'Global Distributive Justice', *Metaphilosophy*, vol. 32, no. 1/2 (2001): 58–78.

Hobbes, T. [1651], *Leviathan*, edited by J.C.A. Gaskin (Oxford: Oxford University Press, 1996).

Hudson, W.D. *Modern Moral Theory*, second edition (Houndmills: Macmillan, 1983).

Hume, D. [1739–40] *A Treatise of Human Nature*, E. C. Mossner (ed.) (Harmondsworth: Penguin, 1969).

Hume, D. [1751] *An Enquiry Concerning the Principles of Morals*, J.B. Schneewind (ed.) (Cambridge: Hackett, 1983).

Hurka, T. *Virtue, Vice, and Value* (Oxford: Oxford University Press, 2001).

Huseby, R. 'Duties and Responsibilities Towards the Poor', *Res Publica*, vol. 14 (2008): 1–18.

Husserl, E. [1907] *The Idea of Phenomenology*, trans. William P. Alston and George Nakhnikian; introduction by George Nakhnikian (The Hague: Nijhoff, 1973).

Ignatieff, M. *Human Rights: As Political and Idolatry* (Oxford: Princeton University Press, 2001).

Irwin, T. 'Tradition and Reason in the History of Ethics', *Social Philosophy and Policy*, vol. 7, no. 1 (1989): 45–68.

James, S.M. 'Good Samaritans, Good Humanitarians', *Journal of Applied Philosophy*, vol. 24, no. 3 (2007): 238–254.

Johnson, J. 'Communication, Criticism, and the Postmodern Consensus: An Unfashionable Interpretation of Michel Foucault', *Political Theory*, vol. 25, no. 4 (1997): 559–583.

Kant, I. [1785] *Groundwork for the Metaphysics of Morals*, trans. H.J. Paton, third edition (London: Hutchinson, 1956).

Keat, R. *Cultural Goods and the Limits of the Market* (Basingstoke: Palgrave Macmillan, 2000).

Keat, R. 'Anti-Perfectionism, Market Economies and the Right to Meaningful Work', *Analyse und Kritik*, vol. 31, no. 1 (2009): 121–138.

Knight, K. *Aristotelian Philosophy: Ethics and Politics from Aristotle to MacIntyre* (Cambridge: Polity, 2007).

Knops, A. 'Debate: Agonism as Deliberation – On Mouffe's Theory of Democracy', *The Journal of Political Philosophy*, vol. 15, no. 1 (2007): 115–126.

Kuhn, T.S. *The Copernican Revolution* (Cambridge, MA: Harvard University Press, 1957).

Kuna, M. 'MacIntyre on Tradition, Rationality, and Relativism', *Res Publica*, 2005, vol. 11, no. 3 (2005): 251–273.

Kymlicka, W. 'Two Dilemmas of Citizenship Education in Pluralist Societies', pp. 47–63, in Andrew E. Lockyer, Bernard Crick, John Annetto (eds), *Education for Democratic Citizenship: Issues of Theory and Practice* (Aldershot: Ashgate, 2003).

Laclau, E. and C. Mouffe, *Hegemony and Socialist Strategy* (London: Verso, 1985).

Larmore, C. 'The Moral Basis of Political Liberalism', *Journal of Philosophy*, vol. 96, no. 12 (1999): 599–625.

Larmore, C. 'Public Reason', pp. 368–393, in Samuel Freeman (ed.), *The Cambridge Companion to Rawls* (Cambridge: Cambridge University Press, 2003).

Levi, P. [1958] *If This Is a Man*, in *If This Is a Man / The Truce*, trans. Stuart Woolf (London: Abacus, 1998).

Lutz, C. *Tradition in the Ethics of Alasdair Macintyre: Relativism, Thomism, and Philosophy* (Lanham, MD: Lexington Books, 2004).

Lyotard, J.-F. *The Post-Modern Condition* (Manchester: Manchester University Press, 1984).

Macedo, S. 'Liberal Civic Education and Religious Fundamentalism: The Case of God v. John Rawls', *Ethics*, vol. 105 (1995): 468–496.

MacIntyre, A. *Marxism and Christianity* (London: Duckworth, 1968).

MacIntyre, A. [1984] 'Is Patriotism a Virtue?' pp. 209–228, in Ronald Beiner (ed.) *Theorizing Citizenship* (Albany: State University of New York Press, 1995).

MacIntyre, A. *After Virtue: a Study in Moral Theory*, second edition (London: Gerald Duckworth, 1985).

MacIntyre, A. *Whose Justice? Which Rationality?* (Duckworth: London, 1988).

MacIntyre, A. 'I'm Not a Communitarian, But...', *Responsive Community*, vol. 1, no. 1 (1991): 91–92.

MacIntyre, A. [1992] 'Plain Persons and Moral Philosophy: Rules, Virtues and Goods', pp. 136–152, in Kelvin Knight (ed.) *The MacIntyre Reader* (Cambridge: Polity Press, 1998).

MacIntyre, A. [1994a] 'a Partial Response to My Critics', pp. 283–303, in John Horton and Susan Mendus (eds) *After MacIntyre: Critical Perspectives on the Work of Alasdair MacIntyre* (Cambridge: Polity, 1994).

MacInytre, A. , [1994b] 'Moral Relativism, Truth and Justification', pp 202–220, in Kelvin Knight (ed.) *The MacIntyre Reader* (Cambridge: Polity Press, 1998).

MacIntyre, A. [1994c] 'The Theses of Feuerbach: A Road Not Taken', pp 223–234, in Kelvin Knight (ed.) *The MacIntyre Reader* (Cambridge: Polity, 1998).

MacIntyre, A. 'The Spectre of Communitarianism', *Radical Philosophy*, 70 (1995a): 34–35.

MacIntyre, A. [1995b] 'Natural Law as Subversive: The Case of Aquinas', pp. 41–63, in Alasdair MacIntyre, *Ethics and Politics: Selected Essays, Volume 2* (Cambridge: Cambridge University Press, 2006).

MacIntyre, A. [1997] 'Politics, Philosophy, and the Common Good', pp. 235–252, in Kelvin Knight (ed.) *The MacIntyre Reader* (Cambridge: Polity, 1998).

MacIntyre, A. *Dependent Rational Animals* (London: Duckworth, 1999a).

MacIntyre, A. [1999b], 'Toleration and the Goods of Conflict', pp. 205–223, in Alasdair MacIntyre, *Ethics and Politics: Selected Essays, Volume 2* (Cambridge: Cambridge University Press, 2006).

MacIntyre, A. [1999c] 'Social Structures and Their Threats to Moral Agency', pp. 186–204, in Alasdair MacIntyre, *Ethics and Politics: Selected Essays, Volume 2* (Cambridge: Cambridge University Press, 2006).

Mackie, J.L. *Ethics: Inventing Right and Wrong* (Harmdondsworth: Penguin, 1977).

Mackie, J.L. *Hume's Moral Theory* (Routledge: London, 1980).

Marx, K. [1844] *Economic and Philosophic Manuscripts of 1844*, D.J. Struick (ed.) trans. M. Milligan (London: Lawrence and Wishart Ltd. 1973).

Marx, K. [1859] 'Preface to a Critique of Political Economy', pp. 424–427, in D. McLellan (ed.) *Karl Marx: Selected Writings* (Oxford: Oxford University Press, 2000).

Marx, K. [1875] *Critique of the Gotha Programme*, pp. 340–360, in D. Fernbach (ed.), *Karl Marx. The International and After. Political Writings: Vol III* (London: Penguin, 1992).

McCabe, D. 'Knowing about the Good: A Problem with Antiperfectionism', *Ethics*, vol. 110, no. 2 (2000): 311–338.

McKeever, S. and M. Ridge, *Principled Ethics: Generalism as a Regulative Ideal* (Oxford: Oxford University Press, 2006).

McMylor, P. *Alasdair MacIntyre: Critic of Modernity* (London: Routledge, 1994).

Melville, H. [1851] *Moby Dick; or The Whale* (London: Penguin, 1988).

Mieth, C. 'World Poverty as a Problem of Justice? A Critical Comparison of Three Approaches', *Ethical Theory and Moral Practice*, vol. 11 (2008): 15–36.

Mill, J.S. [1859] *On Liberty*, ed. Gertrude Himmelfarb (London: Penguin 1985).

Mill, J.S. [1861] 'Utilitarianism', in J. Grey (ed.) *On Liberty and Other Essays* (Oxford: Oxford University Press, 1991).

Miller, D. *On Nationality* (Oxford: Oxford University Press, 1995).

Miller, D. Principles of Social Justice (London: Harvard University Press, 1999).

Miller, D. 'National Responsibility and International Justice', pp. 123–146, in Deen K. Chatterjee (ed.) *The Ethics of Assistance: Morality and the Distant Needy* (Cambridge: Cambridge University Press, 2004).

Miller, R. W. 'Moral Closeness and World Community', pp. 101–122, in Deen K. Chatterjee (ed.) *The Ethics of Assistance: Morality and the Distant Needy* (Cambridge: Cambridge University Press, 2004).

Mouffe, C. 'Radical Democracy: Modern or Postmodern?' *Social Text 21, Universal Abandon? The Politics of Postmodernism* (1989): 31–45.

Mouffe, C. 'Deliberative Democracy or Agonistic Pluralism', *Social Research*, vol. 66, no. 3 (1999): 745–758.

Mouffe, C. *The Democratic Paradox* (London: Verso, 2000).

Mulhall S. and A. Swift, *Liberals and Communitarians* (Oxford: Blackwell, 1992).

Murphy, M.C. 'MacIntyre's Political Philosophy', pp. 152–175, in M.C. Murphy (ed.) *Alasdair MacIntyre* (Cambridge: Cambridge University Press, 2003).

Nietzsche, F. [1887] *The Genealogy of Morals*, trans. Horace B Samuel (New York: Dover, 2003).

Nietzsche, F. [1888] *Ecce Homo*, trans. R. J. Hollingdale (Harmondsworth: Penguin, 1979).

Nisbet, R.A. , *The Sociological Tradition* (London: Heineman, 1967).

Noggle, R. 'Special Agents: Children's Autonomy and Parental Authority', pp. 97–117, in David Archard and Colin M. Macleod (eds), *The Moral and Political Status of Children* (Oxford: Oxford University Press, 2002).

Norton, D.F. 'Hume, Human Nature and the Foundations of Morality', pp. 148–181, in Norton (ed.), *The Cambridge Companion to Hume* (Cambridge: Cambridge University Press, 1993).

Nozick, R. *Anarchy, State and Utopia* (Oxford: Basil Blackwell, 1974).

O ' Neill, O. 'Children's Rights and Children's Lives', *Ethics*, vol. 98, no. 3 (1989): 445–463.

O' Neill, O. *Towards Justice and Virtue: A Constructivist Account of Practical Reasoning* (Cambridge: Cambridge University Press, 1996).

Pogge, T. '"Assisting" the Global Poor', pp. 260–288, in Deen K. Chatterjee (ed.) *The Ethics of Assistance: Morality and the Distant Needy* (Cambridge: Cambridge University Press, 2004).

Pogge, T. 'World Poverty and Human Rights', *Ethics and International Affairs*, vol. 19, no. 1 (2005): 1–7.

Pogge, T. *World Poverty and Human Rights*, second edition (Cambridge: Polity Press, 2008).

Popper, K.R. [1966] *The Open Society and Its Enemies, Vols I & II*, first published 1944, revised edition (London: Routledge and Kegan Paul, 1974).

Porter, J. 'Openness and Constraint: Moral Reflection as Tradition-Guided Inquiry in Alasdair MacIntyre's Recent Works', *Journal of Religion*, vol. 73, no. 4 (1993): 514–536.

Rawls, J. *A Theory of Justice* (Oxford: Oxford University Press, 1971).

Rawls, J. 'Kantian Constructivism in Moral Theory', *Journal of Philosophy*, vol. 77, no. 9 (1980): 515–572.

Rawls, J. 'Justice as Fairness: Political not Metaphysical', *Philosophy and Public Affairs*, vol. 14, no. 3 (1985): 223–251.

Rawls, J. [1987] 'The Idea of an Overlapping Consensus', pp. 421–448, in S. Freeman (ed.), *John Rawls: Collected Papers* (London: Harvard University Press, 2001).

Rawls, J. 'The Priority of Right and Ideas of the Good', *Philosophy and Public Affairs*, vol. 17, no. 4 (1988): 251–276.

Rawls, J. *Political Liberalism* (New York: Columbia University Press, 1993a).

Rawls, J. [1993b] 'The Law of Peoples', pp. 529–564, in S. Freeman (ed.) *John Rawls: Collected Papers* (London: Harvard University Press, 2001).

Rawls, J. [1997] 'The Idea of Public Reason Revisited', pp. 573–615, in S. Freeman (ed.), *John Rawls: Collected Papers* (London: Harvard University Press, 2001).

Rawls, J. *The Law of Peoples* (Cambridge, MA: Harvard University Press, 1999).

Raz, J. *The Morality of Freedom* (Oxford: Clarendon Press, 1986).

Raz, J. 'Facing Diversity: The Case of Epistemic Abstinence', *Philosophy and Public Affairs*, vol. 19, no. 1 (1990): 3–46.

Rousseau, J.-J. [1762] *The Social Contract*, trans. G.D.H Cole. Available online at: http://www.constitution.org/jjr/socon.htm (accessed January 2010).

Rorty, R. *Contingency, Irony, and Solidarity* (Cambridge: Cambridge University Press, 1989).

Rorty, R. 'Justice as a Larger Loyalty', pp. 139–151, in R. Botenkoe and M. Stepaniants (eds) *Justice and Democracy: Cross Cultural Perspectives* (Honolulu: University of Hawaii Press, 1997). Available online at: http://www.kuleuven. be/ep/viewpic.php?LAN=E&TABLE=EP&ID=440

Sandel, M. [1984] 'The Procedural Republic and the Unencumbered Self', pp. 12–28, in S. Avineri and A. De-Shalit (eds), *Communitarianism and Individualism* (Oxford: Oxford University Press, 1992).

Sangiovanni, A. 'Justice and the Priority of Politics to Morality', *The Journal of Political Philosophy*, vol. 16, no. 1 (2008): 137–164.

Scanlon, T.M. 'Fear of Relativism', pp. 219–245, in R. Hursthouse, G. Lawrence, W. Quinn (eds), *Virtues and Reasons* (Oxford: Clarendon, 1995).

Scanlon, T.M. *What We Owe to Each Other* (Cambridge, MA: Harvard University Press, 1998).

Scanlon, T.M. 'Reasons, Responsibility, and Reliance: Replies to Wallace, Dworkin, and Deigh', *Ethics*, vol. 112, no. 3 (2002): 519–520.

Scheffler, S. 'The Appeal of Political Liberalism', *Ethics*, vol. 105, no. 1 (1994): 4–22.

Schmitt, C. [1927] *The Concept of the Political*, trans. George Schwab (New Brunswick: Rutgers University Press, 1976).

Shue, H. 'Thickening Convergence: Human Rights and Cultural Diversity', pp. 217–241, in Deen K. Chatterjee (ed.) *The Ethics of Assistance: Morality and the Distant Needy* (Cambridge: Cambridge University Press, 2004).

Simmons, L. (1994) 'Three Kinds of Incommensurability Thesis', *American Philosophical Quarterly*, 31(2) 119–131.

Singer, P. *Practical Ethics*, second edition (Cambridge: Cambridge University Press, 1993).

Singer, P. *One World: The Ethics of Globalization* (London: Yale University Press, 2002).

Singer, P. 'Outsiders: Our Obligations to Those Beyond Our Borders', pp. 11–32, in Deen K. Chatterjee (ed.) *The Ethics of Assistance: Morality and the Distant Needy* (Cambridge: Cambridge University Press, 2004).

Solzhenitsyn, A. [1973] *The Gulag Archipelago 1918–1956*, trans. Thomas Whitney and Harry Willets (London: The Harvill Press, 2003).

Talisse, R.B. 'Can Value Pluralists be Comprehensive Liberals? Galston's Liberal Pluralism', *Contemporary Political Theory*, vol. 3 (2004): 127–139.

Tasioulas, J. 'The Moral Reality of Human Rights', pp. 75–102, in Thomas Pogge (ed.) *Freedom from Poverty as a Human Right* (Paris: Unesco; Oxford: Oxford University Press, 2007).

Tawney, R.H. [1921] *The Acquisitive Society* (London: Fontana, 1966).

Taylor, C. *Sources of the Self* (Cambridge: Cambridge University Press, 1989).

Taylor, C. [1992] 'The Politics of Recognition', in A. Gutmann (ed.) *Multiculturalism: Examining the Politics of Recognition* (New Jersey: Princeton University Press, 1994).

Taylor, C. 'Justice after Virtue', pp. 16–43, in J. Horton and S. Mendus (eds), *After MacIntyre* (Cambridge: Polity, 1994).

Taylor, C. *A Catholic Modernity* (Oxford: Oxford University Press, 1999).

Thunder, D. 'A Rawlsian Argument Against the Duty of Civility', *American Journal of Political Science*, vol. 50, no. 3 (2006): 676–690.

Tinterow, G. and Lacambre, G. , with contributions by Juliet Wilson-Bareau and Deborah L. Roldán, *Manet/Velazquez: The French Taste for Spanish Painting* (Yale University Press, 2003).

Unger, P. *Living High and Letting Die* (Oxford: Oxford University Press, 1996).

Vatter, M. 'The Idea of Public Reason and the Reason of State: Schmitt and Rawls on the Political', *Political Theory*, vol. 36 (2008): 239–271.

Walzer, M. *Spheres of Justice: A Defense of Pluralism and Equality* (Oxford: Blackwell/ Basic Books, 1983).

Walzer, M. *Thick and Thin: Moral Argument at Home and Abroad* (South Bend, IN: Notre Dame Press, 1994).

Waugh, E. *Unconditional Surrender* (Harmondsworth: Penguin, 1961).

Weithman, P. 'Deliberative Character', *Journal of Political Philosophy*, vol. 13, no. 3 (2005): 263–283.

Wenar, L. 'Contractualism and Global Economic Justice', *Metaphilosophy*, vol. 32, no. 1/2 (2001): 79–94.

Westheimer J. and J. Kahne, 'What Kind of Citizen? The Politics of Educating for Democracy', *American Education Research Journal*, vol. 41, no. 2 (2004): 237–269.

Williams, B. *Moral Luck* (Cambridge: Cambridge University Press, 1981).

Wittgenstein, L. [1953] *Philosophical Investigations*, trans. G.E.M Anscombe, third edition (Oxford: Blackwell, 2001).

Wolf, S. 'Moral Saints', *Journal of Philosophy*, vol. 79 (1982): 419–439.

Wolin, R. 'Carl Schmitt: The Conservative Revolutionary Habitus and the Aesthetics of Horror', *Political Theory*, vol. 20, no. 3 (1992): 424–447 (425).

Young, I.M. [1993], 'Together in Difference: Transforming the Logic of Group Political Conflict', pp 155–178, in W. Kymlicka (ed.) *The Rights of Minority Cultures* (Oxford: Oxford University Press, 1995).

Index